W9-COT-572

The SPIRITUALITY of COMEDY

The
SPIRITUALITY
of
COMEDY

Comic Heroism in a Tragic World

CONRAD
HYERS

Transaction Publishers
New Brunswick (U.S.A.) and London (U.K.)

Copyright © 1996 by Transaction Publishers, New Brunswick, New Jersey 08903

All rights reserved under International and Pan-American Copyright Conventions. No part of this book may be reproduced or transmitted in any form or by any means, electronic or mechanical, including photocopy, recording, or any information storage and retrieval system, without prior permission in writing from the publisher. All inquiries should be addressed to Transaction Publishers, Rutgers—The State University, New Brunswick, New Jersey 08903.

This book is printed on acid-free paper that meets the American National Standard for Permanence of Paper for Printed Library Materials.

Library of Congress Catalog Number: 95-499
ISBN: 1-56000-218-2
Printed in the United States of America

Library of Congress Cataloging-in-Publication Data

Hyers, M. Conrad.
The spirituality of comedy : comic heroism in a tragic world / Conrad Hyers.
    p. cm.
  Includes bibliographical references and index.
  ISBN 1-56000-218-2 (acid-free)
  1. Characters and characteristics in literature. 2. Comic, The. I. Title.
PN56.5.C65H94 1995
809'.917—dc20   95-499
                                                          CIP

The more thoroughly and substantially a human being exists, the more he will discover the comical. Even one who has merely conceived a great plan toward accomplishing something in the world will discover it.

—Søren Kierkegaard
Concluding Unscientific Postscript

Contents

Acknowledgments

Biblical quotations are from the *Revised Standard Version of the Bible*, copyright 1946, 1952 and © 1971, 1973 by the Division of Christian Education, National Council of Churches, and are used by permission. Acknowledgment is also made to the following publishers for material cited: To Simon & Schuster, Inc. for quotations from *Zorba The Greek* by Nikos Kazantzakas, copyright © 1953 by Simon & Schuster, Inc. Copyright renewed © 1981 by Simon & Schuster, Inc. Reprinted by permission of Simon & Schuster, Inc. To Liveright Publishing Corporation for an excerpt from the poem "i thank You God for most this amazing" from E. E. Cummings, *Complete Poems, 1904–1962*, edited by George J. Firmage. Copyright © 1950, 1978, 1991 by the Trustees for the E. E. Cummings Trust. Copyright © 1979 by George James Firmage. Reprinted by permission of Liveright Publishing Corporation. To Harcourt Brace Jovanovich, Inc. for a quotation from T. S. Eliot, *Four Quartets*, copyright © 1943 by T. S. Eliot, renewed 1971 by Esme Valerie Eliot. Reprinted by permission of Harcourt Brace Jovanovich, Inc., and Faber & Faber, Ltd., London. To Prentice Hall for permission to use a quotation from *W. C. Fields by Himself: His Intended Autobiography*, by Ronald J. Fields. copyright © 1973. Reprinted by permission of Prentice Hall/A Division of Simon & Schuster. To Liveright Publishing Corporation for an excerpt from "Chaplinesque" from *Complete Poems of Hart Crane*, edited by marc Simon, with the permission of Liveright Publishing Corporation. Copyright 1993, © 1958, 1966 by Liveright Puyblishing Corporation. Copyright © 1986 by Marc Simon. Some of the material in the book is based on essays by Conrad Hyers in *Theology Today:* "Prometheus and the Problem of Progress" (October 1980) and "Comedy and Creation" (October 1982), copyright © 1980, 1982, and are used by permission. Some material is also based on essays by Conrad Hyers in *The Christian Century:* "The Recovery of Simplicity" (August 7–14, 1974), "Farewell to the Clown: A Tribute to Charlie" (February 22, 1978), and "The Comic Vision in a Tragic World" (April

20, 1983), copyright © 1974, 1978, 1983 by the Christian Century Foundation and used by permission. Some material is further developed from some of the essays in *The Comic Vision and the Christian Faith* by Conrad Hyers, copyright © 1981 by The Pilgrim Press and used by permission. The Epilogue is an expansion of a contribution by Conrad Hyers to the International Symposium on Reversal Theories of Play, "Education as Play: A Paratelic Perspective," published in *Adult Play: A Reversal Theory Approach*, edited by Michael Apter and John Kerr, Zwets and Zeitlinger, Amsterdam, copyright © 1990, and used by permission.

Grateful appreciation is due the National Endowment for the Humanities for providing two research fellowships to explore the spiritual and symbolic significance of the comic tradition. The first fellowship resulted in a previous work, *The Laughing Buddha: Zen and the Comic Spirit*, with its oriental setting. The second fellowship has resulted in the present work, with its largely occidental setting.

I am indebted to various sources of inspiration and guidance in the preparation of this book: to Chad Walsh who encouraged me in the fledgling stages of my study; to Nathan Scott, Jr., who has written the finest single essay on the subject; to Mircea Eliade who first engaged me in the analysis of myth, ritual, and symbol; to John Hick, my former mentor, who led me into philosophical issues that have now born this unusual and unexpected fruit; to Bardwell Smith who provided needed moral support and his own kindly sense of humor; to Northrop Frye and Wylie Sypher whose essays on comedy have been of special help; to Doug Adams who embodies the spirit of this material in such a delightful manner in his person and teaching; and, not least, to my paternal grandmother whose rollicking laughter and bubbling disposition—into her eighty-seventh year—have stayed with me.

I also wish to recognize the many students of two decades who have mused with me, and been amused and bemused, over the many masks and faces of the comic muse. This book had its beginnings in a course I first ventured to offer at Beloit College and have continued at Gustavus Adolphus College, as well as in lecture series, workshops, and seminars under various auspices. The participants in these many contexts have contributed much through their enthusiasm and suggestions. Their reception has persuaded me of the importance of cultivating that side of the human spirit that expresses itself in humor and comedy.

Introduction

Comic Hero With A Thousand Faces

...a little valiant nonsense, some divine service
and ass festival, some old joyful Zarathustra fool,
some blusterer to blow your souls bright.

—Nietzsche, *Thus Spake Zarathustra*

To understand comedy is to understand humanity. Among the defining characteristics of the human spirit is a capacity for laughter, humor,
revelry, and setting things in comic perspective. Informally this spirit is
expressed in joking, banter, punning, horseplay, and the general refusal
to take matters with absolute seriousness—or to absolutize them. More
formally this spirit is expressed by comic figures such as the jester, clown,
fool, humorist, comic hero, rogue, and trickster. These figures both symbolize and incarnate the comic spirit. And they "officiate" in comic rituals as mock priests whose public role is to encourage the comic spirit
and its vision of life.

Human existence at its best, both individually and collectively, is a
running interplay between seriousness and laughter, sense and nonsense,
sacred concerns and comic interludes. On the one side we are sober,
solemn, somber, grave, intense, and perhaps tense. On the other side we
are lighthearted, mischievous, jolly, playful, nonsensical, and perhaps
silly. We also have the capacity to move suddenly from the one mode to
the other—a phenomenon that psychologist Michael Apter has analyzed
as the ability to switch back and forth between *telic* and *paratelic* consciousness and behavior.[1]

If one of the purposes of the humanities and social sciences is better
to understand the human world, the resulting picture is often skewed by
a presentation that largely ignores the playful and comic side. Indeed a
survey of academic literature in any field would hardly lead to the specu-

1

lation that this side of humanity even existed. As Peter Berger once complained with regard to the social sciences, the overwhelming tendency among academicians is to depict human relationships solely in the *dramatic* mode to the virtual exclusion of the *comic* mode, giving a very distorted view of human existence.[2] We have often been like the envious composer Salieri in Peter Shaffer's *Amadeus* who did not know what to do with a Mozart who combined high intensity and a divinely inspired music with raucous laughter and a love of foolishness.

When, further, the serious side of humanity is seen as the hallmark of maturity and profundity, and the humorous side (and aside) as an indication of immaturity and triviality, we have the makings of tragedy. The tragic mode is the dramatic mode untempered and unqualified by the comic mode—not only in literature and theater but in real life. Tragedy is human seriousness carried to the extreme, and the objects or subjects of that seriousness absolutized. When the comic sense is, correspondingly, pushed aside as inappropriate and threatening, much that is human is lost. It is little surprise that the tragic spirit often results in such destructive consequences.

In exploring the richness of the comic repertoire, I am indebted to the variety of fields in the humanities and social sciences, with the focus being in comparative mythology and religion. The specific orientation is around "myth, ritual, and symbol" in the comic tradition, and thus its spiritual significance. We will consider the mythic background of both tragedy and comedy, and myths associated with figures such as the clown, fool, and trickster. We will examine the many comic forms as rituals of the human spirit, with the various comedic figures seen as comic equivalents of "prophets, priests, and sages." And we will explore the profound symbolism and special wisdom embodied in the various comic figures and ritual forms. The result, therefore, is not only an academic inquiry but a philosophy of life.

The Hero

Among the many sources of influence that bear upon this book, two people deserve special recognition, and their acknowledgment gives a preliminary clue as to the method and character of the study. Their names have probably never before appeared on the same page—unless by alphabetical happenstance in an index. They are Joseph Campbell and Charles Chaplin.

My first reading of Campbell's *Hero With a Thousand Faces*[3] was at a time when I began to reflect "seriously" upon laughter, humor, and comedy. While admiring the way in which Campbell integrated an array of heroic myths and literatures from many cultures and eras, I found myself asking about the relationship of the *comic* hero to all this heroism and heroic journeying. Not only did the comic hero seem to be on a different kind of journey, but to display a different sort of spirituality over against, or at least counterweight to, the kinds of heroism represented by the mythic hero, or tragic hero, or military hero—even the rags to riches heroism of an Horatio Alger. What does the comic hero have to do with any of these heroics? Upon what quest is the comic hero embarked, and what does comic heroism discover along the way, or at the end of its particular rainbow? Of what insights and values and aspirations is the comic hero the bearer? What is the meaning of this "valiant nonsense"—as Nietzsche called it—which "blows souls bright"?

The tales and escapades of comic heroes do bear many resemblances to those of epic or tragic heroes. Perhaps this is part of what Socrates meant in the *Symposium* when he persuaded Agathon and Aristophanes (with the help of large quantities of wine and the lateness of the hour) that the genius of comedy is the same as that of tragedy. Unfortunately the discourse put even the comedian Aristophanes to sleep. So we do not have the full benefit of his response—unless that was it! Yet if the genius is the same, the point of noting any similarities between comic and other heroisms lies in the accompanying differences. Comedy offers certain little additions and subtractions, alterations, twists and turns, overstatements and understatements, curious coincidences, miscellaneous reports, gossipy asides, raised eyebrows, ironic observations, tongue-in-cheek interpretations, winkings and whisperings. In fact, comedy employs a great variety of techniques and a vast repertoire of signals and cues—some blatant, some quite subtle—which indicate that even the same circumstances are being understood in a different spirit and seen through a different lens.

These were not the only questions I had of Campbell's heroes, or of his theses and methods in presenting them.[4] But the relevance of the comic hero to the problem of heroism was the focus of our discussions. In various conversations and correspondences Campbell, with his customary graciousness, encouraged me to pursue the comic hero, and offered some examples that were of special delight to him. I recall one lively discussion over dinner on the symbolic differences between the heroics of Superman—who flew everywhere by virtue of the supernatural powers that lay beneath his assumed identity as Clark Kent, and the heroics of Batman who was really the mortal Bruce Wade, and who would laboriously climb tall buildings in order to jump in the window and give the illusion of flying!

While this is hardly the grand tradition of literature and drama, there is some affinity between comic heroes and comic books, as well as their newspaper and cinematic version, cartoons. Granted, most comic books are not comic at all, but bloodthirsty adventures. Yet the use of the term "comic" is analogous to one meaning, at least, in Dante's use of the term *Commedia* for his cosmic drama of Inferno, Purgatorio, and Paradiso: it was written in the "lax and humble" language of home, street, and tavern, rather than the formal and stately language of scripture, scholarship, law, and liturgy; in short, Italian rather than Latin. Comic figures, after all, even when making an appearance in great literature and drama, have the irritating habit of debunking human greatness and grandeur, of mocking heroic attempts at supernatural flying, and of speaking in the vernacular.

Out of such discussions and reflections has emerged a kind of "Comic Hero with a Thousand Faces," organized around the principal types of comic figures: humorist, jester, clown, fool, comedian, simpleton, underdog, trickster, rogue, and—in the narrower sense of the term—comic hero. In one form or another—the hats, coats, and disguises change infinitely—such figures are found in all cultures and throughout recorded time in what might be called "the comic tradition." There is some overlapping between the various types of comic figures, yet each type suggests a different emphasis, as the terms themselves indicate. The fool specializes in foolishness; the clown in clowning; the trickster in trickery; the simpleton in simplicity; the rogue in roguery. The approach will be to underline commonalties of spirit and function, and shared elements of "myth, ritual, and symbol," but also the peculiar emphasis and wisdom of each.

Some might wish to make a longer list; others a shorter list, or a list that combines figures differently. This list, obviously, relies upon English terms commonly in use. One could further subdivide each type, like a biologist, into additional subspecies, since all clowns or fools or tricksters are hardly identical. There are also significant differences from period to period and culture to culture. The Italian *commedia dell 'arte,* for example, used its particular array of five stock characters—braggart, *zanni,* pedant, parasite, and rustic—and was followed in this by Shakespeare's *Love's Labour's Lost:* Armado, Moth, Holofernes, Nathaniel, and Costurd. Certainly other characteristics and combinations are possible, as they were for Shakespeare in other plays. A variety of comic figures are recognizable, one way or another, across time and place. Sometimes a single comic figure can transcend cultural boundaries and absorb many of the traits of other types, eliciting a universal response—as did Chaplin's pantomimed Tramp who worked his magic for decades on all continents.

I have drawn on a variety of examples: from ancient Greek comedy to twentieth century literature and drama; from medieval jesters to modern humorists; from the Shakespearean fool and rogue to contemporary film comics; from American Indian myth and ritual to circus clowning and the animated cartoon; from the archaic trickster figure to recent play theory and chaos theory in the social and natural sciences. It will be apparent from the foregoing that the context of the terms "comic," "comic hero," and "comedy" will extend beyond literature, theater, art, cinema, and television into any arena where comic figures and forms may be found. Like life itself, the comic spirit seems to burst forth into an irrepressible infinity of shapes and situations. Not for naught was the ancient trickster called the shapeshifter.[5]

The Tramp

If ever there was a comic figure that approached universality it was Chaplin's Tramp. I had not seen a Chaplin film until I was several years into my professional career, yet I have learned more from him than from any other source. With good reason. For several decades Charlie was one of the most widely known and beloved figures in the world, second in name recognition at one time only to Jesus and Coca-Cola. This was not only because he was a master clown communicating through the universal language of pantomime, but also because he was the archetypal comic hero, grappling with universal human problems—not just cream pies and sight gags. The range of emotions to which he appealed also gave universality to a figure that so deftly interlaced pathos and humor. In Charlie the whole of the human condition was represented symbolically, not just an excerpt from it of the most admirable or entertaining aspects. And he dared to deal comically with tragic themes and circumstances.

With clipped mustache and soulful eyes set in a pallid face, his shabby but once elegant clothes, his jaunty penguin gait, his dusty dignity, Charlie touched the heart of the human predicament in a way that was as profoundly wise as it was delightfully humorous. He had little formal education or any learned counsel on human affairs. His schooling had been the streets and music halls, the tenements and orphanages and park benches of London. Yet, intuitively, he displayed a deeply human sensitivity that offered much more than a slapstick performance and laughter of the moment. Though in most of his films from 1914 to 1940 he played only one character—the Tramp—he was the quintessential "comic hero with a thousand faces." He was humorist, jester, clown, fool, comedian, simpleton, underdog, trickster, comic hero, and rogue all rolled into one.

Charlie the Vagabond didn't seem to belong anywhere or to anyone. He had nowhere to call home and nothing to call his own. Yet he seemed to fit in everywhere and belong to everyone. We could identify with him. He was vicariously human in a way that few figures in literature, theater, or cinema have ever been. In all those little rituals played out again and again on silent screen he stood for us, represented us. He made us laugh, and he made us cry. Not necessarily in equal proportions. He insisted on interrupting crying with laughter, and surrounding sadness with mirth.

Haloes and awards, however, do not become comic heroes. They are too iconoclastic and blatantly human for that. Even Chaplin's belated Academy Award, and his even more belated knighthood, sat rather awkwardly on a figure whose greatness lay in his portrayal of a tough but tender little tramp who stood at the bottom of the social order, if not quite outside of it, and who in real life had come from the slums of London. Sir Charlie had appeared before us in dust and rags—a knight of sorts perhaps, but a knight without armor come to battle without sword and disarm us all.

Chaplin's parents had been small-time performers, separated by the time he was two. His mother was, at first, able to provide a meager existence for Charlie and his older half-brother Sydney. But before long she lost her voice by performing during bouts of laryngitis. The climax came one winter night when Charlie was four. His mother ran off the stage in tears, unable to continue. Unknown to anyone, little Charlie, who always accompanied his mother in the wings of the theater, had memorized her lines and songs. Seeing his mother's plight, he ran out on stage and assumed her role, to the wild applause of the audience. It was the beginning of his stage career; for his mother it was the end.

Charlie's father, whom he rarely saw and who drank heavily on the theater circuit, provided only sporadic support. His mother was reduced to sewing costumes for pennies, with Charlie and his brother doing odd jobs. As their situation continued to decline, they were forced to live in an unheated attic apartment. Finally, his mother had to pawn her sole means of support, her sewing machine. Two weeks later, when the money ran out, she committed herself to the workhouse and Charlie—now five and his brother seven—were placed in an orphanage. The circumstances were not far from the world of Dickens' *Oliver Twist.* Within two years his mother suffered a mental breakdown. His father was to die four years later with *delirium tremens.*

When Charlie was eight he and his brother ran away from the orphanage and tried to go it alone, with simple jobs and bit parts and handouts in the only other world they knew, the theater. Charlie began to receive minor roles and eventually became a member of a touring group which came to the U.S. where he was discovered by comedy filmmaker, Mack Sennett, in 1912. Charlie was now twenty-three, and within three years he became a leading comic film actor with control of his own productions.

Such a background gave to his comic artistry something more than an occasional tickle on the periphery of existence, and more than the pratfall and mayhem simplicity of other comedies of the day, such as the Keystone Cops. Chaplin plunged his character into the most difficult social issues of the time: immigration, unemployment, poverty, homelessness, crime, alcoholism, drug addiction, slum neighborhoods, sweatshops, war—not the conventional themes of situation comedy, let alone the slapstick that dominated early cinema. Chaplin took on the individual Goliaths (as in *Easy Street*) and the gargantuan forces (as in *Modern Times*) that tend to overwhelm us or dehumanize us. As Chaplin said of the figure he had created: "In emergencies he even triumphs over those imposing characters whom the average man has always visualized with so much awe." In the process he revealed to us, in the comic hero's inimitable way, certain truths about ourselves and the universe. He poked fun at our pride and pretension, celebrated the simple joys of life, expressed our hopes and fears, while reconciling us to one another and to a common humanity.

When Chaplin developed his Tramp character in 1914 he was composing a figure out of his childhood, a rough but sentimental little hobo possessed of great buoyancy in a flood of adversity. In the process of putting the Tramp together, he was also putting himself together. Chaplin the now-successful and highly paid actor and Charlie the poor, undernourished, lonely little boy were being reunited. In the process he was reuniting the extremes of the social order, and of the human condition. Beauty and ugliness, wealth and poverty, success and failure, perfection and imperfection, dignity and indignity, joy and sadness, hope and despair, and a host of other antinomies were there, contained and unified in one slender figure. Even midst the dregs of life and society, he gave a renewed sense of importance and value to the most forlorn insignificance.

The comic ritual was played out in many ways. In *City Lights* a rich man, who in his drunkenness has decided that life is not worth living, is rescued from suicide by the Tramp who presumably should be the one contemplating suicide, but who ironically lectures him on hope. In *The Pilgrim* Charlie is an escaped convict who has disguised himself as a clergyman, and under this assumed identity has successfully traveled by train to the Southwest. But when he alights from the train, free at last, he is greeted by a congregation eagerly awaiting the new pastor of their church which insists on his conducting a service immediately. In *The Great Dictator* Chaplin split himself into the ruthless, mad Führer and a defenseless Jewish barber, united by virtue of being look-alikes. Through mistaken identity the Jewish barber, fleeing his burning ghetto, is thought by check-point guards to be Der Führer on his way to a Nazi rally, where "he" delivers an impassioned oration against hatred, greed, and war.

These were not the only juxtapositions with which Chaplin grappled. Part of his genius was the embodiment of so many of the confusions and contradictions of our lives—which is a further reason why Charlie had such universal appeal. He was such a nobody, yet everybody all at once. He was aristocrat and bum, convict and clergyman, dictator and innocent victim. He was sophisticated and uncouth, graceful and awkward, courageous and cowardly, bold and bashful. He was what the Middle Ages would have called "Everyman." And he masterfully moved back and forth, abruptly, between these many opposite identities. It is this paradoxical figure of Charlie that will always be remembered and loved, along with the clown rituals and fool's feasts and comic heroisms that he celebrated.

Sir Charlie? It was the final, crowning contradiction. It was, in fact, the very contradiction that gave birth to the little tramp some sixty years before, a contradiction that he continued to reenact in the ingenious multitude of its comic variations. He was, as Nathan Scott said of him, "a richly particularized and wonderfully eccentric human being living out his life—a little hobo whose every gesture somehow managed to redeem the human image."[6] It is a fitting epitaph for a rags-and-riches comic hero who always seemed to start over again in the difficult world of a small boy from Kennington, with his playfulness and dreams, his resiliency in the midst of personal disaster, and, above all, his rock bottom humanity.

The Art of Comedy

This eulogy of Chaplin and his Tramp character should not be taken to imply that he offers the sole definition of comedy and depiction of the comic hero. If for no other reason, every instance of comic heroism is colored and molded by its own singularities and the singularities of its time and place. Chaplin's Tramp is certainly very different from Al Capp's Li'l Abner or Shakespeare's Sir Toby or Aristophanes' Lysistrata—to pick a few random names out of the hat. Robert Corrigan is, I think, moving in the right direction in criticizing the "formalistic fallacy" which assumes that a certain theme or structure can be identified which strings together all the varied beads of comedy.[7] The "string" here, if anything, is more a matter of spirit than form, as we might expect, identified by terms such as "comic spirit," "comic sense," and "comic perspective." Since this spirit, sense, and perspective can attach itself to any thing, person, or situation, and can express itself in an unlimited variety, the attempt to associate comedy with one part of that variety is doomed to failure by exception. What is most important is not the particular devices, techniques, characters, themes, and so on, that are employed by a comic sensibility, but that sensibility itself: its introduction to any situation, what it can add to the situation, and its ongoing preservation.

If one were inclined to do so, one might feed the plots and themes of all comedies into a supercomputer and arrive at an array of percentages. 90 percent of all comedies have to do with human survival; 62 percent contain an element of romance; 30 percent result in weddings; in 24 percent nothing of any great importance happens—whatever. This would, of course, presuppose general agreement on what constitutes a comedy—which is the question at issue. One could also take the item with the highest percentage; eliminate all comedies that did not have that item; declare that item to be present in 100 percent of the cases; and, presto, we have in hand the theme or structure that identifies a comedy. Comedies no longer fitting that criterion are no longer comedies.

Paul Grawe, for example, in his *Comedy in Space, Time and the Imagination,* makes a concerted effort to define comedy in terms of a basic patterning that conveys "the assertion of a faith that the human race will survive...(and) the celebration that the human race is destined to survive."[8] It comes as a considerable surprise that what all comedies are said to share is not the comic or comedic, but some sort of credo and its celebration. As common as these elements may be in comedies, they are not necessarily central or even universal. The result is that a great many comedies are set aside as marginally comedic, or poorly comedic, or not comedic at all because they do not fit the definition now used to sort things out.

The cartoon comedy of Al Capp, for example, is jettisoned as having "something to say about what is not comedy, but goes by the same name." The reasoning? "In the modern world, we have two different creatures, both going by the name comedy. One is . . . what we are considering comedy. The other . . . should properly be called a form of satire."[9] Similarly, the comedies of Aristophanes, awarded many prizes in Athens in the category of comedy, considered by critics then and since as fine comedies—albeit of the Old School—are put to one side as "accidentally comedic," for none "displays any systematic comedic patterning."[10] Note that now the patterning has to be systematic in order to be comedic, when characteristics often associated with comedy are happenstances, digressions, asides, miscellania, and the episodic. Note also that we are 2400 years too late in getting a retraction of his awards!

It is also possible that one might isolate some structural element said to characterize comedy, and then discover that such an element is also to be found in cases that no one has ever wished to consider as comedies. That, too, becomes a problem for Grawe's definition, since survival and its celebration is also a characteristic of romances, many fairy tales, sundry detective stories, and *The Wizard of Oz.* Even the classical tragic trilogy—as will be argued in chapter two—is very much concerned with survival and its celebration. The problem we then confront is reminiscent of the scene at the end of Monty Python's *Life of Brian*, where Brian of Nazareth—who is mistaken throughout the film for Jesus of Nazareth—is being crucified (also mistakenly) along with thirty-two others on the hill of Golgotha. Brian's girlfriend has convinced the Roman authorities that they have the wrong man, and a writ of pardon has been dispatched to the site. As the courier reaches the crucifixion scene, he announces that he has a writ of pardon for a Brian of Nazareth. "Which one of you is Brian of Nazareth?" All thirty-three, of course, respond that they are Brian of Nazareth!

In attempting to deal in an inclusive manner with the comic tradition, it would be preferable to proceed the other way around and say, simply, that certain themes, structures, characters, and endings are to be found in a number of comedies, perhaps quite commonly in comedies, and leave it at that. We shall consider this problem, for example, in chapter eight on the happy ending that is often said to characterize comedy. All comedies do not have a happy ending, unless—as above—one arbitrarily defines comedies as having this ingredient. This, however, issues in some very peculiar results. Some of Chaplin's films have a happy ending, some a sad ending, and some an ambiguous ending. Otherwise, the films have most other characteristics in common, including the Tramp figure. Are some comedies and others not? Or are some comedies up to the last possible moment when they are suddenly transformed into something else?

Wittgenstein's views on the nature of language (*Philosophical Investigations*)[11] would seem to be a safe guide here, at least with respect to defining comedy in terms of a certain form or content. There are "family resemblances" between comedies, but no single feature delineates all members of the family. There is no "essence" of comedy, if we are looking for this in some plot, theme, or character common to all. This includes the comic hero, even in the broad sense suggested for the term in the phrase, "the Comic Hero with a Thousand Faces." Trying to arrive at a simple definition of so complex and encompassing an area might well end up like Mark Twain's story of the boy asked by his Sunday school teacher to give a definition of a lie. "A lie," he ventured, "is an abomination before the Lord, and a very present help in time of trouble!"

If one takes such a position, the question remains whether there is an "essence" of comedy in the area of spirit rather than body, feeling rather than form, perspective rather than pattern. I am inclined to believe that there is, and to refer to this by terms such as comic spirit, comic sense, and comic vision—while acknowledging that here, too, there is considerable variety. The attempt will be made in chapter four to map out this variety, and in doing so the terms comic sense and sense of humor will be treated as synonymous. Both terms have a lowly origin, as we might expect. Humor derives from the Latin *humus* (earth), and therefore is never far from a reminder of dirt and compost piles. The term comic derives from the lesser Greek god, Comus, god of fertility—not in the ecstatic sense of Dionysus but in the ordinary sense of "the birds and the bees." The term comedy derives, in turn, from the comic songs and jests (*komodia*) made in conjunction with the annual parade of the phalli from Athenian towns to the temple festival of Dionysus. And—quite instructive it is—while the grand passions of tragic drama partook more of the spirit of Dionysus, the satyr plays and comedies reveal more of the spirit of Comus. They offer a warning concerning the tragic possibilities of Dionysian frenzy and the dark consequences of extremism and over-zealous heroism.

Myth, Ritual, Symbol

Comic performances are often credited with dealing, largely, in trifles and irrelevancies—a comedians' edition of Trivial Pursuit. Closer examination, however, shows that this is far from the case. Nearly all, if not all, the major issues with which human beings have exercised themselves are touched upon in some manner by the comic spirit. One of the more striking features of a comic sensibility is that nothing stands entirely outside its purview. It is not merely tangential to life, or something from the cellar of life, but all-encompassing. No circumstance is so lowly or inconsequential that comedy will not grant it an audience. Yet neither is any authority so lofty or subject so dear that comedy has failed to approach it in more than fear and trembling.

This, again, is why satisfactory definitions in terms of form or content are impossible. The comic vision brings its own peculiar perspective and spirit to play with and upon all aspects of our lives, including those topics and things of utmost importance to us. The great array of comic figures—humorists, clowns, fools, jesters, tricksters, comedians, and the like—are the officiants of this tradition: its heroes and sages, its prophets, mystics, and priests. They are the caretakers of its myths and symbols, exemplars of its practice, defenders of its faith, and celebrants of its rituals.

Questions of the *function* of the comic sense—psychological, socio-logical, political, biological, and so on—will be touched upon, as well as questions of comic themes and plots. But the larger questions have to do with the relevance of the comic spirit to our perception of any and all aspects of our existence, and to the enhancement of the quality of our individual and collective lives. In short, what are the meanings and val-ues of this "other side" of our existence? What does this angle of vision reveal about human existence, or existence as such? What are the impli-cations of the comic perspective for those peculiarly human issues of "truth, beauty, and goodness"—as the Greeks put it?

Restricting the discussion to the functional level, however sympa-thetic the treatment, would be reminiscent of that encomium of laughter given by the nineteenth-century Prussian professor Gottlieb Hufeland:

> Laughter is one of the most important helps to digestion with which we are ac-quainted; and the custom in vogue among our ancestors, of exciting it by jesters and buffoons, was founded on true medical principles. Cheerful and joyous com-panions are invaluable at meals. Obtain such, if possible, for the nourishment re-ceived amid mirth and jollity is productive of light and healthy blood.

A glut of comic fare is certainly available for the production of light and healthy blood in contemporary television and radio programming, cinema, theater, magazines, advertisements, commercials, and books of cartoons and jokes. Yet without an examined understanding of the mean-ing of this side of our existence and its philosophical, ethical, and spiri-tual implications, we may not be carried very far by a mass production of comic forms. Getting the point of a joke is not the same as getting the point of joking.

When Marcel Marceau divided his pantomime performances into a serious, dramatic program followed by a lighthearted comic one, we were moved in the right direction. The comic side of human nature and perception was given expression and celebration. Yet the relationship between the dramatic Marceau and the comic Marceau remained as unclear on stage as it is in human life generally. What does the latter have to say to or do with the former? What is added to the dramatic Marceau by the comic Marceau? And what are the tragic possibilities if the comic dimension is not added?

1

Tragic Weights And Comic Balances—
The Tragic Hero

*Would that strife might perish from among
gods and men!*

—Homer, *The Iliad*

A posthumously published letter to W. C. Fields from a Catholic niece in Ireland informed him in 1940 of the latest news in the centuries old conflict with Protestants:

> Your cousin Hughie Dougherty was hung in Londonderry last Friday for killing a policeman. May God rest his soul and may God's curse be on Jimmy Rodger, the informer. May his soul burn in hell. God forgive me...
>
> Times are not as bad as they might be. The herring is back...and the price of fish is good, thanks be to God. The Black and Tans [the Protestants] are terrible. They go through the country in their lorries and shoot the poor people down in the fields where they are working. God's curse on them...
>
> Your uncle Danny took a shot at them from the hedge, but he had too much to drink and missed. God's curse on drink...
>
> P.S. Things might be worse than they are. Every police barrack and every Protestant church in the country has been burned down. Thanks be to God.[1]

The letter was not intended to be humorous, and the political and religious conflicts to which it refers are certainly tragic. Yet the inconsistencies displayed are nevertheless humorous, especially because the writer is so oblivious to them. A previous letter had ended even more incongruously: "Your Aunt Maggie from Ireland, who has informed me that more Protestant churches have been burned to the ground, sends her love."

Such a scenario, as we are painfully aware, continues in many places and in many ways to play itself out with similar irony. Tragic confrontations—racial, ethnic, national, political, religious, ideological—persist in destroying human relationships. Tragic polarizations, and the attitudes and idealisms that sustain them, seem to define the natural history of civilization, arousing both the bravest and most brutal possibilities of *civilitas*. In recent years the "nice little war" between Great Britain and Argentina over the Falklands/Malvinas is but one small instance among many: Irish Catholic versus Irish Protestant, Israeli versus Palestinian, Arab versus Jew, Muslim versus Christian and Jew, Iraqi versus Iranian, Iraqi versus American, Serbian versus Bosnian, Central and South American Leftist versus Rightist, white Afrikaner versus black liberationist, Kashmiri Sikh versus Hindu, Capitalist versus Socialist. The list seems interminable.

In such conflicts rarely, if ever, is it a simple clash between good and evil, though that is the way the parties to the conflict are inclined to portray the matter—with both sides, of course, representing themselves as the righteous. Two sets of values, two kinds of aspiration, two different clusters of concern, both of which in themselves may be good, are placed in collision and read by those at either extreme as "irreconcilable differences." While the initial aims may be well-meaning, the opposing virtues laudable, the respective causes just, the results are disastrous. In a tragic situation, not only do certain goods and virtues stand in seeming contradiction, but the painful consequences, the inner torment, and the unleashed evils stand in contradiction to the goods and virtues colliding. So do "The best-laid schemes o' mice an' men gang aft agley, an' lea'e us naught but grief an' pain for promised joy." As John Barbour has characterized the tragic dilemma in its artistic presentation:

> A striking moral situation lies at the heart of tragedy. . . . The highest standard of human virtue sometimes leads to the greatest extreme of suffering and misfortune. . . . Tragedy has revealed something of crucial importance about the human moral condition in an unforgettable way which is at once emotionally terrifying, aesthetically beautiful, and intellectually provocative.[2]

Mark Twain put the problem more humorously and unforgettably. In one of his tall tales he tells how exercised he had become about the considerable amount of discord among God's creatures and how he had decided to take the matter in hand.

> So I built a cage, and in it I put a dog and a cat. And after a little training I got the dog and the cat to the point where they lived peaceably together. Then I introduced

a pig, a goat, a kangaroo, some birds and a monkey. And after a few adjustments, they too learned to live in harmony. So encouraged was I by my successes that I added an Irish Catholic, a Scotch Presbyterian, a Jew, a Muslim from Turkestan, a Methodist from the wilds of Arkansas, a Salvation Army Colonel from Wapping, a Brahman from Benares, and a Buddhist from China—along with a Baptist missionary I captured on the same trip. And in a very short while there wasn't a single living thing left in the cage![3]

The comic tradition deals, among other things, with such incongruities, exposing them, softening them, and hopefully in some measure preventing them. Like anything else of value, however, the comic spirit and perspective must be cultivated. Laughter and humor may be natural to the species, but they do not automatically reach full flower, or grace the whole of life. In some contexts they may even be shunned or sup-.pressed as inappropriate and left quite undeveloped. This is often the case with the great issues that confront us and that commonly result in tragic confrontations.

The Tragic Vision

A poignant modern example of the tragic collision is Ernest Hemingway's *The Old Man and the Sea*.[4] The old fisherman—despite all the satisfactions of his simple life—will not rest until he has conquered the great fish that for so many years has teased his ambition. Again and again the fish has eluded his every effort, always managing to slip away into the mysterious depths of the sea, only to haunt his imagination and taunt his prowess again. The challenge of the great fish becomes an increasing obsession to him, filling his dreams, monopolizing his waking thoughts, driving him on with a relentless passion, sustaining his weak frame with a singleness of purpose. Finally he sets out alone in his frail boat for a last determined effort to pit his failing strength against the sea and the fish. After moving out into the deep, far from shore and the familiar fishing waters, exposing himself to the vagaries of the sea and the weather, he does succeed—in a heroic mustering of flagging energies—in catching the fish. What could never be done had been done.

After a period of exultation at the realization of his grandest dream, and wonder at the magnificence of this old titan of the sea, the fisherman discovers that the joys of his triumph are mixed with the sadness of having defeated a noble old hero in his own right, an almost legendary being who had all these years so successfully eluded his every tactic. His victory is increasingly overshadowed by the realization that the suspense and mystery, the unattainability and fascination, that had enshrouded this great beast like a sacred aura, had been dissipated. A seemingly invincible old warrior, like himself an old man of the sea, was dead.

The fisherman then tries to save the creature now at his mercy, at least to bring back the carcass of so magnificent a specimen, to salvage a trophy for posterity. Yet as he tries valiantly in his little craft to tow the massive hulk to shore, and to beat off the greedy sharks that now vie with each other over it, the sharks reduce it chunk by chunk to a bare skeleton. The venture becomes, even more literally, a hollow conquest. Though he returns with the ragged remains, the death of the great fish, and the loss of his consummate prize, portends his own death. Exhausted, with nothing left to live for, and nothing but a mangled carcass to show for his victory, he, too, is broken and destroyed.

Aristotle, in the *Poetics*, argues that the proper responses to tragedy are pity and fear: pity for an admirable character or characters whose very admirable traits lead to suffering and evil; fear, because one can see the same possibilities in oneself and one's circumstances. Pity, because the tragic action leads to consequences that seem unjust; fear, because the actions are also, in some apparent or hidden way, deemed to be culpable and therefore justly visited. Pity, because circumstances seem to be, or to have gotten, out of control; fear, because there is some point, either in the beginning or along the way, where the downward spiral might have been halted. Pity, because the situation appears to have been destined, determined, or accidental; fear, because it appears to have been freely chosen, and therefore avoidable.

Certainly these emotions and judgments are aroused by Hemingway's tragic hero. But what, if any, might be the proper *comic* responses to the tragic situation? Aristotle so separated tragedy and comedy that they were not to be seen as addressing the same issues, employing the same characters, or referring to the same circumstances. Tragedy and comedy do not speak to one another or use a common language, so one might be led to conclude, even though they were performed on the same stage in the Athenian temple of Dionysus, and back to back.

Many interpreters since have followed Aristotle's lead: proposing comic responses to tragic dilemmas would be quite inappropriate. The tragic catharsis and the comic catharsis belong to different worlds. And, of the two, tragedy is assuredly the nobler, wiser, profounder, and more uplifting—even in the midst of the blood, blindness, anguish, death, destruction, and sorrow it entails. Comedy is a condescension to weakness, coarseness, laziness, deformity, ignorance, superficiality, and the difficulties inherent in sustaining resolute action or rapt attention for long periods of time.

There are comedies, however, that have—in their own way—insisted on dealing with tragic issues, as have an array of humorists, jesters, clowns, tricksters, and fools. An early Laurel and Hardy film, *Big Business* (1927), for example, offers a comic parody of the tragic confrontation. The dimensions are small, as tends to be the case with comedies: Laurel and Hardy are attempting to sell Christmas trees house to house in southern California. A man comes to the door, pipe in hand, who clearly isn't interested in a tree. When he shuts the door, it catches a branch of the tree Stan Laurel is holding, and Oliver Hardy rings the bell for the homeowner to come and release it. The man's irritation level is rising. He slams the door, catching Laurel's coat, requiring another summons. As they are explaining, the door is slammed and catches the tree again; and when the irate homeowner comes to the door this time he brings hedge clippers and cuts up the tree. Laurel and Hardy retaliate by cutting strips of wood from his door frame, cutting his doorbell wiring, and—when he comes to the door, telephone in hand, to call the police—cutting his telephone cord.

The remainder of the film consists of his destroying their truck and trees, piece by piece, while they destroy his home and shrubbery, piece by piece. Hammurabi's ancient code of justice, "an eye for an eye and a tooth for a tooth," is played out in perfect symmetry: shrub for tree, front door for vehicle door, bell for horn, window for windshield, truck for house. A patrol officer does come, when most of the damage is done, and is instrumental in negotiating a truce. But after tears of lamentation are shed on both sides, and handshakes are exchanged, the cigar that Stan Laurel gives to the homeowner as a peace offering turns out to be a trick cigar. It explodes in his face, and the film ends with the homeowner and police officer chasing Laurel and Hardy down the street. History persists in repeating itself.

The story has begun innocently and enterprisingly enough, with a touch of holiday spirit and good cheer. It has ended with two piles of rubble. Laurel and Hardy have depicted, in comic dress, the familiar tragic situation in which two parties, each of whom represents a legitimate right, and both of whom may be well-meaning initially, clash and destroy one another. In this case the ambitions of free enterprise encounter the desires of a homeowner to be left in peace to read his morning paper. The right to solicitation collides with the right of privacy. The seller is willing; the potential buyer is unwilling. Good has not come afoul of evil, though both parties do ill and are morally outraged over the actions of the other. One good has come into conflict with another good, bringing evil in reprisal for evil. Neither side gives ground and the altercation escalates. The result resembles the release of two bulls in a china shop.

This is a *comic* treatment of tragedy. Tragic themes and patterns are employed, but played out in a major rather than minor key. The characters and behaviors are laughable. We do not experience fear or pity but the ridiculous, if not preposterous. We are given small-time, tongue-in-cheek destruction in parody of tragic action and its results. The responses of the participants in the drama are portrayed as foolish and avoidable. The consequences are out of all proportion to the circumstances or the original desires of the parties. The demolition is kept in motion by what is depicted as the folly of pride, anger, revenge, stubbornness, and lack of magnanimity. Without the introduction of some new spirit and perspective into the tragic cycle, history will repeat itself.

The Tragic Paradigm

Thomas Kuhn has given currency to the notion of paradigms and paradigm shifts in the history of modern science.[5] The tragic paradigm has played a considerable role in shaping the way in which Middle Eastern and Western peoples have envisioned life and acted or reacted accordingly. This is the result, in part, of the tremendous influence of Greek tragedy, in part of the influence of Persian dualism on Judaism, Christianity, and Islam, and in part of the influence of warrior classes and a warrior ethic that dominated ancient civilizations generally. The tragic paradigm sees existence individually or collectively as structured in terms of polarities, oppositions, contradictions, and their collisions. The images of this paradigm are those of power clashes, confrontations, and heroic struggles. The tragic conflict may be seen as within the individual, between persons or groups, in the very nature of things, or all three.

Not only has the tragic paradigm had a major influence on the way in which we have been inclined to view relationships on a grand scale: between nations, races, ethnic groups, ideologies, religions, political persuasions, and the like. It has also influenced the way we tend to view smaller scale relationships. The adversarial pattern typifies relationships between litigants, political parties, labor and management, the generations, male and female, advocates and counter-advocates of sundry causes. The dominant metaphors are those of the law courts, crusades, military campaigns, and battlegrounds. Camps of friend and foe, armed with arguments and slogans and placards, urged on by grievances and animosities, prepare to go to war across what both sides are determined to see as a "no-man's land" between: liberal versus conservative, Democrat versus Republican, Pro-choice versus Pro-life, "dove" versus "hawk," radical feminist versus male chauvinist, creationist versus evolutionist, right-to-die versus sanctity-of-life. Whatever the advocacy or the party, tragic action is both centrifugal and centripetal: it leads to polarization and those poles, in turn, tend to collide.

At the individual level, likewise, we have had a predilection for reading the psyche as an internal struggle between contending forces. Robert Heilman sees "the heart of the tragic [as] the divided personality."[6] While that may sound distinctively modern, and while it ignores the social and political forms of the tragic, the theme of the inner torment of the tragic psyche has had a long history. Sophocles' King Oedipus is a tortured soul confronted with the twin revelations of having killed his father and married his mother. For Plato the revelation was that of the soul dragged down and clouded by the dense and imperfect world of matter, haunted by a dim recollection of the pure realm from which it had fallen, and with desires that moved in opposite directions: toward the world of body and time, and toward escape from the "prison-house of the soul." For Paul it was the "wretched man that I am" of Romans 7 who laments: "I delight in the law of God, in my inmost self, but I see in my members another law at war with the law of my mind and making me captive to the law of sin" (vss. 22–24 RSV). In the Middle Ages this interior struggle was represented in many a morality play as the contest between the Seven Virtues and the Seven Deadly Sins, pulling in opposite directions, or the often sketched and later cartooned version of an angel and a demon sitting on opposite shoulders, whispering their contrary bits of advice.

Shakespeare seems to have put a great deal of his own inner conflicts—as well as the social and political conflicts of his day—into his tragic figures, such as Hamlet. In this he both harks back to the individual torment of Oedipus and anticipates the tortured soul of romanticism. The romanticists of the eighteenth and nineteenth centuries saw the tragic hero as one wrestling valiantly with deep, irreconcilable passions that tore the psyche asunder, or as hounded by the disparity between the imagined (or professed) ideal and the real. Others, such as Schlegel (*Lectures on Dramatic Art*) and Kierkegaard (*Concluding Unscientific Postscript*), identified the tragic burden as the unmitigated tension between a longing for the infinite and an agonizing awareness of the pitiful limits of our finite existence. For Kierkegaard, too, it was the lonely individual striving for an authentic subjectivity, always in danger of being swallowed up by the crowd—or by a paragraph of the Hegelian world-historical system. Similar themes were to be pursued by twentieth-century existentialists who saw humanity thrown into an existence marked by anxiety, dread, guilt, nausea, and "being condemned to be free"—as Sartre put it with tragic irony.

For Dostoevski—as for a stream of writers up to the contemporary Graham Greene—the center of the conflict was between faith and doubt, a dilemma that characterized many of his characters from *Crime and Punishment* to *The Brothers Karamazov*. For Melville the conflict centered in the problem of evil, and the struggle of good with evil that could turn the best intentions to evil results, as in Captain Ahab's pursuit of the whale in *Moby Dick*. For Schopenhauer (*The World as Will and Idea*) tragedy centered in the will: the eternal strife of will against will which was in the ultimate nature of things as Will, relative to which the only feasible response was a Stoic contemplation of the process and resignation to its fated inevitability. For Nietzsche, too, existence was fundamentally tragic, and this tragedy was irrational; yet the heroic response was to affirm life in spite of its evils, absurdities, and disharmonies. Nietzsche, in fact, moved toward a *comic* understanding of tragedy in the act of affirmation, and in his seeing conflict in terms of the alternate metaphors of play, game, dance, and musical dissonance.

The Freudian interpretation of the psyche worked out of the same tragic paradigm. Freudian psychoanalysis—unlike Jungian—offered an essentially tragic reading of the psyche as the stage for an interior drama of Oedipus and Electra complexes, as well as id and superego, conscious and unconscious, social norms and inner drives, inhibition and impulse, beleaguered adult and repressed child within.

In the nineteenth and early twentieth centuries biological evolution came to be interpreted in a tragic manner as an unrelenting struggle for the "survival of the fittest" within a nature "red in tooth and claw." The animal kingdom and its ecology were depicted as a state of perpetual war within the great food-chain of being. The relationship of humans to both animate and inanimate nature was, likewise, imaged as one of fighting off competitors and conquering territory with the weapons of technology under the generalship of science.

Laissez-faire capitalism, in turn, legitimated itself in terms of the survival of the fittest, while Social Darwinists welcomed its application to social stratification, racial discrimination, imperialism, and colonialism. Ironically, at the opposite pole, Marxists also interpreted political and economic history tragically—to very different effect—as the history of class conflicts. Accordingly, history could only progress by violent revolution rather than gradual reform. Reform movements were polite compromises with the existing evil order that postponed its necessary destruction.

The Death of Tragedy?

The philosopher, Bertrand Russell, in a celebrated essay at the turn of the century, "A Free Man's Worship," offered the twentieth century yet another tragic vision of human existence: a heroic affirmation of human values unsupported by the aimless forces of nature.

> Brief and powerless is man's life; on him and all his race the slow, sure doom falls pitiless and dark. Blind to good and evil, reckless of destruction, omnipotent matter rolls on its relentless way.... It remains only to cherish, ere yet the blow fall, the lofty thoughts that ennoble his little day; disdaining coward terrors of the slave of Fate...undismayed by the empire of chance, to preserve a mind free from the wanton tyranny that rules his outward life; proudly defiant of the irresistible forces that tolerate, for a moment, his knowledge and his condemnation, to sustain alone, a weary but unyielding Atlas, the world that his own ideals have fashioned despite the trampling march of unconscious power.[7]

George Steiner was a bit premature in announcing "The Death of Tragedy" as having begun with the demise of the medieval hierarchical world order and loss of faith in supernatural being!

W. T. Stace has argued quite the opposite: that such a tragic vision is the result of modern science, with the elimination from its purview of considerations of meaning and purpose—whether Aristotelian first and final causes or religious belief in creation and design—with the restriction of its focus to immediate causation.[8] While this is certainly characteristic of modern science, Russell's interpretation is the result of applying the tragic model to a scientific world-view. Hence the cosmic situation of postenlightenment humanity is read as a collision between an alien and insentient nature and its thinking, hoping, valuing progeny who insists on talking about truth, beauty, and goodness. The language throughout is that of some tragic hero, bravely playing out the role fate has thrust upon him, cherishing "lofty thoughts that ennoble," "disdaining coward terrors," "undismayed by the empire of chance," "proudly defiant," "a weary but unyielding Atlas." Having doomed all things to final extinction, all life to meaninglessness, all human values to the abyss out of which they have aimlessly wandered, Russell nevertheless heroically insists upon a momentary championing of certain meanings and values in defiance of the total disinterest of our "unthinking mother."

Examples of the exploration of the tragic paradigm in the literature and drama of the nineteenth and twentieth century could be multiplied indefinitely: Conrad's *The Heart of Darkness*, Maxwell Anderson's *Winterset*, Faulkner's *Absalom, Absalom*, O'Neill's *Long Day's Journey into Night*, Camus' *The Stranger*, Sartre's *Nausea* and *No Exit*, to name a fraction. *The Tragic Sense of Life* (Unamuno) has been very much a part of our modern sensibility—not surprisingly considering the enormous tragic collisions that have engulfed us, from the American Civil War to the First World War through the Great Depression, the Second World War, the Cold War, the Korean War, the Vietnam War, and the Middle East wars.

Graham Greene's arresting statement in his autobiographical *A Sort of Life*,[9] "Hell lies about them in their infancy," expresses what a lot of people in a lot of places have experienced, despite Wordsworth's assurances to the contrary. Still, one must ask whether this is the *cause*—and continuing empirical verification—of the tragic realities among and within us, or is it the *result* of the considerable influence of the tragic paradigm? Art may mirror and imitate life; yet life in turn mirrors and imitates art.

The tragic understanding has tended to interpret its clashes and conflagrations, struggles and torments, in terms of historical accident, political inevitability, psychological determinism, the ways of nature, the workings of some mysterious fate, or Russell's blind "collocations of atoms." Yet to a large extent we have played out a self-fulfilling prophecy. What we have imagined the drama to be about, individually or collectively, is what we have acted out. If there is a causal determinism in the process it is significantly cultural. Given the prominence of tragic presuppositions and metaphors, we are predisposed to conceptualize existence—whether at the macrocosmic, mesocosmic, or microcosmic levels—as the history of a struggle between contrary forces, a battleground of conflicting values, passions, or camps. The objective is not to achieve a balance (read as a stalemate), or a compromise (read as weakness), or an accommodation (read as subversion), but to defeat the adversary or engage in an heroic stand to the last breath in sublime defeat.

We *could*, however, conceive reality in terms of a very different model: a rhythmic harmony or contrapuntal composition (to use musical analogies), a counterbalancing of forces (to use a technological analogy), or a tidal ebb and flow (to use a natural analogy). Traditional Chinese cosmology did just that by seeing opposites as not being in opposition, but as complementary principles. The *yang* forces of light, masculinity, striving, firmness, reason, law, etcetera, were not at war with the *yin* forces of darkness, femininity, passivity, softness, intuition, compassion, etcetera, but were countermelodies in the symphony of the Tao. The dualism—in the psyche, or the society, or the cosmos—is not denied, but it is not read tragically. The goal is to attain an equilibrium, while suffering and evil is the consequence of imbalance. The fundamental state of things is harmonious, not contentious.

In the West it was Hegel (*The Philosophy of Fine Art*) who undertook to read the tragic paradigm in this way and to this end. The flaw in the tragic collision of opposites was one-sidedness on both sides. One extreme tended to call forth its opposite extreme. Instead of recognizing the corollary validity of the opposing principle, tragic heroes relentlessly pursue a singular claim, as in the *Antigone* of Sophocles where the demands of the state (Creon denying burial to Antigone's traitor brother) collide with the rights and duties of the family (Antigone determined that proper burial must be given). The only way out of the tragic dilemma is through acknowledgment that both values are part of a larger whole and more complete justice. This, for Hegel, was in accord with the proper movement of thought, and history itself, as diametrically opposed ideas and principles worked dialectically toward unifying positions that accommodated both.

Roger Sharrock sees this perspective as anticipated in the *Don Quixote* of Cervantes, though not necessarily aimed toward a synthesis, but satisfied with a juxtaposition and balancing of contraries:

> The essence of comedy in *Don Quixote* is the pairing of significant opposites who complement each other's qualities: they divide the world between their mutual obsessions. Quixotism rejects the world of appearances in favor of the ideal; Sanchism tries to limit its vision to the concrete and the visible. In the course of their unending dialogue they each undergo subtle conversions to the contrary point of view as well as fierce confrontations.[10]

In psychology it was Jung who led the way in a similar reading of the psyche as a balancing of the *animus* and *anima*, the interaction of conscious and unconscious, and the cooperation of individual and collective consciousness. In physics Niels Bohr proposed a principle of complementarity as a way of resolving the wave versus particle dispute over the nature of light, when some experiments suggested wave properties for light while others suggested particle properties. (Whether influenced by comedies or not, both Jung and Bohr were influenced, in part, by Oriental cosmologies.) In biology the study of the interaction of species with other species and with the natural environment has led to a parallel paradigm shift. Ecosystems move toward maintaining or restoring balance and equilibrium. A tragic reading of nature as life preying upon life is, at best, superficial, and at worst inappropriate. If anything, it is human beings who introduce the tragic dimension in exploitation of nature and disregard for delicate natural balances.

The Comic Vision

At the primitive level of hurling sticks and stones and insults, tragic clashes were not particularly lethal. And they could be contained within tolerable limits through diverting bellicose energies into rituals, games, fireside sagas, dances, and the hunt. Tensions could be vented harmlessly, and defeats rendered symbolic—as is also the case with jokes, comic rituals, humorous anecdotes, and taunting contests. What anthropologists have referred to as "joking relationships," for example, are instances of ritualized aggression (and acceptance) traditionally employed as a way of preserving peace between individuals, parties, or tribes. Joking, teasing, and pranks serve to defuse areas of tension and convert the mood to one of playfulness and gaming.

The result of such actions usually has been the maintenance of balance and harmony between competing interests or persons within the group, or between groups. In the modern world, however, given the rapidly escalating advances in science and technology, conflicts have become more and more deadly, while rituals of aggression/acceptance have had difficulty keeping pace—except, perhaps, in sports rivalries, from local teams to the international Olympics. Fanaticism and terrorism have certainly become more potent forces than ever before. Peoples with limited technology could only do so much damage to one another, property, or the environment. Now the introduction of long-range missiles and smart bombs and nuclear armaments into the arsenals of contending powers has brought the whole of human history to the brink of an irreversible tragic finale.

The comic vision has thus become increasingly difficult to maintain, and therefore increasingly necessary. As James Thurber once put it, "It is very hard to sustain humor, or the desire for humor, in a period when we seem to be trying, on the one hand, to invent a pill or a miracle drug that will cure us of everything, and on the other hand to invent machines of instant annihilation."[11] Yet it is even more imperative than ever that we understand and develop the peculiarly human gift of laughter, and the comic sensibilities it may express, if the possibility of greater tyrannies and holocausts is to be averted.

A major strength of the tragic spirit has also been its greatest weakness: namely, its exaltation of *warrior* virtues: courage, loyalty, duty, honor, pride, indomitable will, stubborn determination, passionate involvement, absolute devotion, uncompromising dedication. How brave and wholesome and right these virtues have sounded to us! How pervasively they have shaped our collective and individual consciousness! How indelibly they have colored our common understanding of what constitutes the heroic among us, and what it means to be authentically human!

Yet these virtues have so often led, indirectly if not directly, to all manner of evil. The dreams of one group of people collide with the dreams of another, creating a nightmare for both. The reigning ideology sacrifices all things—including truth—to itself. The just cause becomes the source of unimagined injustice. The holy war unleashes and legitimates a host of demonic forces. What is portrayed as the defense of certain noble concerns and sacred principles eventuates in death and destruction, including the death and destruction of other noble concerns and sacred principles. Perhaps the greatest irony of all in the tragic situation is that the one thing opposing parties agree upon is the very thing that drives the fateful process unremittingly forward: the tragic vision of life, with its tragic claims, its tragic virtues, and its tragic extremism and stubbornness.

In comedy, on the other hand, the warrior virtues of tragedy are critiqued and counterbalanced by another set of virtues: playfulness, childlikeness, humor, laughter, lightheartedness, meekness, humility, flexibility, moderation, willingness to compromise, sympathy and empathy, generosity, nurturing, affection, love. While the tragic hero is interested in law, justice, judgment, and retribution (e.g., Shylock in *The Merchant of Venice*), the comic hero is more inclined toward accommodation, compassion, forgiveness, and mercy (e.g., Portia and Antonio). Comic values are those of romance, courtship, marriage, home, children, family, birthdays, holidays, games, dancing, partying, and the day-to-day preoccupations of life.

One will immediately recognize in these comic virtues and values essentially the same as those identified in traditional Oriental cosmology as the feminine contribution of *yin*. In the comic vision existence is to be seen more in terms of play and game than work or war. Whether sumptuous or not, life is a feast and festival, not a series of battles and barroom brawls. The enjoyment and celebration of life, in its simplest and most fleeting moments, are of greater importance than the abstract principles and judgments to which they so often get sacrificed. The spirit that, untempered, brings with it absolutism, dogmatism, intolerance, fanaticism, terrorism, unconditional demand, and unyielding obstinance is understood as the highest folly—however correct, devoted, and courageous it may seem. The tragic hero insists, with Luther: "Here I stand, I can do no other." The comic hero seeks common ground and not only imagines other standpoints but some place for the other to stand. Accommodation is not viewed as weakness or treason, but as fairness, generosity, magnanimity, and openness. Confrontations are to be avoided in favor of consensus.

The comic vision possesses a greater appreciation for the muddiness of human nature—even in its noblest aspirations and righteous pretensions—and of the ambiguities of truth and goodness. Hence there is an immediate inclination to see truth and goodness in other perspectives, and acknowledge the limitations of one's own. People and circumstances are not so neatly divisible into black and white, light and dark, right and wrong, or superior and inferior, as tragic heroism would suggest as a basis for its sterling commitment and inflexible stand. Comedy mixes and confounds all rigid categories and fixed identities—as Chaplin did for so many years with his tramp figure in ragged and ill-fitting but genteel clothing. The comic hero occupies a kind of neutral zone between competing forces, and reveals a humanity common to both. It is the same logic that makes the best mediators those who are not completely identifiable with either side in a dispute—as in the case of Philip Habib, one-time U.S. mediator between the Israelis and Palestinians in Lebanon, who was himself a Christian Arab from Lebanon, raised in a Jewish neighborhood in New York City!

Comic vision is double-vision, as distinct from the highly focused, riveted, even tunnel vision of tragedy. Sometimes this is literally represented by a comic figure who is cross-eyed or wall-eyed. Instead of the unswerving, singleminded, if not obsessive concentration of the tragic hero, the comic hero has a broader, if less focused, vision. The comic hero entertains other possibilities, offers more than one point of view, wanders this way and that, and is inclined to vacillate and equivocate. Tragic vision has the eyes of the hunter, which conveniently for stalking purposes are directed forward, as in most carnivores. Comic vision has the eyes of the hunted—for example the rabbit—which are usually located on the sides of the head for maximum sight in all directions, and thus are more suited to survival—of the individual and the species. Despite the disadvantages of double vision with its lack of narrow focus, a more peripheral vision can take in all the scenery, tolerate frequent distractions, receive images from opposite positions, and move at a moment's notice in any direction.

The spirit of comic mediation may be illustrated by a story which Robert Benchley told of himself as an undergraduate at Harvard. He was confronted by an examination question in a course on international law concerning a dispute between the United States and Great Britain over fishing rights. The students were asked to discuss the issues from the respective points of view of the two countries. Benchley wrote: "I know nothing about the point of view of Great Britain, and nothing about the point of view of the United States. Therefore, I shall discuss the question from the point of view of the fish!"[12]

The comic vision is, as it were, the fish's eye view. It is a vantage point that stands apart from the immediate circumstances and positions of the fray. It is not totally immersed in the seriousness of the moment, or a particular cause, or the all-consuming struggle. It is, therefore, a perspective from which issues and situations can be seen from an unusual or unexpected angle. The tragic impasse is transcended in order to stand more firmly within the flesh-and-blood of the human condition. Tragic disputants are seen as locked in mortal combat over bloodless doctrines, willing to offer up unlimited persons and properties to intangible concerns, such as pride, honor, duty, or revenge. Comedy counters, accordingly, by parodying tragic action and the tragic passions and values that sustain it, turning attention instead to the immediacies of life and the judgments of common sense.

There are, of course, those ultraserious types who claim not to be opposed to the comic as such but to consider it largely inappropriate—considering, that is, the current state of the union and the universe. This is not the time and place for humor, only for diligence and vigilance. Playfulness of spirit is a frivolous and irresponsible luxury. There are letters to be written to congressional representatives, picket signs to be carried, committees to be organized, politicians to be badgered, votes to be garnered, opponents to be debated, corporations and administrations to be hounded, enemies to be defeated. There is little room for parades and balloons and anecdotes and idle chatter. With steeled jaw and knitted brow, looking neither to the right nor to the left, such humorless crusaders are unwilling and perhaps no longer able to laugh, as long as "the cause" has not been victorious, injustice prevails, poverty and pollution persist, warfare continues, textbooks are inaccurate, magazines are sexist—in short, as long as there is evil and suffering in the world—which is to say that they are not likely to be free to laugh in the near future.

To all such one must say: Blessed are they that can laugh outside the gates of Paradise and the New Jerusalem, and who there can give and receive the gift of laughter. Blessed are they who are not determined to wait until lions lie down with lambs, and who can pray, "O God, though I do not live in the Garden of Eden I am nevertheless still glad to be here."

Among the Kurnai of Australia is a myth in which the waters of the earth had been swallowed by a great frog named Dak. The thirsty animals tried to get Dak to cough up the waters, but their efforts were in vain. Dak greedily remained stubborn and adamant. There was a stalemate between

Dak and the other animals. Finally the snake began twisting and rolling about in a most comical fashion. Dak tried to maintain a straight face with resolute determination, but could not—whereupon Dak burst out laughing, and the waters streamed forth to soak the parched earth.[13]

The Kurnai mythmakers were primarily interested in the water, but for anyone interested in the laughter as well, the imagery of the tale may be given another meaning: Laughter bursts out of the small world of our seriousness and greed and self-importance and allows the water of life to flow freely to all, relieving the dryness and barrenness of our parched spirits. Obstinancy and recalcitrance are relaxed, while energies are diverted from a hostile standoff and an otherwise violent conclusion. Thus does comedy intervene in the tragic seriousness with which we take ourselves, our rights and principles, introducing a different spirit and more inclusive vision. The legless snake dances before the intransigent frog.

2

The Agony And The Golden Mean—
The Comic Hero

*Now what else is the whole life of mortals but a sort
of comedy in which the various actors, disguised by
various costumes and masks, walk on and play each
one his part, until the manager waves them off the stage?*

—Erasmus, *The Praise of Folly* (1509)

As theatrical and literary forms, both tragedy and comedy as we know them came out of ancient Greece, especially in association with dramatic contests at the temple of Dionysus in Athens. It is instructive that the earliest tragedies were not "tragic" in the intractable sense in which we often use the word. As interpreters from Hegel to Walter Kerr have pointed out, one of the goals of Greek tragedy was to achieve a resolution after having worked through the conflicts involved. And if that paradigm had prevailed, perhaps Western civilization would have been less inclined to associate heroism with extreme polarization and confrontation, and more inclined to associate heroism with accommodation and reconciliation. Early tragedies began, to be sure, with a collision of forces and values. The first two plays in a tragic trilogy identified these "worlds in collision" (the *agon*), with the first play representing the conflict from the side of one party (the pro*tagon*ist) and the second play taking the position of the other party (the an*tagon*ist). The dilemmas involved were *agon*ized over, injustices decried, lamentations made. Truth, goodness, and justice (as well as error, evil, and injustice) were seen in both positions. Then, in the final play the opposing forces and values were brought into some sort of resolution.

Thus, in the third play of Aeschylus' *Oresteia* justice is said to be achieved, compensation made, and parties reconciled. In the first play Clytemnestra murders her husband Agamemnon in vengeance for the sacrifice of their daughter. In the second play their son Orestes avenges his father by murdering his mother. In both cases some measure of justice, and injustice, is attached to the murders. In the third play, justice is visited on Orestes for murdering his mother by the Furies who drive him to the brink of madness. Yet, since there was also some justification for his actions, aided by Apollo and Athena, he is absolved and freed.

When comedies were added to the theatrical venue at the temple of Dionysus in Athens and performed following the tragic trilogy, they had something to celebrate. Comedies expressed the sense of resolution and release achieved in the tragic compromise. With conflicts and tensions reduced, there could be a season of laughter, playfulness, and good cheer. Nonsense, foolishness, and lighthearted banter were appropriate to the resolution achieved. The agony of the *agon* was replaced by a festival atmosphere.

The Tragic Compromise

Perhaps Hegel saw the triadic movement of tragedy so clearly because it corresponded to his philosophy of history, with its pattern of thesis, antithesis, and synthesis. Or did Hegel's study of early tragedy suggest this dialectic as the pattern of historical movement? In either case, the plays of the early Greek tragedian, Aeschylus, are instructive. In his Promethean trilogy, Prometheus' defense of his theft of fire is established in *Prometheus Bound*—unfortunately, the only play fully extant. Another play (*Prometheus the Firebringer*) presumably presented the case of Zeus and the other gods of Olympus for their punishment of Prometheus, while the third play (*Prometheus Unbound*) effects an accommodation of both sides. The trilogy follows the main outlines of the myth as told three centuries before in Hesiod's *Works and Days* and his *Theogony*. Prometheus stole the sacred fire from the altar of the Olympian gods and gave the fire to mortals. For this rebellious action he has been chained to a Scythian cliff, where the eagle of Zeus comes daily to gnaw at his immortal liver. Prometheus, however, is totally unrepentant and uncompromising. Instead, in *Prometheus Bound* he gives an eloquent defense of his gift of fire—and hence civilization—to mortals heretofore kept in bestial ignorance. Through him have come reason, technology, crafts, mathematics, writing, medicine, agriculture, and metallurgy: "In short, all the arts have come to mortals from Prometheus." For this he has become the suffering savior of humanity. He acknowledges no guilt; instead it is the gods who have been quite unfair in hoarding fire, and unjust in subjecting him to this suffering. He remains defiant.

Prometheus the Firebringer (probably the first play in the trilogy) may well have offered an equally eloquent defense of the prerogatives of the gods, of their warnings concerning the usurpation of divine power by humans, of the dangers of *hubris*, and thus of the justice in the punishment of Prometheus and the visitation of plagues upon mortals. Prometheus is a thief and rebel, not the Robin Hood he claims to be. He is also a trickster. He had helped mortals deceive the gods by giving disguised bones and fat in sacrifice to the gods, keeping the meaty portion for themselves, whereupon the gods had withheld fire from humans—so they would have to eat their meat raw!

In the third play, judging from the title alone (*Prometheus Lyomenos*: "unloosed"), Prometheus is released from his agony and banishment. He and Zeus are reconciled, perhaps through an ancient form of plea bargaining! And the effects of his gifts to mortals—making them more like the gods in knowledge and power—are effectively countered by the gift to mortals of Pandora and her jar of plagues. Thus, a compromise is achieved, and the cosmic balance restored, both among the gods and between gods and mortals.

With playwrights such as Euripides and Sophocles, however, we see an ominous shift in the tragic drama. We are given tragic collisions for which there are no compromises or resolutions forthcoming. Conflicting parties or principles or forces are left in mortal combat and mutual destruction. And it is this view of tragedy—both in real life and in theatrical or literary drama—which has dominated Western self-understanding ever since. Euripides' *Trojan Women* begins with Troy devastated and all the heroes slain, leaving the widows, mothers, and daughters to pick up the broken pieces of their lives. As with other holocausts, it is unclear whether it is better to be among the survivors or the dead. Great is the lamentation over past glories and persons, and anxiety for the seeming bleakness of the future. The play ends more or less where it has begun: in the midst of the *agon*; in the midst of suffering and despair. The drama was left at that stark and bleak point, without another play to bring about some more satisfying resolution of the agony—without even a few pious platitudes, or suggestion of larger meanings in the wanton death and destruction.

Sophocles' plays tended in this direction. *Antigone, Electra, Oedipus Tyrannus* depict conflicts largely in their unredeemed and unredeemable agony. The plays are almost entirely focused in the pathos of the tragic *agon*. A certain course of action is carried through tenaciously to the bitter end. A certain heroism is displayed, but it is purchased at great expense and with great suffering. A certain justice is achieved, but it is harsh and hard-won. If Aeschylus had produced only the first two plays of his Promethean trilogy, we would have had a similar result: a dramatic action, deadlocked in antithesis, with no synthesis offered or seemingly offerable. Stalemated by colliding and uncompromising opposites, the conflicting courses of action would carry irrevocably through to their shattering conclusions.

To this day Western civilization seems to have been destined—or determined—to read human conflicts in such tragic terms, and to derive a bittersweet catharsis out of re-enacting a heroism in the midst of tragic clashes and "inevitabilities." Shakespeare's *King Lear* and *Hamlet*, and Sartre's *Nausea* and *No Exit*, seem fated to come to inexorable ends, moving however nobly down a descending staircase into regions of darkness, destruction, death, and decay. For all the heroics, "head bloody but unbowed," and all the nobility of character, the prevailing tragic mood becomes one of anguished lamentation, defiant resignation, forlorn despair. So *Lear* ends with Albany saying, mournfully, "the weight of this sad time we must obey." So *Romeo and Juliet* ends even more sadly:

> A glooming peace this morning with it brings;
>   The sun for sorrow will not show his head:
> Go hence, to have more talk of these sad things;
>   Some shall be pardon'd and some punished:
> For never was a story of more woe
> Than this of Juliet and her Romeo.

"The master image of tragedy," in the words of John Jones, "is that of playing with fire." Tragedies are left attempting to salvage something from the ashes. Often the chorus or a god or one of the actors delivers a word of warning concerning untoward action, dangerous pride, or vindictiveness— usually unheeded or too late. Some word of consolation, also, is generally offered in the end, like hope stuck in the lid of Pandora's jar of plagues. There needs to be a minimal resolution, or thread of purpose, or dim prospect, so that life can go on again. Some lesson is said to be learned, some knowledge gained, some wrong righted, some guilt assuaged. Some truth, however horrible, is revealed; some murder avenged (often by another murder). Whether it is worth all the suffering and carnage and sorrow, it is the best that can be gleaned from the field of circumstances with which the tragedy begins and by means of which it proceeds. No matter how great the bloodbath and the anguish, tragedies are still inclined to conclude the ritual performance with a benediction.

So does Sophocles' version of the *Oresteia* (*Electra*) end abruptly with Orestes' vengeful murder of his mother and her lover, while the chorus, in the final lines of the play, sounds the benedictory chant: "O house of Atreus, through how many sufferings hast thou come forth at last in freedom, crowned with good by this day's enterprise!" And there is blood all over the place!

Of course, tragedians are not necessarily recommending tragedy or the tragic hero or tragic heroism. They may be realistically portraying what has occurred historically; or what often does occur, but might be avoided in the future through the bitter lessons of tragic rehearsal—as in Shakespeare's tragedies where the fool performs the function of commenting on the foolishness of those in tragic conflict, while attempting to introduce some saving elements of playfulness and humor. There are those modern tragedians, of course, for whom existence as such is so fundamentally tragic, or given to the tragic, that such a lesson itself is what is to be learned from tragedy, along with its corollary, that tragedy therefore is inevitable, and we must face the stark realities as bravely as we can—a point to which, at least, some modern tragedians seem to come: Conrad, Kafka, Mann, Malraux, Sartre, and others.

In Greek tragedy the purpose of the tragic drama was to work through the tragic *agon* and, if possible, wrest from it something of lasting value. Even if a natural resolution of the conflict did not present itself to the dramatist, a device such as the *deus ex machina* might be used, as in the *Oresteia* of Euripedes. In the third play of the trilogy, a god or goddess (here Athena) descends to the stage in a basket and sorts things out like a federal mediator. Divine arbitration had the authority and prerogative of the "arbitrariness of the gods." The highest court of appeal was not human reason or an earthly tribunal but the "will of the gods." Perhaps that is where the tragedies of life end, after all, in a kind of divine mystery, and, if not in a reconciliation of parties or forces, a reconciliation to the situation.

The Comic Alternative

Where does comedy fit into all of this? At least in ancient Greece comedies, along with the (also humorous) satyr plays, were placed after the tragic performance. Interestingly, this was (and is still) done in Japan, where the equivalent of the tragedy, the *Noh* drama, with its similar background in the warrior virtues and conflicts of the Samurai class, is followed by the *Kyogen* play (literally, "crazy words"). Traditional performances would last most of a day and evening, interspersing three to five *Noh* plays with *Kyogen* skits. At the minimum, this association of comedy with tragedy, whether in ancient Greece or in medieval to modern Japan, has provided a comic release from the tension and weightiness of the tragic drama. Comedies, thereby, offer an emotional counterbalance to the emotions elicited by tragedy. One can breath a sigh of relief, and a bit of fresh air. Laughter replaces tears.

Comedies have also offered a renewed sense of the celebration of life. In the case of those tragedies that achieved a significant resolution and reconciliation, the comedies that followed could function as celebrations of the rapprochement, like the shouting and dancing in the streets at the end of a war. Comedy expressed the liberation and newfound harmony that had been worked out. The satyr play in Greece expressed this, too, with its parody of some heroic legend or myth, as in Euripides *Cyclops* which *satir*ized an episode from Homer's *Odyssey*. Quite humorous, for example, is the scene in which Odysseus gets the Cyclops drunk, and the Cyclops comes to the conclusion that his stomach, glowing with wine, is the "greatest of gods."

With the development of tragedies which left matters in a tragic collision, it then fell to comedies and comic satire to do something more. Comedies begin to propose alternative scenarios; they introduce a different spirit; they recommend other kinds of virtues; they insist on another scale of values, with very different things given value. Some comedies begin to lead the way toward bringing reconciliation about. Even more ambitiously, some suggest ways of avoiding the tragic landscape in the first place. Writers of comedy, very early in the genre, began to debunk tragic extremism, its heroic virtues, its demand for vengeance, its burden of guilt, its gigantic passions, its absolutism and absolute seriousness. In the face of the tragic labyrinth, comedians offered comic solutions to tragic dilemmas.

Aristophanes, for example, suggests a charming comic compromise in one of his plays, *Lysistrata* (414 B.C.E.). Two cities have been involved in interminable warfare. The allusion is to the long-standing conflict between Athens and Sparta, a rift in Greek civilization which was one of the likely sources of the Greek attraction for the tragic. The women of both cities have grown weary of seeing their husbands or lovers always going off to the battlefield, sacrificing the normal joys of life and home for patriotic ideals and military codes of honor. Many have also returned wounded or maimed, or have been killed in the name of loyalty, duty, pride, and manliness.

Led by Lysistrata, the women of both cities agree to a common course of action. They go on a "sex strike." An ultimatum is delivered to both sides for unconditional surrender. No more sex, and no more bag lunches, will be forthcoming until the men of both sides give up their foolish flag waving and vain bravado and heroic talk. At first the men are determined to tough it out. They don't really need women, and they would rather fight than anything else. They refuse to be threatened or intimidated by mere womenfolk. But by the end of the comedy the men of both sides give up and come home, "tails" between their legs. "Make love, not war" wins the day. And life returns to the simple pursuits of wife, children, friends, job, and yard work. These are the people and things most important after all.

Tragic heroism makes dogmatic claims for itself, its virtues and principles, its immutable laws and eternal ideals, and takes great pride in doing so. Its system of values and beliefs is absolute and closed, like the law of the Medes and the Persians that cannot be changed. In comedy, however, the rule of law is better understood as the rule of thumb or the rules of the game. There are other ways of playing the game, and other games to be played. The comic vision protests against all finite claims to the infinite. Pride and pretension are gleefully derided, along with the rigidity of person and regulation that accompanies an intractable spirit. All claims to unquestionable truth and all aspirations to godlikeness are as vanity and a chasing after the wind. "Pride goes before destruction, and a haughty spirit before a fall" (Proverbs 16:18). And comedy wishes to help that fall along a bit. Comedy effects pratfalls in the hope of avoiding devastating falls and avalanches.

Consider a contemporary comic tale. For decades two cities in Mexico have been claiming to have the skull of the revolutionary hero, Benito Juarez, who died of apoplexy in 1872 while serving as president of Mexico. Both cities had set up shrines, and could offer passionate, if not completely convincing arguments as to why theirs was the one true skull of Juarez. Finally, after decades of wrangling and ill feelings, the Mexican government decided to try to settle the dispute once and for all. Physical anthropologists were brought in to examine the skulls and determine which claim could be substantiated. One of the anthropologists, realizing they were in a no-win situation, whichever city they agreed with, proposed an ingenious solution. In measuring the skulls it had been observed that one of the skulls was larger than the other. The solution: the larger skull is indeed that of Juarez when he died of apoplexy at the age of sixty-six; however, the smaller skull is also that of Juarez as a boy of thirteen!

While this might be said to be an unlikely solution, and literally preposterous, it is a good example of the comic impulse. The tragic inclination would be to see the dispute in either/or terms. Certainly that is the way the two cities, and the government, saw it. But the comic inclination is to change the rules, in this case of logic, so that neither side would lose and both would be included in the final determination.

The Comic Middle

This spirit and approach leads to a comic inclusivism, in contrast to the exclusivism of the tragic view. Competing canons and claims must be relativized, and both incorporated in a larger, more flexible world view. In the comic society both vertical exclusivisms (e.g., superior/ inferior) and horizontal exclusivisms (e.g., rival claimants, friend and foe,) are moderated in favor of a complementary and more equalitarian view of relationships. Shakespeare, though anything but an egalitarian, nevertheless creates in Falstaff a marvelously mediating figure who stands (and falls) between nobility and the populace. So does Sir Toby Belch in *Twelfth Night,* who combines the "Sir" of the gentleman with the belch of the tavern bumpkin. Owing to such mediation, comic relationships are marked by a strong sense of fellow-feeling, with an air of openness and freedom. Those who are puffed up are deflated, while those who have been deflated by the proud are defended. The words reported of Jesus could well serve as the motto of such comedy: "Everyone who exalts himself will be humbled, and he who humbles himself will be exalted" (Luke 14:11 RSV). What is taken from the one is given to the other, freely and to all.

The tragic figure is prevented from such generosity because of a consuming interest in nobility, honor, prestige, and rectitude. Heroism, superiority, number-one-ness, saving face, national pride, vengeance, tenacity at all cost: these are tragic concerns. Comedies counter by paying particular attention to ordinary affairs—including the ordinary affairs of the high and the mighty—and to ordinary people. Comic concerns are simple and mundane. Relative to the sublime heights to which tragic heroism often aspires, this may seem ridiculous. But relative to the abysmal depths to which tragic heroes sometimes fall, and cause others to fall, here there is wisdom and grace.

In ancient Greece, while the tragedians were representing humanity in terms of gods and kings *(Prometheus, Oedipus)*, the comedians often responded by making heroes of average people or improbable people *(Lysistrata)*, or by reminding those with godlike aspirations of our affiliation with the animals (Aristophanes' *Birds, Wasps,* and *Frogs,* or the horse-men and goat-men of satyr plays). Similarly, Shakespeare's tragedies dwelt on the affairs of a host of kings and queens, princes and princesses, noble lords and ladies, military heroes: *Lear, Macbeth, Othello, Hamlet, Romeo and Juliet, Antony and Cleopatra, Julius Caesar.* His comedies, on the other hand, belong more to the world of merchants, moneylenders, taverns, and bedchambers: *The Taming of the Shrew, The Merry Wives of Windsor, All's Well That Ends Well, The Merchant of Venice, Comedy of Errors, As You Like It, Much Ado About Nothing.*

Even though Shakespeare passionately defended the status, privileges, and responsibilities of royalty and nobility, which he saw as threatened—and was in this sense an arch-conservative loyalist of the feudal order—the very character of comedy itself drew his comedies toward the social middle. The center of gravity for comedy is in the more basic, common, and therefore universal human concerns of daily life, as evident in Falstaff's lack of enthusiasm for fighting but considerable enthusiasm for lovemaking, victuals, wine, and poaching. Because of Shakespeare's aristocratic bias, and with the primary audience of his plays being the

Elizabethan elite, his comedies were heavily predisposed to include the lowliest folk as the butt of jokes. So we are given a myriad of proletarian figures with quite unflattering names: Bottom, Wart, Snout, Mouldy, Simple, Pinch, Elbow, Dogberry, Dull, Sly, Bullcalf, Puck, Starveling, Snug, Speed, Moth, Gobbo, Froth. On the other hand, there are clowns such a Feste and Touchstone who are quite gifted and wise and whose names suggest positive features. There are also knighted figures who are comic characters: Sir John Falstaff, Sir Toby Belch, Sir Andrew Augecheek.

For all of Shakespeare's love of nobles and nobility, it is surprising—and suggestive of the larger sympathies of comedy—that in *All's Well That Ends Well* he departs from the tale in the *Decameron* on which the comedy is based. Instead of the heroine Helena being daughter of a rich physician attached to the court, Shakespeare makes Helena the daughter of a poor physician, and she is in love with a man well beyond her station: Bertram, Count of Rousillon. There is some upward mobility, even in Shakespeare, available through the lighter, freer world of comedy.

Shakespeare's comic world, to be sure, is hardly the comic world of Chaplin's Tramp. They come to comedy from opposite ends of the social spectrum. Yet through comedy both tend toward the "comic mean" as they deal with fundamental, and therefore universal human concerns, and as they create comic characters that mediate the extremes of the human hierarchy. Chaplin's Tramp is the paradoxical union of gentleman and bum; Sir John is a gentleman, and associate of princes and noblemen, who is also a quite "regular fellow." Shakespeare comes down to comedy from above; Chaplin up from below—as did Shakespeare's younger contemporary, Ben Jonson, who caricatured the foibles of the aristocracy with such sobriquets as Sir Epicure Mammon, Lady Haughty, Sir Eitherside, Sir Amorous La-Foole, Sir Diaphanous Silkworm! As medieval and Renaissance fool literature suggests, there is enough foolishness to go around. Fools and their folly neither know nor obey class distinctions.

Given Chaplin's lowly origins, it is understandable that he would have had some difficulty with the Shakespearean world. Even as *Sir* Charles Chaplin, and a right wealthy gentleman of leisure living on his Swiss estate, he wrote in his *Autobiography*: "I dislike Shakespearean themes involving kings, queens, august people and their honor.... In my pursuit of bread and cheese, honor was seldom trafficked in. I cannot identify myself with a prince's problems."[1] Still, these concerns, while fundamental to the Shakespearean histories and tragedies, are much softened in the comedies, their place taken by more ordinary concerns, such as bread and cheese, and a different set of problems, such as bed and breakfast.

One is put in mind of the passage in Cervantes' *Don Quixote* where Sancho is invited, somewhat patronizingly, by his knight to eat at his table, "that you may be even as I who am your master and natural lord." To which Sancho replies:

> Many thanks...but if it is all the same to your grace...I can eat just as well, or better, standing up and alone as I can seated beside an emperor. And if the truth must be told, I enjoy much more that which I eat in my own corner without any bowings and scrapings, even though it be only bread and onions, than I do a meal of roast turkey where I have to chew slowly, drink little, be always wiping my mouth, and can neither sneeze nor cough if I feel like it.

A Comic Embrace

Theorists, from Aristotle on, have contended that tragedy portrays the actions of noble and superior people, displaying great dignity and determination in the face of seemingly insuperable odds or inexorable fates. Comedy is seen as portraying those who are common, inferior, if not vulgar, as they confront the ordinary, even trivial, issues of the marketplace, courtship, home, job, and neighborhood. In the *Poetics* Aristotle classified tragedy with beauty, while comedy was classified with ugliness. Tragic action is sublime; comic action is ludicrous. Tragedy depicts people as above the average; comedy as below it. The result ever since is, as Maurice Charney has argued:

> We have been thoroughly indoctrinated in the belief...that tragedy is "more serious" than other genres and, therefore, more significant, more profound, more meaningful as an imitation (or "mimesis") of human experience. In Shakespeare studies there is a whole subindustry of criticism devoted to discovering dark implications, tragic overtones, ironic undercutting in otherwise lighthearted romantic comedies.[2]

This is to measure comedy by the standards of tragedy. Comedy measures tragedy from the standpoint of comedy. From the perspective of comedy, it is precisely such values and assumptions, and their bleak and bloody consequences, that are being challenged. Fools in their foolishness unmask the foolishness of the wise. Simpletons in their simplicity have a solid grasp of those earthy matters that life is mostly about: food, fun, sex, love, family, friends, and a good night's sleep. Clowns positively delight in confounding and collapsing all those aristocracies of status, profundity, or worth with which we establish our various elites. Ordinary values are not superficial but basic; ordinary people are not ignoble, but the salt of the earth. The considerable tragic interest in the honorable and the heroic is seen as participating in the ludicrous, while the ludicrous may be found to contain something of honor and heroism. As in the modern tale of *The Elephant Man*, out of the most horrible deformities may shine forth the noblest of spirits.

Comedy is the great leveler. Kings become servants, and servants become kings. The hypocrisies of the self-righteous are exposed, and the virtues of rogues are revealed. Malicious gossips become victims of their own malicious gossiping. Beautiful people are splattered with mud, and Cinderellas are fitted with glass slippers. Even an Archie Bunker, who was a veritable fountainhead of racial and ethnic slurs, was embraced by comedy for all the warts on his soul; and, in turn, he could embrace real polacks and real blacks and real draft-dodgers in a shared humanity. When comedy is blatantly elitist or prejudiced it is usually in parody—like Basil Fawlty expressing his hopes for a finer clientele in *Fawlty Towers*: "a better class of people...not the riff-raff we get in here."

In comedy the very distinctions that separate us into our various social, racial, ethnic, and religious battlements and our vain hierarchies of relative worth are moderated, suspended, or turned upside down. Valuational discriminations, likewise, are challenged: sacred and profane, important an unimportant, wise and foolish. Beggars are invited to the banquet table; slaves are set free; privates behave like generals; children are proclaimed king and queen for the day; the last person to cross the finish line receives the trophy; the clever are outwitted by innocents; swaggerers get their come-uppance; former enemies forgive and forget; fools specialize—as in *King Lear*—in "taking one's part that's out of favor" (I.iv.100). Such is the peculiar fare of comedy. The result of all this is that people are brought closer together in a spirit of camaraderie and the celebration of a common existence. The revelations of tragedy may lead to alienation, guilt, rage, and horror; the revelations of comedy lead to humility and good humor.

In Shakespearean comedy, as Northrop Frye notes, the most roguish and marginal characters are included in the celebration, rather than excluded:

> When we find Falstaff invited to the final feast in *The Merry Wives*, Caliban reprieved [in *the Tempest*], attempts made to mollify Malvolio [in *Twelfth Night*], and Angelo [*Measure for Measure*] and Parolles [*All's Well That Ends Well*] allowed to live down their disgrace, we are seeing a fundamental principle of comedy at work. The tendency of the comic society to include rather than exclude is the reason for the traditional importance of the parasite, who has no business to be at the final festival but is nevertheless there.[3]

One might also add that at the end of *Two Gentlemen of Verona* the Duke pardons the robber band that has captured him, restoring them to citizenship.

"Comedy," argues Walter Kerr, "at its most penetrating derives from what we normally regard as tragic."[4] While in an extrinsic sense this may be true of those comedies that have a direct relationship to tragic dramas, in an intrinsic sense this suggests a misleading "second fiddle" or parasitic image of comedy. Comedy is seen as derivative, with its themes and impetus and substance originating in tragedy. Yet to speak of "comedy at its most penetrating" already presupposes the terms and values of tragedy, which comedy is questioning. Apart from the happenstance that comedies were officially introduced in Greek theater and competition in 486 B.C.E. fifty years after tragedies (535 B.C.E.), comedy *derives* from a fundamental joy of life, delight in life, celebration of life. The source and inspiration of comedy is not tragedy but playfulness and lightheartedness—a certain spirited friskiness that human beings refuse to give up entirely, regardless of how old they are, and even in the midst of suffering and tragedy. Comedy is not a subspecies of ugliness, but of play.

Tragedies, in fact, are often very threatening to that life, and buoyancy of life, that comedies hold so dear. Tragedies lay down all sorts of conditions that might make life worth living, yet as a result of which life is subject to guilt, grief, and despair. Comedy reaffirms the unconditional value of life itself. Tragic heroes are willing to kill and be killed for all sorts of reasons extraneous to life and survival, like Medea in the horrendous climax of Euripides' *Medea*, who torches Jason's intended bride and slaughters the children she has had by Jason. Comedies are biologically and psychologically sound. Tragedies spin out tales of threat to life, limb, and sanity.

What defines the tragic figure is not, as Aristotle would have it, that the hero is better than the common run of people, but is one given to greater extremes pursued with admirable, yet fanatical and foolhardy, tenacity. As Henry Myers puts it:

> To reach his goal, whatever it may be, he is always willing to sacrifice everything else, including his life. Oedipus will press the search for the unknown murderer, although he is warned of the consequences; Hamlet will prove the King's guilt and attempt to execute perfect justice, whatever the cost may be to his mother, to Laertes, to Ophelia, and to himself; Ibsen's Solness will climb the tower he has built, at the risk of falling into the quarry; Ahab will kill Moby Dick or die in the attempt.[5]

Comedies, too, can make a considerable mess out of most any situation; yet the messes of comedy are hardly to be compared with the catastrophes of tragedy. Thus, while it may be true that some comedies draw upon similar themes and conflicts to those found in tragedies, this is in order to return tragic extremism to the joy of life and the basics of life. When the burdens of life come, and innocence is shattered, comedy still insists on affirming life, renewing life, playing with life, delighting in life, and is not easily overwhelmed. Comedy also insists that the tragic spirit has to work through so much suffering and woe because it has abandoned the comic spirit in the first place.

Tyrannosaurus Rex

These aspects of the comic vision have, perhaps, never been stated more succinctly than by Chaplin at the end of his last "silent" film, *The Great Dictator* (1940). As a refugee Jewish barber who is fleeing the burning ghettos and Nazi roundup of Jews, he is mistaken for the German dictator. Instead of being taken to a prison camp, he is chauffeured to a nearby Nazi rally where the Führer has been scheduled to speak. Hesitantly and haltingly "he" begins, to the consternation of the audience:

> I'm sorry, but I don't want to be an emperor. That's not my business. I don't want to rule or conquer anyone. I should like to help everyone—if possible—Jew, Gentile, black men, white. We all want to help one another. Human beings are like that. We want to live by each other's happiness—not by each other's misery. We don't want to hate and despise one another. In this world there is room for everyone. And the good earth is rich and can provide for everyone.[6]

The film was conceived in 1937, produced during 1938 and 1939, and finally released in 1940 before the United States had gotten into

World War II. Ironically, it was immediately opposed by Americans who were variously pro-German, anti-Semitic, pro-Nazi, antisocialist, and/or anti-Stalinist. The *New York Daily News* accused Chaplin of being a communist sympathizer and of preaching socialism. Hitler, after all, was an avowed enemy of communism and Stalinism. The social message of this, like almost all of Chaplin's films, seemed suspiciously Marxist in lampooning the rich and powerful, while defending street vendors, blue collar workers, the unemployed, orphans, and homeless tramps. Chaplin was hauled before zealous officials of the Hays Office (precursor of the House Un-American Activities Committee). He became the target of the political right, which wanted to make a public example of him.

The charges continued to haunt him after the war, into the Cold War and the McCarthy era. Even more ironically, he was refused reentry into the United States in 1952, when he had taken his family on vacation to Europe, unless he would agree to stand trial for un-American activities and moral turpitude! Chaplin declined and after forty years of success and acclamation in the U.S., made Switzerland his permanent home. Such are the occupational hazards of comic heroes in entering an otherwise tragic arena, or in targeting the rich and powerful, while elevating the lowly in their stead. But Chaplin the multimillionaire, Chaplin the renowned actor and producer, Chaplin the world-celebrity, had never forgotten what it meant to be penniless and homeless and orphaned.

This was Chaplin's first sermon. It was a long sermon, and one quite out of character for Charlie who had previously only broken silence by singing in French as a waiter in *Modern Times* (1936), and by speaking in mock-German at an earlier point in *The Great Dictator* as the Führer addressed a mass rally. Perhaps it was not the best of sermons, or—from the standpoint of the aesthetics of filmmaking—the best of endings. Yet it was Charlie, trying bravely to put into words what, for twenty-five years, he had been saying through pantomime. Essentially, and at its best, it is the credo of the comic hero. And we are indebted to a great comic artist for putting it so simply, as in his pantomime he put it so eloquently.

W. H. Auden was of the opinion that tyrants such as Hitler were not fit subjects of humor, because the extremities of fear, suffering, evil, and hatred that center in such figures remove them from the possibilities of humor or comic representation.[7] Chaplin himself expressed misgivings about *The Great Dictator*, following the war, when the extent of the devastation and the horrors of Nazi concentration camps and gas chambers were revealed. Yet comic heroism in such a context becomes even more heroic for taking on the darkest and hardest and most sinister situations, not just providing after-dinner entertainment.

· "Comedy thrives on tyranny," argues Daniel Gerould. "Even in the depths of secret prisons and concentration camps, the comic spirit under tyranny emerges as a positive force, necessary for survival and, indeed, liberating and heroic."[8] Gerould documents this from a number of twentieth-century plays: Brecht's *The Resistible Rise of Arturo Ui*, Toller's *Wotan Unbound*, Romains' *Dr. Knock*, Ferrero's *The Naked King*, and so on. The greatest of tyrants are also the greatest of fools, and as such they are not only fit but necessary subjects of comedy. Going back to medieval plays, tyrants were held up for deserved ridicule and indirect political warning. Using historical examples, Pharaoh, Caesar, Herod, and Pilate were portrayed as braggarts, blusterers, and pompous idolaters, speaking nonsense with great authority, ordering impossibilities, or flying childishly into uncontrollable rages and tantrums.

In all this we can see clearly represented the effect of what Peter Berger has called "the humanizing quality of the comic perspective on the social drama." Berger then adds:

As little men put on their terrifying masks and headgears and war rattles, and march into the arena with solemn chants, there is always some old lady who smiles at them, not unkindly, and suggests that the boys go play elsewhere where they cannot hurt anybody.[9]

3

Tragic Castles And Comic Cottages— The Rogue

*It is told of Saint Maurus that when the pagans put
him in boiling water, he complained that the bath
was too cold; the pagan governor foolishly put his
hand in the water to test it, and burned himself.*

—Umberto Eco, *The Name of the Rose*[1]

According to a medieval collection of tales, King Solomon was once visited by a wandering fool from the east named Marcolf. He is described as a dwarf with carrot-red hair, the lips of a horse, the ears of an ass, and the beard of a goat—in short, ugly. He announced himself before the king by giving a mock pedigree: "I am of the kindred of the Churls. Rusticus begat Rustam; Rusta begat Rustum; Rustus begat Rusticellu; Rusticellus begat Tarcum; Tarcus begat Tarcol; Tarcollus begat Pharsi; Pharsus begat Marcuel; Marcus begat Marquette; Marquat begat Marcolphu, and that is I." His lineage having been established— a lineage with no links between generations, and sounding more like a declension in Latin—Marcolf announced that he had come to witness the celebrated wisdom of Solomon and test it for himself.

A series of confrontations ensued in which Marcolf persisted in besting the king every time. He topped Solomon's proverbs, or discovered some flaw in them. He solved his toughest riddles, or posed riddles that Solomon could not solve. He confounded Solomon's authority by playing various pranks and tricks that ran rings around the less agile official wisdom. While Solomon was reputed to be the wisest man in all the kingdom, Marcolf demonstrated the larger wisdom of the fool.

As one might expect, after a time the royal dignity and patience wore thin. What really got to Solomon, however, was Marcolf's questioning of the wisdom of having 700 wives and 300 concubines. Furthermore, in the king's harem Marcolf had even suggested that the wives and mistresses organize themselves and go on a sex strike. While Solomon might have been willing to give a little on his wisdom, he was not willing to give on his women, and he ordered that Marcolf be brought to trial for subversion of the kingdom. Marcolf was tried, convicted, and sentenced to hang. As Marcolf stood before the king, however, he asked if it were not fitting that he, but a poor fool, be granted at least one dying request. Solomon in all his wisdom acknowledged the justice of the request and granted him one last wish. Marcolf then said, "O king, my desire is that I may be able to choose the tree from which I am to be hanged." To Solomon this seemed fair enough, and the wish was granted. The legend then concludes: "So Marcolf and the king's soldiers traveled throughout Jerusalem, and through the valley of Josaffat, and over the hill of Olivet, and from thence to Jericho, and over the river Jordan, and through all Arabia, and over the Grand Desert to the Red Sea, and *never* did Marcolf find the tree from which he chose to be hanged."[2]

Comic Freedom

The difference between tragic heroes and comic heroes is sometimes difficult to define, but one suspects it has something to do with hanging. From King Oedipus to King Lear, tragic heroism has had a penchant for defining the tree from which it might be hung. In the name of freedom it often builds its own prison-house. In the name of knowledge it increases sorrow and vexation. In the name of empowerment it offers new forms of bondage. In the name of courage and conviction it pushes recklessly ahead without regard for consequences. In the name of justice it reaps further injustice. In the name of duty and loyalty, honor or prestige, God and country, it sacrifices the very people involved on the altar of principle and virtue. In the name of dedication to truth or worthy causes, it turns its salvations into Pyrrhic victories. In the name of transcending human limitations it results in opening up new abysses for itself and others.

The warning comes from Greek tragedy itself:

Unwise are those who aspire,
Aiming to go beyond the limits of humanity...

He that seeks glory, he who pursues
Some unbounded, superhuman dream,
May lose the harvest that he has,
And reap death instead.[3]

While tragic freedom has a habit of getting itself chained like Prometheus or blinded like Oedipus or murdered like Hamlet, comic freedom offers a liberation and transcendence of its own. There is no tree from which it chooses to be hanged.

The tragic problem is not so much one of necessity or fate, militating against human freedom, but one of a loss of perspective and balance, as the tragedies themselves would often remind their audiences. Freedom, tragically conceived, for all its nobility and promise of glory, so easily becomes its own undoing. Freedom is a precarious blessing, as are all the other capacities and virtues that tragedy extols: courage, loyalty, duty, pride, power, authority, determination, conviction, justice, aspiration, perfection. Whenever such virtues lose their flexibility and their concrete humanity, and freedom locks itself into an invariable commitment, tragic freedom becomes tragic inevitability.

All the noblest ideals of tragic inspiration so easily turn into something less than, or even opposite, their intention. This is the irony that Sophoclean tragedies such as *Oedipus Rex*, *Electra*, and *Antigone* explored in masterful torment very early in the genre. A tenacious pursuit of aspirations, however lofty, and an unswerving obedience to principles, however admirable, can lead to tortuous and destructive consequences. Hence the necessity for the tragic vision to be tempered and humanized by the comic vision. If there is a "tragic flaw," it lies at least in part in the absence of the comic spirit and perspective. How many are the trees from which we propose to hang ourselves and others!

Comic heroes, like Marcolf, are thus exemplars of a special human freedom and flexibility—which, after all, is the real genius of the race. Naked as we are, and bereft of physical endowments comparable to the higher animal orders, the secret of human survival over the past million years or so is that we are adaptable. We are endowed with a brain that— along with the capacity for imagining all sorts of paradises and utopias for ourselves, and an equal number of holocausts and hells for our enemies—is capable of imagining an endless variety of alternative modes of being, believing, and doing. We are not locked into an unvarying set of biologically imprinted behavioral patterns. Instead, we have developed an unending variety of cultural elaborations and alternatives. While these superadditions can in turn become as rigid as a biological imprint, and thus violate the very freedom that gave them birth, it has been the task of the comic hero to remind us of our intrinsic freedom and flexibility.

Unlike the rest of the animal kingdom, and more like the ancient trickster and shapeshifter, we are not easily pinned down and defined, whether in our nature or our behavior or our symbolic repertoire. We are tricky little devils. To be sure, our unpredictability and amorphousness can at times be threatening to a sense of our own clear and solid identity or to the rudiments of a common order. Yet it makes possible our peculiar capacity for survival under the most difficult and diverse circumstances. We have lived in caves and palaces, deserts and fertile valleys, igloos and tropical huts, monasteries and harems. We have been patriarchal and matriarchal, monarchists and anarchists, capitalists and communists. We have been animists and polytheists and monotheists and atheists and even Presbyterians. And we have survived.

This flexibility and freedom has another side, which is also taken into the province of comedy. By virtue of having a mental capacity well in excess of what is normally needed for survival, humans have to have something to do, if it is only a matter of *decorating* this survival. To be sure, we are inclined to speak of the matter in more lofty terms, such as creativity, imagination, reason, spirit, perhaps "divine image and likeness." But it is this cerebral "having to have something to do" that opens up the whole range of human culture, and specifically human preoccupation. We organize not only pastime activities like sports and entertainment, but also art, music, crafts, education, science, politics, parades, myth and ritual, stories and jokes. We *play* with our existence. Having satisfied the barest necessities, we invent new "necessities," more and more intricate and elaborate games with which to occupy our time, engage our minds, keep our hands busy, flatter our fragile self-consciousness, and give meaning and direction to our lives.

Animals have enough brainpower to get by and get the job of survival done, given their ecological niches. But humans have such a considerable surplus to play with that one of the most basic problems is that of boredom. Mentally we are like the small child who must constantly be squirming, wiggling, jumping, singing, dancing, chattering, and in general producing astounding amounts of noise and confusion for its size. We are not satisfied simply to tear off chunks of the carcasses of gazelles and then lie in the sun or shade until the pangs of hunger begin to stir us again. Whether primitive or modern hunter, we feel compelled to surround our hunting with all sorts of symbols, ceremonies, customs, and meanings. We must decorate the hunters, decorate the weapons, decorate the meat, decorate the eating place, and decorate the trophy, or decorate with it. We must cook the kill, and in a certain way. We must eat it in a certain manner, with certain instruments, at certain times, in certain places, with certain people, supplemented by certain other foods, consumed in certain orders and combinations, and accompanied by certain kinds of conversation, dress, etiquette, furniture, music, lighting, and prayers.

Well does Claude Levi-Strauss characterize this as "The Raw and the Cooked." Even the simple requirement of eating for survival is turned into an elaborate aesthetic, ethical, social, and religious game, with rules and styles and mannerisms as varied as the variety of human cultures. None of this has anything directly to do with the physiology of digestion and absorption. And, to compound the issue, after we have eaten we consider ourselves to have replenished our energy for all sorts of *other* activities, most of which also have little to do with the basic necessities of life and survival.

This superabundance of playful mental energy, under whatever name, is our Promethean nature. Understandably the Prometheus of Aeschylus claims that "all the arts come to mortals from Prometheus." This seemingly infinite capacity for play is the source of our flexibility and adaptability and freedom. But it may also be turned into the source of our inflexibility and bondage, like Prometheus defiant and in chains. When the games that we have developed become absolutized in a rigidity of forms and dogmatized in an inerrant justification of those forms—like insisting that there is only one right way to play poker—we destroy the very imagination and playfulness and freedom that made possible those enrichments of human existence. Human beings seem to have the peculiar habit of organizing the most ingenious cultural games and then throwing themselves into those games with a singleness of purpose and passionate involvement that quite forgets the game and the playfulness. The new vistas that have been opened up by our capacity for playing with our existence are closed off again and sealed by seriousness and the desire for security. This forgetfulness and closing and sealing is at the root of tragic conflict and results in the tragic contradiction of a freedom that issues in bondage and death.

The Picaro

In literary terms, the themes of comic freedom, adaptability, and survival are the special emphasis of the picaresque hero, like the sixteenth-century Lazarillo de Tormes or Grimmelshausen's seventeenth-century Simplicius Simplicissimus. The picaro is generally an ordinary citizen having no political power, wealth, or social status, a relative nobody caught in a world of competing forces or faced with a world of indifference. Lazarillo does not belong to a noble line or a prominent family or a great cause or the "mainstream of history." But like an orphaned street urchin who is wise and wily because of the necessity to do or die, Lazarillo has learned to use his intelligence to survive, to remain free of spirit, and to maintain a kind of rugged, self-reliant identity.

The picaro is not an idealist or ideologue but a pragmatist, indeed a bit of a rogue (*picaro*) with an irrepressible sense of life as a game. For the picaro, the real problem is how to keep from being trampled by or enlisted in the tragic fray of conflicting powers (whether religious, political, or nationalistic). Simplicius Simplicissimus comes forth out of the insane carnage of Protestant/Catholic Europe during the Thirty Years' War. His own village is in ruins, and "Christian civilization" is in apparent ruins. But he comes with a determination to make his own way, and with the droll observation that "this introductory entertainment almost spoiled my desire to see the world."

Among the English, the number-one rogue is Shakespeare's Sir John Falstaff, that "huge bombard of sack" who moves so merrily outside the conventional honesties and dishonesties of his time with a great love of wine and life and laughter. As Morgann said of him, "He is a man at once young and old, enterprising and fat, a dupe and a wit, harmless and wicked, weak in principle and resolute by constitution, cowardly in appearances and brave in reality, a knave without malice, a liar without deceit, a knight, a gentleman, and a soldier without either dignity, decency, or honor."[4]

Falstaff *is* a bit of a rascal and ruffian, but that is not because of some streak of meanness in him. Rather, it is because he has such a zest for living that human orders and human ideals are always getting in the way. Whereas others may put their lives in the enlisted service of some great cause or ambition, Sir John is primarily enthusiastic about life itself. His largeness of heart and frame and his raucous laughter would embrace all in a common contagion. Falstaff is, that is, the very opposite of the historical character to which Shakespeare alludes: Sir John Oldcastle, who was a zealot in the Lollard cause. Falstaff is zealous about keeping alive and focused on the simple pleasures of the day. He is, as Susanne Langer expresses it, "the personified *élan vital.*"[5] Whereas Sir John Oldcastle is a tragic figure, involved in many conspiracies—including a plot to kill King Henry during the Twelfth-night mummery—and eventually hanged, Sir John Falstaff is his comic opposite. Though Shakespeare changed the name to Falstaff to avoid offense and carried the comic contrast even further in Falstaff's double, Sir Toby Belch of *Twelfth Night*, Shakespeare's implied commentary on the respective fortunes and fates of tragic and comic heroes is quite transparent.

Tragic heroes—at least from Sophocles on—so easily destroy themselves and others. They crush and are crushed by their own stubborn idealism and vain pride. They take the game, whatever the game, so seriously and uncompromisingly. And though tragic heroes may die in a blaze of glory or a final shout of defiance, or be awarded some posthumous vindication, even martyrdom, comic heroes live on in their playful, middling-muddling manner. They imagine a considerable variety of options between being "red or dead."

Flexibility is, after all, the characteristic of life; rigidity is the sign of death. Flexibility is even the secret of airplane wings and skyscraper technology. Because comic heroes do not lose themselves in absolute seriousness, rigid principles, and unwavering pursuit, they are better adapted for survival—theirs, and those who are associated with them, and even those who are opposed to them. Because they do not refuse to walk anything but a straight line, do not insist on barricading themselves within unchangeable systems, and do not always believe their own rhetoric, they are not easily trapped. They wrestle with life, to be sure, and rather valiantly. But they wrestle like greased pigs. As Hegel observed:

> In tragedy individuals are thrown into confusion in virtue of the abstract nature of their sterling volition and character.... What on the other hand is inseparable from the comic is an infinite geniality and confidence capable of rising superior to its

own contradiction, and experiencing therein no taint of bitterness or sense of misfortune whatever.[6]

Some comic heroes, however, *are* hanged. The freedom and flexibility of the comic vision—if too threatening to the powers that be—may result in crucifixion or burning at the stake. Clowns and fools, at least symbolically, have often suffered for their license by being flogged or driven from the ritual arena. The liberty available to jesters to parody the king and to dance outside the protocol of the court always involved the risk of being beheaded for their pains. Comic iconoclasm in particular may offer the dual reward of freedom and imprisonment. The comic hero, by virtue of playing the mediator and occupying a no-man's land between antagonists, may get shot at by both sides.

The redheaded McMurphy, in Kesey's *One Flew over the Cuckoo's Nest*, swaggers into the asylum to which he has been committed with a laugh so free and loud that it reverberates through the hollow halls, and with a determination to teach fellow inmates how to loosen up and live a little. But he runs squarely into Big Nurse, whose therapeutic ordering has all but suffocated the last breath of self-respecting humanity in her charges and reduced them to the numbed submission of automatons. Though the "gambling fool" teaches the "loonies" to play once more and to laugh with something more than nervous, squeaky bird chirps, he is eventually sent up for shock treatments and finally for a frontal lobotomy on a cruciform operating table. Still he is the victor in the end, for through him others have been given courage and hope, found new faith in themselves, and been set free.

And You Shall Be as Gods

From the lofty standpoint of tragedy or any drama of high seriousness, comedy and the comic hero no doubt appear as pale and shifting seconds, on the order of moonlight to solar radiance. Certainly a formidable array of literary scholars have insisted that comedy comes after tragedy, after the sublime, after the ideal. Tragedy therefore presents itself as more fundamental and profound than comedy, the real substance of which comedy is the mock reflection—or, as James Thurber put it, "the tragic is the robust wine, the dramatic the champagne of the arts, while comedy is the ginger ale."

But a partisan of comedy could just as well argue the contrary. Human beings share seriousness with the animals, but in laughter they laugh alone. The comic sense goes beyond taking things "straight" and univocally, in that remarkable human capacity for seeing words and situations in double and even multiple senses. Tragic heroism has a Promethean/Oedipal air of adolescence about it. Comic heroism, with its flexibility and inclination to compromise, its playfulness and delight in ambiguity, its knowing winks and lighter countenance, is the more mature form. If comedy comes from tragedy—as in the Dionysian performances—it comes as a reaffirmation of those aspects of the human condition which tragedy has neglected, and therefore as the larger perspective and fuller spirit. Jonathan Swift, the Anglo-Irish author of *Gulliver's Travels*, stated it boldly: "In Comedy the best actor plays the part of the droll, while some second rogue is made the hero or fine gentleman. So, in this farce of life, wise men pass their time in mirth, while fools are only serious."

To attempt a comparison between tragedy and comedy for the purpose of declaring which is superior and more profound is not a very helpful exercise. We would do well at most to come with Christopher Fry "to the verge of saying that comedy is greater than tragedy"—or any other dramatic form. Even in the Dionysian theater, a comedy was placed in competition not with a tragedy but with other comic entries. Shakespeare wrote both great tragedies and great comedies, suggesting not only that it can be done, but that the two genres serve different purposes and aim at different effects.

If in tragedy the praises of humanity are sung, it is clearly exceptional individuals and their exceptional acts who, even when they sin, sin in a grand manner. Comedy is more modest and magnanimous. It is in comedy that humanity is celebrated and enjoyed and laughed over, more or less as it is. If there are comic sins, they tend to be on the order of roguish pranks and tricks. Comic crimes are petty crimes, deserved crimes, crimes that backfire or are of doubtful result. Perhaps they are crimes that are wildly successful, then abysmal failures because of the most trivial omission—like being apprehended for failing to put a nickel in the parking meter next to the getaway car.

When one speaks of praise-singing relative to human enterprises, however, one senses that we are in the world of rhetoric, rhapsody, eulogy—the world of commencement speeches, political conventions, national holidays, funeral orations, corporation meetings, and paid commercials. "Numberless are the world's wonders," sings the chorus of *Antigone*, "but none more wonderful than man." Then recounted, as in the *Prometheus Bound* of Aeschylus, are all the marvels of human achievement. Carefully omitted, of course, are a number of other, less glorious marvels. Or, when they are included, and the conflict and irony begins to build, we move toward tragedy in the darker sense. Even Hamlet, in the midst of the monumental miseries and injustices he suffers and sees strewn about him, clings tenaciously to the heroic vision of the species:

> What a piece of work is a man! How noble in reason! How infinite in faculty! In form and moving, how express and admirable! In action how like an angel! In apprehension, how like a god! The beauty of the world! The paragon of animals!
>
> *Hamlet*, II.ii.311-15

Tragedy is selective in what it chooses to admire about human nature and accomplishment. And it is just this tension between eulogy and actuality, its incredible irony, and frequently its darkly tragic consequences as well, that comedy immediately notices and puts on display. Not that tragedy always fails to note the contradiction; it is a part of the torment of tragedy. So Hamlet continues: "And yet, to me, what is this quintessence of dust? Man delights not me; nor woman neither..." But comedy deals with the matter quite differently. The terms of the tragic juxtaposition are placed by comedy in a more relative and congenial light.

In comedy, after listening to hymns of praise for the species, one has the choice of either gagging, throwing up, or laughing. The comic impulse being what it is, comedy counters with any of several devices. It may exaggerate the praise and its object even further—though in some cases this seems hardly possible. It may exaggerate the act and gestures of praising, depicting as infinitely praiseworthy some creature that is anything but, like a eulogy of a mule. Or it may confront head-on the contradiction between the panegyrics and the circumstances. As W. C. Fields put it in *Tillie and Gus* (1933), "There comes a time in the affairs of man when he must take the bull by the tail, and squarely face the situation!"

For Hegel, "the true theme of primitive tragedy is the godlike." And whereas tragedy exemplifies "the godlike manifestations of the human heart," comic figures "make visible the general perversity of mankind" (*Philosophy of Fine Art*). While there is some truth in the distinction, its terms are quite ambiguous. And that ambiguity comedy goes out of its way to detail, to play with, and to enjoy. A part of what comedy makes "visible" is the folly of this very aspiration or claim to godlikeness itself, and the perversities to which even the most well-meaning heroism and nobly heroic virtues are subject. This is its prophetic-iconoclastic function. Comedy shares in something of the same insight that led the Yahwist author of Genesis 3 to credit the promise "You shall be like God" to a snake.

Adolf Hitler, after all, had lofty aspirations for uniting Europe, vindicating a humiliated Germany, reestablishing strong leadership, breaking down class and economic bonds, and revitalizing old Germanic values. He came as a savior (*Führer*) of his people and of Western civilization, bringing a new enthusiasm and promise and hope. And he evoked a deep sense of loyalty and commitment, self-sacrifice, and exalted destiny. Yet in the grandiose visions and god-playings, as well as the various personal and ideological idiosyncrasies that accompanied this godlikeness, Hitler became a perverse fool among fools. As such he was appropriately depicted in Chaplin's comedy *The Great Dictator*, and especially Bertolt Brecht's tragicomedy *The Resistible Rise of Arturo Ui*. The tragedy of Hitler and of the world that came tumbling down with him had much to do with the prior lack of any refined comic sensibility relative to such "godlike manifestations of the human heart." Godlikeness is a self-image that we have played with for a good part of our history, in one form or another.

"You shall be like God"—how much human energy has been expended in working on that fantasy or being destroyed by it or bemoaning its unattainability. For Plato the supreme goal was "to become like God, as far as this is possible for a mortal" (*Republic* 10.613a-b). For Pindar, though humans have a kinship with the gods—by virtue of the belief that "from one mother both came forth"—humans have received, as it were, the short end of the stick. "The powers have been so divided that the one is as nothing, while the other is securely established in the eternal heavens" (*Nemean* 6:1). Thus in reason, imagination, creativity, and foresight, humans have certain affinities with the gods. But those powers are very limited and partial, are mixed with mortal flesh, and are often the source of their own undoing. Epimetheus (afterthought) is the brother of Prometheus (forethought).

Nowhere is this problem more painfully rehearsed than among the Greek heroes, for the hero is the superlative instance of human strength, beauty, and intellect. How like the gods! And yet how quickly the youthful flower of vigor and virtue fades! How suddenly the mighty hero is slain in battle and becomes a rotting corpse! How overnight the labor of the years is reduced to rubble! The dramatic effect of this pathos is further heightened by mythologically accounting for the splendor of the hero by crediting the hero's birth to a mixed divine/human marriage. This was no ordinary human, but a god-man. Yet in the end, as with the heel of Achilles, the hero too proves vulnerable and mortal. No matter how close to divinity, no matter how carefully drawn the hero's plans or how relentless the hero's struggles, still, like the hair shorn from Samson in his weakness for Delilah, the human element eventually brings life and dreams crashing down upon the hero and those around. Tragedy, then, as for Chaucer's monk in *The Canterbury Tales,* is the story

> Of hym that stood in greet prosperitee,
> And is fallen out of heigh degree
> Into myserie, and endeth wrecchedly.

Prologue, Monk's Tale 1975–77

Out of this vision of human existence comes a sense of tragic conflict between human realities and divine aspirations, mortal flesh and dreams of immortality, finite limitations and infinite imaginings. But the same conflicts are also the source of comedy. If tragedy deals with oppositions, tensions between contrarieties, worlds in collision, so does comedy, though more in the manner with which the queen in *Alice's Adventures in Wonderland* disposes of them. When the queen orders the Cheshire cat beheaded, the executioner makes bold to suggest, "You can't cut off a head unless there is a body to cut it off from," while the queen insists, "If something isn't done about it in less than no time, I'll have everybody beheaded!" Similarly, the Red Queen in Lewis Carroll's *Through the Looking-Glass* practiced believing in impossible things for at least a half hour each day, and claimed to have accomplished as many as six, on a good day, before breakfast!

The comic hero playfully incarnates the essential contradictions of our natures, and the awkwardnesses and bewilderments of being human. Basic to the various forms of comic heroism is the same thesis—comically understood—that we are creatures of very diverse, and often opposite tendencies. We are suspended, as it were, between heaven and earth, eternity and time, the infinite and the finite, spirit and flesh, rationality and impulse, altruism and selfishness, pride and insecurity, life and death. We are compounded of sunlight and stone, intelligence and ignorance, the divine image and the dust of the earth, the cleverness of Prometheus and the foolishness of Epimetheus. And if there is any "salvation" forthcoming, it comes in the candid—rather than tortured—acceptance, and even enjoyment, of this ambiguousness.

We prefer, of course, to flatter ourselves with images of idealized heroes, or at least tragic ones. And there is a certain inspiration and catharsis to be had from their heroism. Yet it has always been the task of comic heroes to identify our pretensions and self-deceptions, our inconsistencies and incongruities, if need be by exemplifying them. In their antics and adventures, their fancies and follies, we are gently reminded that, despite all the grandeur of our dreams and accomplishments, we are finite, fallible, mortal, and frequently foolish creatures of the earth. Even when our heads are in the clouds, our feet walk on the ground and are made of clay.

For the comic protagonist, life is never so simple, so sensible, so logical, or so organized as our inspirational visions, our theatrical plots, our historical reconstructions, or our great works of art might wish to suggest. There everything may be neatly arranged, sorted out, pieced together, all wrapped up, as so many tightly woven stories with a beginning, a progression, a climax, and an end—or as so many paintings with a theme and structure and composition, forming an ordered whole, finished and complete. The comic artist knows life to be otherwise and people to be otherwise. The world is seen, as Pirandello put it, "if not exactly in the nude, then as, so to speak, in its shirt-tails. It is in his shirt-tails that he sees the king, who makes such a fine impression on you when you see him 'composed' in the majesty of enthronement, with his crown and scepter and mantle of purple and ermine."[7] In the latter form the king is a composition, an appearance, an illusion of reality. Actually such a king, like such a hero or such a world, does not exist.

Hence comes, in the art of humor, all that seeking after more minute and intimate details, even details that may appear trivial and vulgar when set alongside the idealized syntheses of art in general; hence that seeking after the contrasts and contradictions on which the humorist's art is based, as opposed to the consistency sought by others; and hence all that breaking down, that unraveling, that whimsicality, all those digressions that mark the work of the humorist, as opposed to the ordered piecing together, the "composed" nature, of works of art.[8]

The result, however, is not simply a breaking down, an unraveling. It is a putting together of a different sort: the silly is mixed in with the sublime, the simple with the sophisticated, the miscellaneous with the monumental, because that is the way the totality of the picture, the whole of life, really is. Out of the comic "composition" an odd sort of wholeness and unity results, a kind of *coincidence of opposites* without entirely losing the opposition. In such comic realism, human limitations and aspirations, follies and successes, are gracefully welcomed in all their awkwardness. Instead of becoming the torment of Tantalus, comic revelations became tantalizing: they beckon us back to the adventure of life and the celebration of life.

Here, paradoxically, comedy approaches its own form of heroic greatness relative to which even the tragic catharsis is the simpler and easier way out. One approaches, and quite unprepossessingly, the very sphere of the divine, the transcendent laughter of the gods. For comedy, in the course of being frankly human and refusing to be trapped by frustrating aspirations and wrenching conflicts, has something of the divine—the truly cosmic—perspective in it. It proceeds from a higher and larger vantage point in which mountains become molehills, tyrants do not loom as large as gods, and the greatest deeds for good or ill are but ripples on the waves of a limitless cosmic sea.

On the one hand, comedy laughs from a position that is totally *within* the human condition, for it accepts that condition and sees itself as a part of that condition, even offering itself as the vehicle for laughter. Yet in the act of espousing and identifying with the human condition, comedy expresses its peculiar freedom. At the same time, it views the human condition from *beyond* itself, as it were, *sub specie aeternitatis*. In both senses comedy has a capacity to ameliorate and reconcile and redeem what the tragic hero cannot. In Enid Welsford's words,

> The serious hero focuses events, forces issues, and causes catastrophes; but the Fool by his mere presence dissolves events, evades issues, and throws doubt on the finality of fact.
>
> The Stage-clown therefore is as naturally detached from the play as the Court-fool is detached from social life. And the fool's most fitting place in literature is as hero of the episodic narrative, or as the voice speaking from without and not from within the dramatic plot.[9]

Tragic Wars and Comic Games

The dramatic presuppositions and controlling metaphors of heroic/tragic literatures are, after all, very much the legacy of warrior cultures and the warrior ethos. The element of struggle in all life for survival is abstracted and amplified as the central key to reality. And this key is further understood in terms of that peculiarly human form of struggle, *war*. Thus the divine and the human, higher and lower natures, old and new orders, male and female, family and state, parent and child, civilized and savage—all are read as being in fundamental conflict with one another. These antagonistic and sometimes violent relationships, in turn, provide the dramatic plot. Drama is the narration of conflict, as history is the record of triumphs and defeats.

For several millennia this stirring image of heroes and their war cries and their bloody battles has dominated the great civilizations, and their myths and literatures as well. The martial scenario of Greek gods and heroes is but one instance among many. The Babylonian god of order, Marduk, is perennially besieged by Tiamat, goddess of watery chaos. The Canaanite fertility god, Baal, is annually slain and dismembered by Mot, god of death and desolation. The Hebraic "Lord of Hosts," "mighty in battle," destroys the enemies of Israel, smashes "high places" and other "abominations," and commands the genocide of conquered peoples. The Zoroastrian spirit of light (Spenta Mainyu) is at war throughout history with the spirit of darkness (Angra Mainyu), and blessed are they who choose to fight on the side of light. A Christian mythology appropriates the same cosmic conflict between God and Satan, angels and demons, heaven and hell, culminating in a final battle of Armageddon. Muslims actively enlist in the cause through declarations of holy war, crushing infidels and idolaters, and often one another, in the name of Allah and "the struggling" (*jihad*).

In Asia the Aryan war-god Indra, recipient of more hymns than any other divinity in the Rig-veda, is hailed as the powerful "destroyer of fortresses" and "slayer of the foe"—the defeated Indus peoples. The beloved Bhagavad-gita has as its setting the war chariots and bloodbaths of the Indian Mahabharata. The great mother-goddesses of India, Kali and Durga, are depicted with necklaces of skulls, girdles of severed arms, swords in hand, lapping from bowls the blood of decapitated victims. Even a quietistic Zen Buddhism becomes heavily involved with the martial arts and the samurai class.

A seemingly endless list of examples could be produced from the religions of the world, so deeply and almost universally has this tragic vision "captured" the human imagination. Whether the commandment has been to "utterly destroy" every Hittite, Amorite, Canaanite,

Perizzite, Hivite and Jebusite—man, woman, child, infant, and beast (Deut. 20:17) or to "put on the whole armor of God" (Eph. 6:11) and "fight the good fight of the faith" (1 Tim. 6:12), the dominant images and metaphors through which life is to be perceived and lived are those of warfare and conquest.

In varying combinations, corresponding warrior qualities have also been extolled, from Homer's *Iliad* to Nietzsche's *Zarathustra* and Kierkegaard's *Training in Christianity:* unquestioning loyalty and obedience, inflexible conviction, unswerving dedication, indomitable will, passionate involvement, uncompromising determination. Religious, nonreligious, and antireligious alike have stirred to the rallying cry of such qualities as these. And how quickly and easily the more spiritualized reinterpretation of the old warrior ethic and world view slips back into a literal and political application. The knight and the "knight of faith" become practically indistinguishable. War and Holy War become synonymous. The way of the Buddha and the way of the warrior (*bushido*) coalesce.

Surely there is something admirable, as well as rousing, about these warrior traits. And there is an obvious historical reality to conflicting principles and forces—much of it in fulfillment of such a world view itself. Yet the comic hero enlists in the army, if enlisting at all, as one come to introduce a certain amount of confusion in the ranks and chaos on the battlefield. In the presence of such a figure, distinctions between friend and foe, the righteous and the unrighteous, generals and privates, tend to become fuzzy and confounded. The comic soldier does not quite fit in, even when making a valiant effort to do so. Whether in the officers' quarters or the supply depot or on the front line, the comic soldier comes bringing a combination of cleverness and ineptness that tends to collapse the military hierarchy, and cancel out the effectiveness of both sides in the conflict. Such soldiering is frequently out of step and seems to be marching to a different set of signals.

Comic heroism does not manifest a reckless determination to die in one's boots, weapon in hand, with a look of defiance stamped on one's face. It seems more inclined to the view that "they that take up the sword shall die by the sword." Other things may well be taken up instead, as Laurel and Hardy and the Three Stooges and the Marx Brothers were particularly noted for doing: hammers, pitchforks, broom handles, china vases, hat pins, squirt guns, flowerpots, itching powders, and the like.

While the comic intent may not always wear the halo of turning swords into plowshares and spears into pruning hooks, the result is at least that of dulling or misplacing swords and turning spears into fishing poles.

The drift of comic fights is that of nobody getting seriously hurt. A considerable amount of cleanup may be necessary following the battle, but there is a distinct preference for replacing lethal missiles with mudballs and spitballs and gooey cream pies. As in the many post-World War II comedies that dealt in a farcical manner with war—*Sergeant Bilko, At War with the Army, McHale's Navy, Hogan's Heroes, Gomer Pyle, M.A.S.H.*—the fighting is transformed into a sport, a rivalry, perhaps a schoolyard fracas. Conflicts are returned, as it were, to that time before humans picked up even sticks and stones, a time of shouts and growls and raw strength. Fighting is redirected toward that pretechnological level of bluffs and fisticuffs, where human power is rarely deadly and not so grossly out of proportion to the need to vent anger, defend territory, obtain food, or protect home and family.

Even when the comic setting is that of the most advanced technology, disputes are usually settled in the most natural and least damaging manner. Thus in the Batman television farces of the late 1960s, despite the fact that the "dynamic duo" had access to the most sophisticated technology, its use was restricted to detection and apprehension. The forces of evil—Joker, Riddler, Penguin, Iceman, Catwoman, and company—were almost invariably vanquished by conventional barroom brawling: Bam! Whap! Bonk! Socko!

Insofar as comic heroism participates in the ethic of the hero, it does so in a fundamentally different way. From the start it insists on adding another set of virtues: flexibility, freedom, compromise, playfulness, lightheartedness, childlikeness, celebration of life, survivability. Thus "armed," comic heroes are more inclined toward mock battles than real ones. They exhibit honest fear, cowardice, squeamishness, bewilderment, a preference for going AWOL, and a special talent for running and hiding. They are masters of elusiveness. The early Keaton in *Cops* (1922) managed to escape the entire police force of New York City for half an hour by ingenious trickery, acrobatic agility, and Olympic speed. Like Don Quixote, comic heroes occasionally take on a windmill or two. But they are not so eager to die, or to propose hanging-trees for themselves and others, or to consign anyone either now or in the hereafter to the flames.

The resoluteness of comic heroism is as pre-ideological as it is pre-technological. Its commitment is to life and to the basics of life. Only secondarily is it concerned with the fine points of custom, mores, legal codes, social hierarchy, political arrangements, or religious doctrines. It is far more concerned with saving skin than with saving face. And its defense is of persons more than principles, the spirit rather than the letter. "The Sabbath was made for man, not man for the Sabbath" might well serve as a comic motto. The ethic of comedy is situational. Moral codes are in the service of people and their circumstances. Hunger supercedes Mosaic Law. Comic heroes are therefore not disposed to prostituting individuals to bloodless ideas and ideals or to bloody pride and honor. Rhetoric, flag-waving, and fanaticism do not become them— except by way of exemplifying such in parody.

For comic heroism, existence is to be seen under a different set of metaphors and images. The various competing forces, whether of natural or human orders, are to be viewed more in terms of a *game* than a battle. Life is a *contest* more than a conflict, a *play* of forces, a *sporting* proposition, an inter*play* of opposites, a cosmic *dance*. Life is not intrinsically a quarrel or titanic confrontation, any more than nature is simply "red in tooth and claw." Life flows, as rivers flow, sometimes lazily in the summer sun, sometimes in a raging spring torrent; sometimes fertilizing, sometimes eroding; sometimes building up, sometimes tearing down; but not necessarily at war with anything or anyone.

We are often deceived by our metaphors. There is an almost total inappropriateness in applying military imagery to plant and animal kingdoms, the physical order, or the universe at large. War is a specifically human phenomenon, and with great injustice is it applied outside the human sphere. Does light have a quarrel with darkness? Does the volcano seek to ravage the forest, or the earthquake to molest the land? Is the wolf at enmity with the caribou? Must the lion lie down with the lamb to usher in an era of peace? Is death the "last enemy to be destroyed" (I Cor. 15:26)?

Life is not out to vanquish death, or death out to eliminate life. They only exist and have meaning relative to one another. Life needs death, and death needs life. They are two aspects of the same biological process, each requiring and interpenetrating its opposite. Otherwise the game would be over. The drama would cease. Solitaire.

The comic-heroic venture, accordingly, is not that of conquest and victory, but of compromise and mediation. The goal is not to win a war at all cost, but to play the game of life, accepting its risks, its winnings, and its inevitable losings. While the dynamic of the hero is still there, it is a different sort of dynamic. And while there is a rhythm to the action, it is not from the beat of a war drum. It is more like the dynamic rhythm of meandering streams, springtime and autumn, the tidal ebb and flow, the waxing and waning of the moon—and in this sense, too, of light and darkness, life and death, cosmos and chaos. As in the dynamic of music, point and counterpoint, melody and countermelody, major and minor, euphony and dissonance juxtapose themselves, compete with one another, and in the tension between them form a higher unity, not a pitched battle.

> Meeting, they laugh and laugh—
> The forest grove, the many fallen leaves.[10]

Are the summer leaves—as we might be inclined to phrase it—"fallen" as in battle, "felled" by the "relentless onslaught" of an "advancing march" of winter? Or is this the metaphorical trap? Meisetsu touches the heart of the comic understanding:

> Butterflies swarm in delight
> upon the floral wreath,
> adorning the coffin.

Amid human grief and wailing, there is rejoicing in butterfly land!

A similar point is expressed—with less poetry and sentiment—in a Gary Larson cartoon. Vultures are flocking around a dead carcass on the hot African plains. One vulture is saying to another: "Just think, here we are in the warm afternoon sun, a dead, bloated rhino underfoot, and good friends flying in from all over. I tell you, Frank, this is the best of times!"

4

A Voice Laughing In The Wilderness— The Humorist

That's the first thing that got me about this place,
there wasn't anybody laughing. I haven't heard a
real laugh since I came through that door.... Man,
when you lose your laugh you lose your footing.

—Randall Patrick McMurphy in
One Flew over the Cuckoo's Nest[1]

The last person known to have laughed in the United States was Robert Ketchum in 1984 in Salem, Massachusetts. As a result of his lack of seriousness and his bold impropriety, he was publicly burned at the stake by the local authorities. All three television networks covered the event.

Such was the tongue-in-cheek Orwellian prophesy offered by Art Buchwald in the midst of the radicalism of establishment and antiestablishment confrontations in the decade of the 1960s. It was the humorist's warning. Unqualified seriousness is dehumanizing and dangerous. It is the crucifier of freedom and the human spirit. And this is true whether one has in mind radicals of some right or left, or the more or less acquiescent middle. Humanity cannot live by seriousness alone.

In some respects it might seem that the prophecy had already come true, if the enormities perpetrated in the twentieth century in the name of racial purity or national superiority, ideological truth or political necessity, are any index. And perhaps in a much longer view of history one would come to conclude that the problem is coterminous with the species. The prophecy was fulfilled in the beginning. The biblical fall of Adam and Eve was a fall into seriousness; and we have taken ourselves, our circumstances, our achievements, and our beliefs very seriously ever since! As Oscar Wilde put it in one of his more theological moments: "It's the world's Original Sin."

Friedrich Nietzsche, in the same passage of *Thus Spake Zarathustra* in which he said he "would only believe in a god who could dance"— though he was never able to locate such a god—nevertheless went on to identify Satan as the one who is "serious, thorough, profound and solemn...the spirit of gravity, through whom all things fall."[2]

C. S. Lewis comments to similar effect in the preface to his diabolical correspondences from Hell, *The Screwtape Letters:*

> Humor involves a sense of proportion and a power of seeing yourself from the outside. Whatever else we attribute to beings who sinned through pride, we must not attribute this...We must picture Hell as a state where everyone is perpetually concerned about his own dignity and advancement, where everyone lives the deadly serious passions of envy, self-importance and resentment.[3]

There is a contemporary urgency about the question of humor, if for no other reason than that we, more than any previous generation, have eaten so much more of the fruit of Adam's tree. An unparalleled knowledge and power is available to us for dehumanizing and destroying, as well as benefiting, one another. The four horsemen of the tragic Apocalypse—Absolutism, Dogmatism, Fanaticism, Terrorism—are more potent forces than ever before, given the latest technological capabilities. It is more imperative than ever that we understand the peculiarly human gift of laughter, and the comic sensibility that it expresses, if the prospect of greater tyrannies and holocausts is to be averted.

As Konrad Lorenz suggests in concluding his important study *On Aggression*, the survival of civilization depends to a significant degree upon our capacity for humor.[4] People who laugh together are less inclined to kill one another. Humor, among other things, is a valuable mechanism for ritualizing aggressive impulses in substitution for the more violent and destructive means available to us. And it can provide a larger perspective in relation to ourselves, our scientific accomplishments, and our ideological persuasions. Sanity and humanity, as McMurphy the affable rogue in Ken Kesey's *One Flew over the Cuckoo's Nest* understood the moment he entered the insane asylum, are impossible apart from humor.

The Seriousness of Humor

Nearly a century ago William Austin Smith made bold to suggest:

> Every Divinity School might well have in its senior year, along with courses in systematic divinity and homiletics, a course in the great masters of comedy; and, to arouse our sluggish wits and keep us on our guard, it might not be amiss to carve upon our pulpits, side by side with the lean Gothic saints, the figure of Aristophanes or Molière with warning finger.[5]

The suggestion has not been diligently pursued in our seminaries or other institutions of higher learning. The prevailing attitude, if anything, has inclined in the opposite direction. And the calumny and vehemence that often characterize human conflicts are continuing testimony to the failure to understand the fundamental importance—indeed, necessity— of the comic vision.

The situation is hardly improved by the fact that though our educational systems sponsor innumerable courses in the appreciation of art, music, and literature, as well as gardening, cooking, and tennis, little is offered in the way of *comic* appreciation. This remarkable side of our existence as human beings, which actually tempers and qualifies everything else, is left adrift as a light distraction from more important concerns, a playful interlude whose justification is that it may help us let off a little steam now and then or provide a cheap vacation of the mind from which we will return to work more industriously and fight unquestioningly. To the most soberminded, humor may even be seen as—in Chad Walsh's phrase—a kind of "wart on the human soul."

Yet the ability to see the humor in things, or to create comic tales and rituals, is among the most profound and imaginative of human achievements. The comic sense is an important part of what it means to be human and humane. Without it we return to brutishness, and the Philistines are upon us. The dark possibilities of even the highest ideals and noblest aspirations is part of the terrible irony of tragedy and the seriousness of humor.

Revealing of traditional understandings is the eighteenth-century treatise by Richard Blackmore ironically titled *Satyr Against Wit*. In his "satire" Sir Richard saw unbridled wit and humor as the enemy of true religion, stalwart virtue, and right reason—a form of insanity and a seducer of young people. Later in the preface to his *Creation* he saw a definite link between witticism and atheism—and no link between creativity and humor. Extending his argument further in a subsequent essay, he concluded that

> wit has no place in history, philology, philosophy, or in the greater lyric or epic poems.... Lofty and illustrious subjects, such as the foundation, rise and revolution of kingdoms, commotions of state, battles, triumphs, solemn embassies, and various other important actions of princes and heroes, are exalted above the sphere of wit and humor.

It is an ancient and venerable viewpoint with respect to the more serious subjects that affect and concern us deeply. The similar warning of the German philosopher George Friedrich Meier is representative of the misgivings of more than German philosophers:

> We are never to jest on or with things which, on account of their importance or weight, claim our utmost seriousness. There are things...so great and important in themselves, as never to be thought of and mentioned but with much sedateness and solemnity. Laughter on such occasions is criminal and indecent.... For instance, all jests on religion, philosophy, and the like important subjects.[6]

Yet our failure to entertain the jester "on such occasions" may be one of the primary sources of the "criminal and indecent" behavior that our "utmost seriousness" so often produces. The endemic weakness that accompanies the intensity of our more sacred concerns is a predilection for translating that intensity into intolerance, aggression, and violence. In this lies the seriousness of humor. The barbarous chronicle of inquisitions, heresy trials, witch hunts, book burnings, religious persecutions, political imprisonments, holy wars, and even acts of genocide—justified by the most respected elements of society and sanctified by pious interests—is sufficient testimony to the stark possibilities of sincerity without humor. Truth without laughter, and the sacred apart from the comic, are easily twisted into a perverse self-caricature. It is difficult to imagine people with a profound sense of humor in relation to their own most ultimate convictions participating in the burning of other people at the stake—as was Michael Servetus in John Calvin's Geneva—because of a failure to subscribe to a certain formulation of the doctrine of the Trinity!

The problem is not peculiar to religion. It is found in all areas of human endeavor, including science and academia, and among people of all persuasions. Russian communists, in the name of official atheism and with the goal of eliminating the "opiate" of religion, destroyed art and architecture, burned books, denied freedom of speech and assembly, imprisoned or coerced thousands of religious leaders, and sent dissidents of many stripes into Solzhenitsyn's Gulag Archipelago. Or, for a change of pace, one could read the acrimonious debates among the various schools of psychology, or the history of the literature on Shakespearean authorship.

The same debilities beset the radical enthusiast of whatever persuasion who, in certainty over the righteousness or rightness of a particular cause, zealously pursues some grand program or vision. Whether a fiery exponent of Marxism, free enterprise, socialism, nationalism, feminism, minority rights, nuclear preparedness, pro-choice, or anti-abortion, the predisposition of the advocate is to absolutize some scheme for saving the world and rectifying the ills of society. Ideologies, like religious dogmas, have a high level of missionary—and military—zeal but a low level of comic awareness. Unqualified and untempered, the mentality and morality of the zealot is fundamentally tragic.

There is a marked affinity between absolutisms of every sort. All share in the attempted abolition of humor in relation to themselves. A common trait of dictators, revolutionaries, reactionaries, and authoritarians alike is the refusal both to laugh at themselves and to permit others to laugh at them. Charles de Gaulle once threatened a Parisian cartoonist—whose specialty was caricaturing the French president—with imprisonment by invoking a law instituted in the time of Napolean. In totalitarian countries, humor and satire directed at the official ideology are the nearest equivalents to treason. Humorists who turn wit and wisdom in the direction of the functionaries and policies of the ascendant regime are open to the charge of unpatriotic, if not subversive, behavior—as in the religious sphere they are open to the charge of heresy or blasphemy.

In Stalinist Russia, comedies were permitted and even encouraged by the government. But they were of a certain type, namely, comedies that targeted capitalistic, imperialistic, democratic countries and that reinforced Leninist-Stalinist viewpoints. It was only in the less repressive and more liberal atmosphere, however modest, which entered after the death of Stalin that comedy and humor were permitted greater room to breathe. The Soviet magazine *Krokodil* signaled the change in 1953 by running a full-page advertisement for the best political joke, satire, or anecdote of the year. The promised award for the winning entry: "A free, one-way trip to Siberia!"

A part of the pretension of orthodoxies of whatever sort is the claim to have elevated themselves beyond the requirements and qualifications of humor. Such an exemption, however, is equivalent to the claim to have transcended the human condition, to have become "as God," knowing in some final sense the difference between good and evil. Various attempts have been made historically to minimize the human element in matters of fundamental concern, and thereby the necessity for the comic perspective, through dogmatic positions and absolutist presumptions. But like the proud who stumble in their moment of glory, or the foolish whose disguises fool no one but themselves, the very claim to have risen above the finiteness and fallibility of human nature is itself comic-pathetic and in its consequences so often tragic. In this sense, far from humor being a sign of fallenness or a trespass upon some holy ground, the absence of humor signifies the pride symbolized by the myth of the fall, and comedy a reminder of paradise lost. Humor acknowledges that "we see in a mirror dimly" and that we "know in part" and "prophesy in part" (I Cor. 13:9, 12 RSV). The alternative to humor is the arrogance and idolatry of those who profess to see clearly, know absolutely, and prophesy inerrantly.

The criterion by which one judges the importance an individual attaches to something is not necessarily the degree of unwillingness to laugh about it, to make it the grist of comedy or the target of puns and jokes. While such an attitude has been a common prejudice surrounding our most cherished opinions and convictions, it is the mark of pseudoseriousness—in fact, the mark of what often becomes an inhuman and inhumane seriousness. Seriousness is human; it is the seriousness of this or that human being. Insofar as we remember our humanity, the play of humor is not irreverent or irresponsible but a moral and spiritual necessity. Without humor we become something less, not more, than human. We become not more divine but more demonic.

Though the playfulness of humor may jar our Calvinistic-Puritan-Capitalistic sensitivities, seriousness alone is stultifying and creates its own sterile forms of bondage, as well as violent forms of oppression. We need not only to be serious about certain things, but to laugh, to laugh even at our seriousness, to laugh at the things about which we become so serious and in which we become so seriously involved. We cannot be deadly serious about law, for instance, without suffocating the spirit of the law in the process—as the natural history of legalism abundantly demonstrates. In George Santayana's words,

> Where the spirit of comedy has departed, company becomes constraint, reserve eats up the spirit, and people fall into a penurious melancholy in their scruple to be always exact, sane, and reasonable. . . . Yet irony pursues these enemies of comedy, and for fear of wearing a mask for a moment they are hypocrites all their lives.[7]

Seriousness also intensifies anxiety. As long as one is completely immersed in and therefore circumscribed, defined, and determined by the little drama of the finite self, its opinions and situations, everything is quite sober and serious. A hushed mood of pontifical gravity and regal solemnity prevails, and trespassers on this holy ground must be punished, beaten off, or crucified. The comic perception, however, no matter how brief the glimmer, is itself an emancipation from the prison-house of the self, its opinions and its situations. One is free to laugh. And in that freedom, life opens up to a different light and a larger perspective.

"High" and "Low" Laughter

Not any laughter will serve the purposes of humor, to be sure, as is well illustrated in the epitaph for the notorious Billy the Kid provided by his nemesis and biographer, Sheriff Pat Garrett: "Those who knew him best will tell you that in his most savage and dangerous moods his face always wore a smile. He ate and laughed, drank and laughed, rode and laughed, talked and laughed, fought and laughed—and killed and laughed."[8] The observation is reminiscent of Hamlet's exclamation over the ghostly revelation of his father's murder by his uncle, who has in turn married his mother and usurped the throne:

> O villain, villain, smiling, damned villain!
> My tables—meet it is I set it down,
> That one may smile, and smile, and be a villain.
>
> *Hamlet* I.v. 106–8

This gives some credence to the common suggestion that laughter is born of antagonism and aggression. Certainly executions, lynching parties, torture chambers, and the like have always provided their own sadistic merriment. Nero, we may presume, laughed as well as fiddled while Rome burned. The mocking laughter of the mob at the crucifixion of Jesus was of this baser sort: "He saved others, he cannot save himself." Laughter per se is hardly a reliable indicator of the comic spirit. Laughter can be arrogant, taunting, scornful, contemptuous, sneering, vulgar, cruel, nervous, giddy, hysterical, malicious, bitter, and insane. Laughter can be both sadistic and masochistic. For that matter laughter may also be the result of tickling and laughing gas.

The most primitive form of humor is laughter at the misfit, the deformed, the outcast, the nonconformist. For all their aspirations to high civilization, and their vaunted emancipation from the "dark ages" of medieval life, the exemplars of the Renaissance often engaged dwarfs, midgets, hunchbacks, and imbeciles for their entertainment. Even bishops, cardinals, and popes provided themselves with collections of less fortunates. There is a childish quality in such humor, for children can be quick to ridicule those who deviate from the norm, a departure experienced as threatening and anxiety-producing. Children are seeking an identity for themselves and a structure to their world, needs which can find expression in laughter at differences from oneself or differences from some accepted order of things. In the extreme, such laughter can take cruel delight in the mistakes and misfortunes of others, supposedly thereby enhancing one's own self-worth by diminishing others.

The Oklahoma humorist Will Rogers, after a trip to Rome and a visit to the Coliseum, offered a professional assessment of Roman humor: "If we see a fellow slip and fall and maybe break his leg, that's a yell to us; or if his hat blows off and he can't get it. Well, that's the way the Romans were.... These Romans loved blood.... A Roman was never so happy as when he saw somebody bleeding. That was his sense of humor."[9] The same seems to be true of the English who, for some reason, find the word "bloody" extremely funny.

Aristotle distinguished between a "liberal" and an "illiberal" laughter. Surely an illiberal laughter has effects opposite to those that Konrad Lorenz sees humor as encouraging. Rather than harmlessly releasing aggression, laughter may serve as the tool of aggression, and even incite it, as teasing schoolchildren and skillful propagandists know very well. Or instead of developing a larger perspective and a humbler posture, laughter may be used to reinforce one's prejudices and sense of superiority, as sexist and racist and Polish jokes do quite successfully.

To some extent we are thrown back on Anthony Ludovici's theory that the smile has its origin in the animal's baring its teeth in a threatening or threatened pose, just as the handshake is credited with having its origin in a gesture that stopped hands and bodies short of a less happy collision.[10] If so, the smile is a significantly redirected expression that moves from hostility to friendliness, from the tension of strangers meeting to a relaxed atmosphere of congeniality. And the accompanying laughter likewise moves from aggression to acceptance and goodwill. On this line of interpretation an "illiberal" laughter is a laughter that moves back toward the original baring of the teeth. It is laughter retrogressing to the growl and the snarl. "Liberal" laughter moves forward into more playful, pleasant and convivial surroundings, and it is liberating both to ourselves and others.

Laughter may also be used in excusing oneself by "laughing it off," where change or restitution might otherwise be in order. It may be a way of refusing to look candidly at oneself, so that instead of unmasking pride and pretension they may only be masked more effectively. Laughter, too, can become an easy path of escape from intellectual labor, moral accountability, and profound commitment. It can degenerate into a frivolous diversion from the tortuous and seemingly intractable issues that confront us. And laughter can simply be trivial, dealing as many comics do with clever gags and word tricks, witticisms of the moment that are quickly forgotten because they do not touch us at the core of our being. They provide only a convenient diversion, a momentary chuckle, a false sense of security.

Because of the variety of illiberal forms of laughter, it has been easy for sensitive souls to see it as a dangerous and volatile gas that must be tightly bottled up. Plato rejects a comic art that so easily arouses the "rebellious principle" in the populace, especially at public festivals, and counsels the guardians of his ideal republic not to indulge in laughter or to play the clown. Ecclesiastics have been known to have similar misgivings over the value of laughter, usually preferring to keep it at a respectable distance from holy things, if not to eliminate it altogether, after the manner of the Rule of Saint Benedict: "As for coarse jests and idle words or words that lead to laughter, these we condemn with a perpetual ban." Or, as the seventeenth century religious writer Robert Barclay in his *Apology for the True Christian Divinity* (1676) insisted: "It is not lawful to use games, sports, plays, nor among other things comedies among Christians, under the notion of recreation since they do not agree with Christian silence, gravity and sobriety."[11] Even

Baudelaire argued that there is a "violent" and "satanic" element in laughter, and that it is so closely associated with feelings of pride, superiority, and defiance that it may be said to be "intimately linked with the accident of an ancient Fall."

Though such examples of uneasiness about the comic could be multiplied indefinitely, and though many forms of "fallen" laughter do serve to support such views, the humorist does not trade in any and all sorts of laughter. The laughter of humor *may* strike out at persons or circumstances as a substitute for more violent alternatives and as a harmless escape-valve for tensions and frustrations. But it does so particularly when the laughter is justified by the object—for example, laughter at a haughty individual caught in a ridiculous pose, or at someone whose pretensions have suddenly been exposed. Laughter at an oppressor, similarly, is a way of converting defeat into victory and the grimace of suffering into a smile. Or the laughter of an inferior toward a superior is a way of momentarily reversing and equalizing their relationship. Such uses of laughter are not "fallen" but are aimed at a restoration of balance and a renewed sense of dignity and fair play. Comic *justice* is served.

Yet at its highest, the laughter of humor is a laughter in which, if one laughs at others, one is also willing to laugh at oneself. Even in laughing at others one vicariously laughs at oneself, for humor sees all as sharing in a common human nature and the common predicaments, embarrassments, and temptations of life. The humorist laughs *with* and not just *at* other people. The laughter of humor is thus able to function relative to those things which we may hold dear and cherish, including ourselves, as well as all those things which others, in ways that may seem foolish and therefore funny to us, hold dear and cherish. Humor is not aimed solely outside the self or the in-group. It circles back upon our own postures and claims, foibles and failings. Humor is like the bauble carried by the fool in medieval and renaissance Christendom which might be used to mock and caricature others or simply to hit other people over the head, but which also bore a likeness of the fool in comic miniature.

Once this step is made, humor is opened up to sympathy and goodwill. Those who are able to include themselves in their laughter are also able to include others in their generosity. A humor that heretofore has moved within the context of comic release and comic justice now moves within a context of empathy and kindred feeling. Humor is freed to become the humor of humility and compassion.

Such a comic sensitivity is much more than a keen wit, quick repartee, ingenious word-play, or the wag's talent for making others laugh—all of which might take place completely outside a sense of humor with respect to oneself, as an examination of the biographies of certain well-known clowns and comics would clearly reveal. The ability to be funny and get laughs has nothing directly to do with gaining a comic understanding of one's own existence, or of human existence as such. The technique of the comic twist is not identical to the art of humor. One may make mirth daily for the admiring masses yet not necessarily have succeeded in personally existentializing the comic spirit and perspective.

Humor at its best is a comic sensitivity in this more mature, internalized form. The perspective it provides is a perspective on one's own life, not just other people's lives, and on the whole of life, not just occasional and peripheral moments. The humorist, as the specialist in humor, is therefore to be distinguished from the satirist, the ironist, the wit, and the comic. The humorist may use satire, irony, wit, and a variety of comic devices, yet speak and act out of a more profound spirit and a more all-embracing vision. In humor dwells the truth of Kierkegaard's dictum: "The more thoroughly and substantially a human being exists, the more he will discover the comical. Even one who has merely conceived a great plan toward accomplishing something in the world will discover it."[12] The wit and the comic may offer entertainment and diversion, along with a means of elevating ourselves at the expense of others, but the humorist offers a kind of salvation. The laughter of the humorist has a redemptive quality.

Limiting Views

The art of humor is, however, forever encountering misunderstandings. The situation is hardly improved by multiplying the number of stand-up comics in nightclubs or the percentage of comedies in cinema, television, and theater. It is probably worsened. When humor is so commonly associated in the popular mind with "illiberal" and immature forms of laughter, humor is that much more easily prevented from becoming internalized and mature and from addressing us in the totality of our lives.

Medieval physiology determined that the seat of laughter was the spleen.[13] This not very intellectually or spiritually promising location may have derived from the abdominal associations of laughter, which seemed to well up and explode in the larynx from some dark, abysmal region. Laughter belonged to the lower levels of our being, in association with the stomach, intestines, sex organs, and bladder. By identifying laughter with the spleen rather than the brain or heart, let alone Platonic psyche or Christian soul, the rational, moral, and spiritual values of a comic sensitivity were easily dismissed.

Yet the belly laugh is not necessarily the disruption of our higher nature by our lower, or the dark descent of spirit into flesh, but may represent the unrestrained laughter of the whole person, the free and unitary expression of the totality of our being. The attempt to locate humor in the province of sensuality misses the fact that humor can just as easily debunk sensualism as intellectualism. As in the comic impulse toward moderation rather than tragic extremism, humor can respond as well to excesses of the left or right, whether the excess is sensuality or spirituality, gluttony or anorexia, the anal or the analytical. The humorist is also inclined to play with the tensions between such extremes, finding sources of laughter in the awkwardnesses of our being, rather than leaving them to tragic anguish and alienation.

An example of good-humored treatment of these troublesome polarities of human nature may be drawn from Laurence Sterne's *The Life and Opinions of Tristram Shandy*. The eighteenth-century novelist— also a priest at Yorkminster cathedral—tells the story of Tristram's Uncle Toby who had been wounded at the battle of Namur: "in the attack of the counterscarp before the gate of St. Nicolas...in one of the traverses, about thirty toises from the returning angle of the trench, opposite to the salient angle of the demi-bastion of St. Roch." This wound, furthermore, had not been received in a particularly glorious and notably heroic place, but rather upon the groin. At home Uncle Toby had become the subject of much interest to his neighbor, the Widow Wadman, including the subject of his wound—purely out of neighborliness and Christian charity, of course. After months, even years, of the most polite and circumspect inquiries, the Widow finally became direct: "'And whereabouts, dear Sir,' quoth Mrs. Wadman, a little categorically, 'did you receive this sad blow?' 'You shall see the very place, Madam,' said my Uncle Toby.... You shall lay your finger upon the place.' Whereupon Uncle Toby drew forth and displayed, for Mrs. Wadman's particular inspection, his map of the battlefield."

Arthur Koestler in his *The Act of Creation* offers a lengthy—but for all that lowly—view of the character of humor. Humor is not only malicious rather than compassionate and rude rather than gentle, but also "emotion deserted by thought" and an inner tension "discarded by reason [which] finds its outlet in laughter."[14] Still, Koestler is forced by further consideration of examples to acknowledge a special kind of wisdom and rationality in the capacities of humor. Humor can stand apart from any situation, no matter how emotional or tense or negatively charged, and can divert energies in less passionate, inflammatory, or violent directions. Koestler, that is, has begun with Aristotle's illiberal laughter and moved to admitting its remarkably liberal capacities. The conclusion to which he comes seems hardly to have been promised by his starting point and general line of argument:

> The sudden realization that one's own excitement is 'unreasonable' heralds the emergence of self-criticism, of the ability to see one's very own self *from outside*; and this bisociation of subjective experience with an objective frame of reference is perhaps the wittiest discovery of *homo sapiens*. Thus laughter rings the bell of man's departure from the rails of instinct; it signals his rebellion against the single-mindedness of his biological urges, his refusal to remain a creature of habit, governed by a single set of 'rules of the game.'[15]

Humorists' interpretations of their own art are also not always helpful, and sometimes they are quite misleading. Even Al Capp—who, if he was not being facetious, should have known better—stated baldly, "All comedy is based on man's delight in man's inhumanity to man...and this has been the basis of all the comedy I have created." The joke or comic performance or cartoon strip portrays people who are uglier, dumber, poorer, hungrier, lonelier, or grumpier than we are, so that we may come away enjoying our superiority and congratulating ourselves on our greater good fortune.[16]

It isn't true, of course, not even of Al Capp's comedy. Daisy Mae was uncommonly beautiful. Li'l Abner's physique was the envy of every red-blooded American body-builder. Mammy Yocum, despite having the stature of a pygmy, had superhuman strength and a firm control of almost every situation. Other Capp characters, such as Lem and Luke Scragg, were definitely beneath us, burning down orphanages to get some light for reading their comic books, and in other like ways endearing themselves. But they also turned out to be better than most of us in dutifully asking their father's permission to perform their dastardly deeds.

On the other hand, Mammy Yocum tended to be bossy. Daisy Mae, for all her charms, was almost totally unsuccessful in gaining the attention, let alone the attentions, of Li'l Abner. Li'l Abner, while seemingly a hunk of ultramasculinity, had no interest in kissing anyone but his mother and his pig. In other words, comic characters are on the average not inferior to us but both better and worse than we are, and a part of the comedy they present has to do with the incongruities this makes possible and the awkwardnesses that result. Comic characters mirror in striking form our own existence.

Even though no less an authority than Thomas Hobbes may be quoted in support of the theory—"laughter is a sudden glory arising at the sight of an inferior"—it is a garbage collector's view of the comic sensibility. Everything is thrown away but the trash. Humor would hardly be worth devoting a career to if this were all laughter amounted to. It would also hardly be worth burning anyone at the stake over. Though Hobbes has been followed in this by subsequent interpreters, including modern theorists, such as Koestler,[17] to see humor as essentially aggressive and self-inflating is to ignore the fundamentally playful character of humor. Humor is first and foremost a form of play, a playfulness that issues in a great variety of comic games: puns, jokes, quips, anecdotes, jests, teasings, gags, witticisms, slapstick, farce, cartoons, comedies, clownings, and so on. Some comic games are less formal, others more formal; but whether impromptu, or well-prepared and programmed, their basic motivation is playfulness.

The Hobbesean view also ignores the fact that a sizable proportion of humor is directed at those seen as guilty of the very characteristics alleged to be the substance of humor: aggression, self-assertion, pride. When the prophet Amos makes fun of rich Israelite women as "cows of Bashan" who will be led forth out of the land with fishhooks in their noses (Amos 4:1–5) it is because they have grown fat on the deprivation of others, and he is defending those who have been oppressed by their selfishness and pride. The "victims" of the humor are those who have made victims of others. Of the thirty-odd references to laughter in the Hebrew Bible, nearly half are in the context of celebration, thanksgiving, and praise; and nearly half are in the context of mockery, derision, and defeat of enemies—as in Psalm 2:3 (RSV).

> He who sits in the heavens laughs;
> the Lord has them in derision.

This laughter, however, is seen as just and deserved because of idolatry, pride, or oppression. It is the laughter of comic justice.

Another common misunderstanding of humor is that it is basically trivial. Gordon Allport refers to the psychological function of humor as that of helping "to integrate personality by disposing of all conflicts that do not really matter."[18] Reinhold Niebuhr, writing in the period of disillusionment following World War II, argued, "Laughter is our reaction to immediate incongruities and those which do not affect us essentially. Faith is the only possible response to the ultimate incongruities of existence which threaten the very meaning of our life.... Man's very position in the universe is incongruous. That is the problem of faith, and not of humor."[19]

Yet this cannot be true, for in the first instance this would mean that somehow human beings were not free to laugh relative to the fundamental incongruities of their nature—a minor difficulty that would soon be dispensed with by but a single small child finding humor therein and laughing. In the second instance, incongruities of every sort are central to the persona of the comic hero, especially in the form of the clown. In the third instance, this interpretation would hardly answer the difficulty that much of "man's inhumanity to man" historically is the result of some faith, some vision or ideal, some intransigent ideology, that has been taken absolutely and with absolute seriousness. When one considers all the "good" that has been done to the human race in the name of one faith or another, faith has considerable incongruities of its own to worry about. If humor without faith is in danger of dissolving into cynicism and despair, faith without humor is in danger of turning into arrogance and intolerance. Indeed, faith without humor is itself an incongruity, for it is inevitably the faith of this or that finite and conditioned group of human beings—as the humorist is quick to point out.

A similar misunderstanding is that humor concerns itself only with issues that are basically unimportant to us. Humor plays in the relative safety and irrelevance of the circumference of our lives. In Harold Watts' words, "It is the trick of comedy to confirm all our superficial judgments; it must make us ignore those which we regard as profound and eternal."[20] While this is no doubt true of some comedy and humor, it is not true of all. In fact, quite the opposite is the case in the most mature and internalized expressions of the comic vision. At first sight the comic sense may seem inappropriate to the seriousness of our most fundamental problems and persuasions. Yet it is precisely here that humor is most needed. It is least needed on the periphery of our lives. And to restrict it to such marginality is to offer a conveniently self-fulfilling prophecy: Humor is trivial and superficial.

Of more than etymological interest is the fact that the words "wisdom" and "wit" have the same root, common to Indo-European languages, *vid*. The term is drawn upon in Sanskrit to refer to the exalted wisdom of the sacred scriptures, the *Vedas*; in Greek it becomes *oida*, knowledge; in Latin *videre*, to see, and *visus*, vision; in German *wissen*, wisdom. The term "wit," from *wis*, wise, did not necessarily refer to humor, as in "have their wits about them" or "being out of their wits." On the other hand the term "wise" takes on associations with humor, not only in the word "wit" but also "wiseacre" and wisecrack." That both wit and wisdom have a common lineage bears a profound insight. Wit is not necessarily frivolous, and certainly is not witless, but may convey wisdom in its own special form. Wisdom, in its fullness, contains wit and, without the perspective and sparkle of wit, leaves something to be desired. The wise man and the wit, the sage and the jester, are twins—not identical twins, but twins nonetheless.

Aristotle reminded the disputants of his day, quoting Gorgias: "Humor is the only test of gravity, and gravity of humor. For a subject which will not bear raillery is suspicious; and a jest which will not bear serious examination is false wit." Such is the intertwining of wit and wisdom. Comic protagonists are often *socially* marginal and, like the fool, may appear to be the very opposite of the wise. But they do not therefore deal only in marginal issues and literal foolishness. Their marginality and foolishness gives them a certain immunity in the precarious business of dealing humorously with matters otherwise held very dear. The philosophy of the humorist may be put quite succinctly: *Anything that is serious is worthy of humorous consideration.*

Three Levels of Humor

If one were to put these arguments in more systematic fashion, three levels of humor might be identified. Humorists are not particularly enthusiastic about systems and charts, being more inclined to parody or frustrate them than espouse them. As Edwards remarked to Johnson in

James Boswell's *Life of Samuel Johnson*, "I have tried too in my time to be a philosopher but, I don't know how, cheerfulness was always breaking in." Still, some initial map is essential for understanding humor—as it is here being interpreted—and for suggesting a more adequate frame of reference than is commonly given to the comic spirit.

From a mythic standpoint, humor may be said to function on three levels, corresponding symbolically to the themes of paradise, paradise lost, and paradise regained. Humor is a playful return to a past innocence and unity, a reflection and release of present tensions and contradictions, or a recovery on a higher level of lost simplicity and amiability. Putting these levels in developmental terms, they are represented by the humor of childhood, adolescence, and maturity.

Childhood: The Laughter of Paradise

We first encounter laughter in response to a pleasant surprise or parental touchings and ticklings or the delighted enjoyment of anything. In mythological terms, this is the laughter of paradise, prior to the awareness of nakedness or sexuality or death, and prior to a divided consciousness. Such laughter is not generated by the tensions and doubts, anxieties and frustrations of life. It springs forth from the exuberance of life itself. It is, as Joseph Campbell put it, a leap into that "wild and carefree, inexhaustible joy of life invincible."[21]

The growing sense of humor that accompanies this laughter plugs into the *elan vital* itself, the energy of life which bursts forth into playfulness, lightheartedness, smiling, and laughter. Humor becomes a form of human life at play: life playing with life, sporting with life, surprised by life, amazed by life, delighting in life. There is no particular purpose, plan, aim, or goal. There are no rules or forms, regulations or genres. One is simply enjoying playing for the sake of playing.

At the simplest and most innocent level, then, humor is the enjoyment of playing for the fun of it—whether with words, concepts, objects, situations, or persons. Fortunately, this level is not closed off to adolescents or adults, as those evicted from the garden of delights. It is one of the ways human beings, of whatever age, may frolic, play the fool, indulge is silliness, enjoy nonsense, act with childlike abandon, and deliver themselves to the caprice of the instant. Through puns and pranks, tall tales and zany absurdities, we may still enter that freedom which resists being fixed in rigid categories or sterile reasonableness or wooden eternal appropriateness. One does not have to be programmed or proper all the time. Like the play of children, humor in this sense is a sheer "waste" of time and energy. It has no aim other than to play and have fun.

One of the *Monty Python's Flying Circus* vignettes shows a family gathered in their living room on a Sunday afternoon, arranged as if watching a television program. Instead they are taking turns, dividing up all the words they can think of according to whether they are "woody" or "tinny"—including the word "woody" which does sound woody and the word "tinny" which does sound tinny. One might ask, in a industrious and industrial society, What is the point of that? Well, there isn't any point. The humor is not going anywhere or taking on any grand issues or relieving any deep disturbances. It is just *being*, playfully, just "horsing around" laughingly.

A book of elephant jokes compiled by a public school student contains the following prefatory note by the publisher: "Warning! Practically no parents will think elephant jokes are funny." An example: "What did Tarzan say when he saw the elephants coming? 'Here come the elephants.' What did Jane say? 'Here come the plums' (She's color blind)."[22] In this exchange no antagonism toward elephants is being vented, no sense of superiority over ponderous pachyderms, no anxiety over the prospect of being run down by a herd of wild elephants, no catharsis for elephant complexes. Nor is there necessarily any implied sexism or tension between the sexes. The joke is just plain fun. One is enjoying being nonsensical for the sake of being nonsensical in a refusal to make sense or progress or money all the time. The "weightier matters of the law" are set aside and the world of playfulness is entered through the peculiar freedom of humor. It is the world of innocence prior to the knowledge of good and evil, outside of shame and guilt, where taboos do not exist and where there are neither things important nor unimportant, sacred nor secular—the world biblically represented by the original innocence of Adam and Eve.

In such a world everything becomes, in a sense, unimportant and profane, and therefore fair game as the object of laughter—a carefree nonsense that David Letterman has used quite successfully. Yet in another sense everything becomes playfully important and indiscriminately endowed with holiness—as in the *Batman* television farces, where

Robin's exclamations announced the most mundane variety of things as holy: "Holy smoke rings," "Holy syllogisms," "Holy hypothesis," "Holy jelly beans." Such humor is most open to the charge of being trivial, frivolous, and irresponsible. Yet this misses the point of comic banter, for the distinctions between significant and trivial, serious and frivolous, holy and unholy, are not available. They have been set aside in the recollected laughter of little children.

Adolescence: The Laughter of Paradise Lost

Humor is not all innocence, however. At a more sophisticated level, it stands more self-consciously in the midst of conflict and anxiety, success and failure, faith and doubt. It is not so much a humor that lays aside the tensions of life in a holiday of innocence as a humor that moves within those tensions in comic reflection of them. It is, consequently, the comic mode that corresponds mythically with paradise lost. And its laughter proceeds from the Adamic "knowledge of good and evil." Psychologically this corresponds to the humor of adolescence. Here humor draws upon the many ambiguities and tensions of our existence that arise from self-consciousness of our nakedness and sexuality and mortality, including self-consciousness itself. Humor plays with all the awkwardnesses of our self-awareness as creatures of both reason and impulse, altruism and selfishness, sense and nonsense, mind and body. Hence so many jokes about sex and food and body wastes; or, for that matter, about mad scientists, goody-goodies, and bespectacled professors. We discover that we are "a little lower than the angels" (Ps. 8) and—on a good day—a little higher than the apes.

Usually human awkwardnesses are presented by the humorist in their least distressing though perhaps most embarrassing forms: a seat collapses under the dignity of the portly mayor; the queen's slip is showing; the preacher's false teeth fall out at the climax of the sermon; the ranting politician gets a pie in the face; a lovemaking scene is interrupted by the sudden cave-in of the bed. Yet these minor awkwardnesses point to a deeper level of awkwardness. There is an intrinsic awkwardness about human nature and its position in the cosmos as such. The glory and pathos of the human situation to which Pascal referred so poignantly in his *Pensées* has its humorous side as well. But instead of leaping out of this "existential predicament" in a temporary amnesia of innocence, or being consumed by the tragic collision, humor remains to confront the situation comically. Humor in fact serves as a reminder of this awkwardness for those inclined to forget it (its *iconoclastic* function, which it shares with satire and irony); and it offers a means of accepting this awkwardness and coping with it (its *cathartic* function).

Though we would prefer to ignore it, we are creatures of enormous potential contradictions which can tear us apart, and tear others apart, and tear us apart from others. These contradictions are the stuff of tragedy, but they are also the stuff of comedy—which may be why Christopher Fry was able to say that he could find himself in one or the other perspective at "the turn of a thought" and that "if the characters were not qualified for tragedy there would be no comedy."[23] These contradictions and their stresses can lead to physical illness, mental illness, violence, and suicide. They can lead to split personalities and alienated relationships. Yet the same tensions can provide humor with its energies. Instead of letting them eat away at our insides or vent themselves by lashing out at others we release these tightly coiled springs humorously.

Humor, therefore, can provide great therapy, or preventative medicine, as Norman Cousins, Daniel Keller, and others have argued.[24] Mark Twain in *Tom Sawyer* credits such healing powers to humor when he writes of the old man who "laughed joyously and loud, shook up the details of his anatomy from head to foot, saying that such a laugh was money in a man's pocket because it cut down the doctor's bills like everything." Humor converts tragic dramas into comic games, and in so doing turns tension into a positive source of healing. Instead of these energies bursting forth in anger or hostility or agony, they burst forth in laughter and enjoyment.

Humor in this context contains a kind of confession, the comic analog to the confession of sin. Through humor we acknowledge the infinite human capacity for getting it wrong, sometimes intentionally, often unintentionally. While our pride and official poses present a different picture, we are beset by all manner of faults and foibles. In humor we confess, as it were, our foolishness, or at least other people's foolishness, and perhaps foolishness as a general human problem of which we are an occasional example. Thus the popularity of the genre of bloopers. Professors, as a case in point, are especially fond of student bloopers, such as the following collection of answers to questions on major inventions:

> Gutenberg invented the Bible;
> Sir Walter Raleigh invented the cigarette;
> Gravity was invented by Isaac Newton in his spare time;
> Benjamin Franklin invented electricity by rubbing cats together backwards;
> Lois Pasteur invented a cure for rabbis.

Or take some of the choice answers reported by religious educators:

> Noah's wife was Joan of Ark;
> Solomon had 700 wives and 300 porcupines;
> Lot's wife was a pillar of salt by day and a ball of fire at night;
> Martin Luther was a martyr who was nailed to the church door and executed by a papal bull.

The humor in the context of paradise lost is also a means of venting frustration, fear, and antagonism. W. C. Fields is credited with saying that "no one who hates children can be all bad." And much of Fields's humor expressed the hostilities we often feel toward children and dogs and salespeople and spouses. There *are* things about children that can be irritating at times. And laughter with respect to those persons or situations that we do not like is a means of disposing of matters symbolically. Whether or not anything is actually disposed of other than our immediate irritations, we feel better about it. The humorist provides us with a ritual triumph. We even manage to enjoy, through the magical transformations of humor, the very sources of our irritations.

Raised to a higher plane, such humor becomes a means of dispensing a kind of poetic justice. Much laughter is *justified*, as in the proverbial example of the proud man falling on a banana peel. Humor can have an ethical dimension to it, which fastens on hypocrisy and injustice. It can delight in bringing down the mighty, counterbalancing inequities, and mocking evils. While it is a laughter at others, it is not the laughter of superior relative to inferior or victor relative to victim, but of justice in relation to injustice or of honesty in relation to hypocrisy. The concern is the opposite of the Hobbesean formula, namely, to put down the mighty from their thrones and exalt those of low degree (Luke 1:52).

Arthur Koestler has tried to associate the comic impulse with malice and the tragic impulse with pity, citing respective responses to "a fat man falling on ice." If one laughs at the spectacle this suggests malice relative to a comic figure, but if one shows sympathy this suggests pity relative to a tragic figure.[25] While it is possible, in such a case, that we might be viewing the lowest form of laughter, the laughter might also be predicated on the assumption that the man was not hurt, only his pride; and the laughter might quickly turn to expressions of sympathy if real pain were evident. The laughter, too, might be an expression of a sense of justice if the man were pompous or arrogant or the source of other people's fallings. Thus, the laughter itself may be an expression of sympathy, namely for those who have been the victims of this man's pride and injustice.

Humor is an important part of the struggle for justice on the part of the powerless. It becomes one of the weapons for those who have no weapons. In the most difficult circumstances, humor also helps maintain at least a modicum of sanity among those who are demeaned, humiliated, downtrodden, dehumanized. Even in the absence of any literal possibility of justice, humor has allowed slaves, at least symbolically, to bring down their masters. Jesters have ridiculed kings, peasants have turned the tables on overlords, and conquered peoples have been victorious over their conquerors. Through humor some small particle of self-respecting dignity has been preserved, like Chaplin's tramp who rose again and again out of dust and destitution, finding moments of mirth in the most godforsaken places.

Far from lacking in sympathy and compassion, humor in the context of paradise lost begins to come to terms with the hard and harsh side of life. Playfulness is still there; lightheartedness is still insisted on; but this is now in the midst of evil, suffering, and death. Part of the heroism of the humorist lies in the refusal to take these features of human experience with absolute seriousness. The humorist does not permit them to have the last word, to be controlled or destroyed by them. Against the "thorns and thistles" or "slings and arrows" of our individual and collective fortunes, humor bursts forth out of the will to live and the courage to be—or not to be.

Consider the comic treatment of death and its distance from the tragic lament. Red Skelton, on reaching the age of seventy, at his birthday celebration remarked: "At my age, if I wake up and don't see any candles or smell flowers, I get up!" Or Woody Allen on the same subject: "I'm not afraid to die. I just don't want to be there when it happens."[26] Here even death is played with; it is not approached in a one-dimensional and univocal way. In such humorous inventions we see the peculiarly human capacity for contemplating the darker side of life, yet in such a way as to accept it philosophically and with some equanimity, while affirming life and the gift of life. When the humorist James Thurber learned that he had a degenerative eye condition and was going blind, he chanced one day to overhear a young woman's offhand remark: "We are not going to hide our heads in the sand like kangaroos." Said Thurber, "This was just what my harassed understanding and tortured spirits needed. I was, it is not too much to say, saved by the twisted and inspired simile; and whenever I think I hear the men coming with the stretcher or the subpoena, I remember those kangaroos with their heads in the sand, and I am ready to face anything again."[27]

The same capacity of the comic spirit is more profoundly visible in the remarkable phenomenon of Jewish humor; for the Jews, like the American blacks, have developed a genius for comedy in the mist of very tragic histories. It is hardly a coincidence that a high percentage of comedians in the United States, especially relative to their proportions in the population statistics, are Jewish or black. Humor is not only possible in relation to the more superficial and inconsequential incongruities of life. As gallows humor or concentration-camp humor will attest, it may also express a certain heroic defiance in the face of life's most crushing defeats, an unquenchable nobility of spirit that refuses to permit a given fate or oppressor to have the last word—to be absolute. The human spirit has not been utterly vanquished. The will to live and the determination to continue the struggle, or the faith that the struggle will be continued, has not been finally conquered. Where there is humor there is still hope.

Maturity: The Laughter of Paradise Regained

There is, however, another level of humor, though it is not as commonly achieved. It is prefigured in the laughter of innocence, yet it is not identical with it. It is the laughter that comes beyond good and evil, rather than before it. It is the laughter of maturity, the laughter in the freedom of a higher innocence and unity, that corresponds mythically to paradise regained. One has now become free in the fullest sense to laugh. Such humor is not centered in the playfulness of childish delight and gay abandon, nor driven by the doubts, anxieties, and animosities of our lives, or even by a noble desire to see justice done. It arises out of a sense of acceptance, resolution, and larger harmonies.

A. C. Bradley found elements of this kind of humor in the figure of Falstaff: "The bliss of freedom gained in humor is the essence of Falstaff.... a humorous superiority to everything serious and the freedom of soul enjoyed in it."[28] Hegel paid similar compliment to the best in comedy: "The keynote is good humor, assured and careless, unconcerned gaiety despite all failure and misfortune, and with this the exuberance and dash of what is at bottom pure tomfoolery and, in a word, fully exploited self-assurance."[29]

The distinctive feature of this form of humor is that it is generated not by inner tension but by an inner harmony. It does not reflect conflict so much as reconciliation. Clearly this is the most dynamic and self-contained humor, for it proceeds not from a position of weakness and turmoil but from a position of strength. It is like the difference between the taunting laughter of adversaries and the relaxed laughter among friends. Whether one sees the context of such humor in terms of faith, trust, serenity, or affirmation of life, the laughter it produces comes from a profound sense of security rather than insecurity, acceptance rather than protest. It does not come from the spleen. It presupposes faith in some sacred order or depth-dimension of being, some common basis of worth and dignity, while at the same time refusing to dogmatize its understanding of that faith and worth.

This makes possible a further relationship between humor and compassion. Instead of moving only in the direction of a laughter at others and their faults and foibles or supposed injustices, humor moves toward a laughter that accepts others in spite of their differences and even their devilishness. Since it is not grounded in a nervous insecurity, it does not need to be self-protective and self-assertive. It is therefore capable of becoming, in the purest sense, the humor of love. The element of judgment in humor (its iconoclastic function) passes over into mercy.

To such a level Wylie Sypher alludes when he speaks of the "radiant peak of 'high comedy'" where "laughter is qualified by tolerance, and criticism is motivated by a sympathy that comes only from wisdom." A victory is won over our absurdities "at a cost of humility...and in a spirit of charity and enlightenment...without despair, without rancor, as if human blunders were seen from a godlike distance."[30] Such a magnanimous humor is not easily realized, but it should not therefore be discounted or ignored. It is, in a sense, the final goal and fulfillment of humor. Humor moves from playful innocence through truth and justice to humility and compassion.

Here there is no suspicion of malice, aggression, or denigration of others. The desire is to share with others something entertaining and enjoyable—as when friends sit around in a convivial atmosphere and exchange stories to the merriment of all. Instead of a discharge of tensions and thwarted energies, what is discharged is good will. The context is one of the celebration of life and the communion of laughter and good cheer. The appropriate benediction for the occasion is that of Tiny Tim: "God bless us, everyone."

In this freedom humor is able to go beyond dispensing judgment upon the follies and hypocrisies of others and dispenses, as it were, a kind of divine grace. Grace, as Northrop Frye has argued, is an important theme in the most mature comedies.[31] Comic grace is grace both in the sense of the graceful courtier or gracious host or hostess and in the sense of a long-suffering, forgiving, and reconciling grace. The humorist, though capable of very pointed criticism and of putting people's faults in bold relief, leads the way finally to acceptance rather than rejection. Instead of the distances between people being enlarged and hardened, they are reduced and softened.

There is a recovery of childlikeness in this, for children have the remarkable capacity to forgive and forget over matters that in the adult world become permanent grudges. Children can have the worst quarrel of which they are capable and in a few hours—or minutes—are back playing together as if every moment were a new moment and nothing quite so important as play. Because children are not given to absolutizing themselves and their situations, reconciliation comes easily and the festival can begin once more.

Here too those other virtues of the child are recovered: spontaneity, immediacy, lightheartedness, playfulness, naturalness. To be sure, a distinction must be drawn between childlikeness and childishness. Many adults quite successfully kill their former childishness but in the process kill also the possibility of a mature childlikeness. Much of what passes for adulthood is therefore not maturity but an advanced and hardened stage of adolescence. The adolescent imagines that adulthood is achieved through a process of forgetting and destroying one's former identity as a child. How else can one be considered adult, be given more freedom and responsibility, stay out late at night, and have the keys to the car, except by getting rid of the child that we once were? Thus the worst comment that can be made to a teenager is that you remember his or her former identity as a child, knee-high to a grasshopper. That is precisely what the adolescent is trying so hard to forget.

The developmental logic seems so impeccable that many never get beyond it. The world becomes more and more serious, less and less playful, with the prize presumably going to the adult who manages to avoid laughter for twenty-five years or more. One may, indeed, become an adult on this basis and succeed in the marketplace, but one does not necessarily become mature. True maturity involves a resurrection of childlikeness. One becomes once again—as an adult, and in full knowledge of good and evil—like the child. Joseph Campbell put it a little differently: "It is the gift of immaturity itself, which has enabled us to retain in our best, most human moments the capacity for play.... It is, in fact, only those who have failed, one way or another [to preserve this gift] in their manhood or womanhood, who become our penny-dreadfuls, our gorillas and baboons."[32]

It is true that children can be selfish and self-centered and short-tempered. They can throw tantrums, be inconsiderate, and make quite a mess of things. And they cry a lot—which is why children have to grow up. Still, there are certain childlike graces that we tend to lose as we do grow up and face the sobering realities of life, which is why adults need to turn and become like children again. Children have a secret. It is the secret of how to live, playfully and lightheartedly—at least the half of the time in which they are not crying and trashing the living room. But they don't yet have it all together.

The world ruled by seriousness alone grows old, faded, wooden, rigid, lifeless. The grave world is indeed the world of the grave. But the world in the reign of the comic spirit grows young again—lively, vital, creative, dancing, joyful. It is a world that is guarded not, like Eden by some angel of judgment with a flaming sword, but by the heralds of good humor who invite all to come in who will lay down their rifles and rattles, their poses and posturings, their stern masks and fierce trumpetings. It is a world which, as Johan Huizinga said of poetry, "lies beyond seriousness, on that more primitive and original level where the child, the animal, the savage and the seer belong, in the region of dream, enchantment, ecstasy, laughter."[33]

5

Will The Real Adam And Eve Please Stand Up?—The Comedian

There are no lavatories in tragic palaces; but from
its very dawn, comedy had use for chamber pots.

—George Steiner, *The Death of Tragedy*[1]

One of the problems generated by tragedy, as with high serious drama and art generally, is the omission of a considerable amount of relevant detail concerning the total human condition. Such an omission comedy sets out to correct, almost with a vengeance. Tragedy is extremely selective, not only in its representation of human types, but also in the information it admits about even those lives and actions it chooses to dramatize. Comedy, however, introduces whole sets of characters and circumstances, attitudes and forms of behavior.

In comedy, devoted attention is willingly given to the many particulars of everyday life which a more heroic sophistication seems determined to dress up, cover up, forget, ignore, or otherwise treat as polite unmentionables. The archaic staples of comedy are thus the earthen trinity of sex, food, and body wastes. Added to this are the basic requirements of clothing, shelter, and sleep—the first two as reminders of our nakedness, the third a reminder of our nightly helplessness, unconsciousness, and irrational dreamings. Mixed in are all those troublesome inevitabilities of burping, itching, scratching, sniffling, twitching, yawning, dozing, stretching, hiccuping, nose-wiping, ear-picking, sneezing, snorting, coughing, choking, spitting, belching, farting—ad infinitum and ad nauseam. There are, indeed more things in heaven and earth than are dreamed of in our philosophies!

95

Already we have much of the basic fare of comic episodes. What, in short, is turned by comedy into a matter of great dramatic consequence is a considerable inconvenience and embarrassment to tragedy. So much is this the case that all this plethora of human activities is almost completely bypassed and suppressed as if such did not, or at least should not, exist. As Bergson has commented on the point: "No sooner does anxiety about the body manifest itself than the intrusion of a comic element is to be feared. On this account, the hero in a tragedy does not eat or drink or warm himself. He does not even sit down any more than can be helped."[2]

The Whole Truth

If tragedy deals with more negative and troublesome matters, as it must, it prefers to do so in a grand manner and for some grand purpose. For all its idealism and exalted opinion of the species, tragedy can admit a considerable array of evil and degeneration. Yet it cannot even begin to handle a simple affair like hiccups. When Chaplin in *City Lights* inadvertently swallows a whistle, just as a pompous soloist is beginning to sing, and starts tweeting with every hiccup, we know that we are in the world of comedy. Tragic heroes simply don't go around swallowing whistles and tweeting.

Tragedy will take on any number of bloody battles and fallen houses, but it would be greatly offended at the proposal to pause over a pesky mosquito. It will grant the existence of certain more "noble" weaknesses of the flesh, such as a craving for power, or the love of a beautiful mistress, but it will not touch an inordinate desire for pickles. Tragedy wants to play only with the fine china and silverware, even if it gets stolen or broken in the process. Comedy gets along very well with kitchen spoons, lunch buckets, and eating with impatient fingers.

The comic sense, as Eric Bentley remarks, "tries to cope with the daily, hourly, inescapable difficulty of being." Comedy persists in noticing the little problems of life that are ignored by those who would restrict themselves to major crises and important decisions. If the dramatic hero refuses to acknowledge even such small matters as the necessity of relieving bladder or bowels at the normal time, we are given to understand that a worse fate can occur. Perhaps in the very midst of slaying dragons the hero will be weighted down by constipation! Or in the triumphal procession our hero will begin to squirm uncomfortably in the chariot and smile painfully at the cheering crowds!

The comic perception in this is the protagonist of all that is natural, however ordinary or lowly, while it is the antagonist of all that is unnatural, artificial, affected, or pretentious. Oscar Wilde's aristocratic title *Lady Windermere's Fan* with only slight alteration becomes "Lady Windermere's Fanny"—a less dignified but considerably more fundamental and essential attribute. Kierkegaard had the audacity to note that Hegel, for all his world-historical categories, world-encompassing genius, and grand philosophical system, went like everyone else to pick up his paycheck on Fridays. The list of such comic reminders is unending.

This is not just a matter of debunking. There is in comedy a kind of rock-bottom faith in the essential goodness of what is *natural* to humankind. What is natural is that we should think. And it is equally natural that we should think about eating, sleeping and sex. What is natural is that we should dream. And what is equally natural is that we must wake up from our dreams, or that if we refuse we shall surely wet the bed. If we bask too long in the sunshine of our createdness in "the image and likeness of God," we will sooner or later be returned to the dust or splattered with mud.

The reasons for tragic delimitations are not hard to come by. Tragedy is inclined not only toward abstracting the more glorious, heroic, and grandly dramatic aspects of human existence, but also toward abstracting spirit from body. The totality of the human condition is avoided as something confusing a singleness of purpose and preventing the exercise and pure nobility of the spirit within. The body gravitates to earth like a great weight, anchoring and restraining a ballooning spirit, eager to make its ascent. The mind soars upward to infinity, the imagination imagines its creative marvels, the spirit floats off toward some limitless bliss, and all the while the body just sits there, finite, lumpy, leaden, and tugging away at the winding-sheet of the ghost within. In the midst of thinking a great thought or dreaming a great dream, we are interrupted by any one of a myriad of petty demands, like a little child insisting on going to the bathroom in the middle of an oratorio.

Such a body easily presents itself as a kind of tragedy befallen the spirit, a wart attaching itself to the soul and growing until it encases the "true self" in a ponderous mass. Such a body, so conceived, so tolerated, so used or abused, becomes in Socrates' unfortunate but revealing metaphor "the prison-house of the soul." Such a body is worthy of representation at all only in its most ideal, virile, and heroic forms: clothed in great deeds and high drama or frozen in incorruptible marble. Otherwise it is at best a damned nuisance.

This ethereal view of spirit and gross view of body very early becomes comic fare at the hands of Aristophanes, whose *The Clouds* puts Socrates in a basket suspended from a cloud balloon, riding majestically, if precariously, in the sky like a god. When asked what he is doing up there in that curious conveyance, he replies that it is necessary for him to suspend his brain in the sky and mix the essence of mind with that of air, which is of similar nature, in order to contemplate the sun and understand the things of heaven. "Had I stayed on the ground, I would have comprehended nothing, for the earth draws to itself the sap of the mind—as is the case with watercress." There follows a discussion of the source of rainfall, the nature of which Socrates understands because his head is in the clouds. His student responds that he always presumed it was Zeus urinating into a sieve! That issue clarified, there still remains the problem of the source of thunder, also attributed to Zeus. Socrates resolves the issue by an analogy with the grumbling stomach that issues in periodic belches: "Consider what sounds are produced by the stomach, which is small. Is it surprising that the boundless heavens should produce such loud claps of thunder?"

Aristophanes has been much criticized for this attack upon such a paragon of humanistic ideals and philosophical acumen. But it is this very mind/body, spirit/flesh dichotomy with which Aristophanes is dealing. Reason, like the best intentions and highest ideals of tragic aspiration, is not the pure, infallible, and trustworthy instrument it often claims to be vis-à-vis the supposed denseness of matter and irrational passions of the flesh. In the hands of a skilled debater or clever defense attorney, and motivated by reward or status or pride or simply the desire to win, reason can be mere sophistry.

By satirizing the "Socratic" training in the sophistic art of "unfair argument," Aristophanes is making the double point that is so much at the heart of comedy. Faith in a reason and virtue somehow emancipated from the restrictions and temptations of the flesh, and returned to the clear light from which it originally came, is unfounded. Reason is not intrinsically pure any more than the body is intrinsically impure. Reason can confuse, twist, distort, trick, and pervert, just as virtue can become self-righteous, proud, and hypocritcal. Genius is no more a guarantee of truth than power is a guarantee of justice or a strong will a guarantee of right choice. Thus, as Meredith insisted, "comedy is the ultimate civilizer," not reason or law or moral order alone.

The implied derogation of the body as impure in any attempt at extracting from it "pure" reason and "pure" spirit, and dropping it off like a dirty rag or an outgrown shell, is a lack of appreciation for the integrity of the body and its natural functions. There are times, in fact, when the natural inclinations of the body and the mundane concerns of everyday life are more to be trusted than those principles and visions to which they are sacrificed. One might well argue that the evils resulting from bodily needs and desires per se are nothing in comparison with the evils brought on by reason and imagination—including moral principles, political ideologies, and religious beliefs.

Even greed will preserve that which it has taken by force, whereas ethical, ideological, and religious considerations are often far less merciful. When the prophet Samuel announces to King Saul that God has ordered an attack on the Amalekites to "utterly destroy all that they have," not sparing but slaying "both man and woman, infant and suckling, ox and sheep, camel and ass," Saul at least saved the best animals on the pretext of offering them in sacrifice (I Samuel 15 RSV). Comedy obeys a different word and a different god and has a different assessment of a righteous spirit that adjusts so well to slaughter. The comic muse might well be more inclined to recommend killing the prophet and sparing the women, children, and camels!

Give Me Your Tired, Your Poor

Comedy goes yet one more step. It points not only to the body but to bodies of all sorts, from handsome to grotesque. If anything, comedy is focused somewhere between the plain and the grotesque, with some preference for the grotesque. A parade of comic characters would certainly be a motley sight: giants and midgets, the fat lady and the thin man, the rubber-legged and the lame, the toothy and toothless, the bulbous-nosed and flat-nosed, the blind and deaf, the bald-pated and bushy-haired, the garrulous and tongue-tied—followed by a middling troop of normally unnoticed individuals who are not distinguished in any particular respect. The whole human circus and sideshow is there in comedy, boldly exhibited like some grand human menagerie.

An 1899 Barnum and Bailey Circus poster for "The Greatest Show on Earth" displayed just such an array of assorted people and attractions, along with the title "The Peerless Prodigies of Physical Phenomena and Great Presentation of Marvelous Living Human Curiosities." One of the characteristics that comedy and circus have tended to share is a willingness to encompass and make use of the whole human spectrum. The costumed beauty rides on the lumbering beast or walks hand in hand with the ugly dwarf. The graceful trapeze artist soars high above the stumbling imitations of the clown in the ring below. Nothing and no one seem to stand outside this circumference, this *circus*.

The motives for inclusion may be mixed. But as even sideshow freaks have often testified, the circus and carnival—like the earlier social niches for fools and grotesques—have been places where they have been wanted and accepted *as they are*. They have been able to hold a job, feel a sense of personal worth, develop friendships, and play a part in this great theatrical mirror-image of human life. Instead of being hidden away in lifelong seclusion, they have been made a focus of special attention. So much was this so at one time, in fact, that circuses had difficulty getting people to move from the sideshow into the main tent—that is until someone at Ringling Brothers came up with the ingenious solution of putting a sign over the exit that read "This Way to the Grand Egress."

When Aristotle classified tragedy with the sublime and beautiful, and comedy with the ludicrous and ugly, there was considerable empirical basis for doing so. Comedy does not restrict itself to, or aim toward, the "best specimens." Any body, and any bodily function or malfunction, that tragedy might spurn as beneath its dignity has been welcomed by comedy with open arms and given a dramatic significance. "Come as you are. Come one and come all." That is the comic invitation and the comic capacity. At the more primitive level, this comic sense may be little more than the combined result of fear of that which is not normal and feelings of superiority over others, along with the necessity of giving some social place to everyone. But the larger result—and at the more sophisticated level, the goal—is that of accepting and admitting this great multitude of human forms, fortunes, and imperfections.

Who could imagine that such delight and camaraderie could be fashioned out of those same abnormalities and subnormalities, or just plain

normalities, that otherwise cause such embarrassment, anguish, or boredom! Who would suppose that so much drama could be gotten out of
such castoffs as nervous twitches, wobbles, peglegs, and stutterings and
stammerings; such miseries as headaches, bellyaches, trips, and falls; such
annoyances as seasickness, a stubbed toe, a dropped hammer, or a sudden
gust of wind; such miscellaneous events as a tear in the seat of the pants,
a butterfly on the nose, pigeon droppings, or an ant in the soup!

Comedy, however, is not just the associate of the ugly and ludicrous.
The wise, the powerful, and the beautiful also become unwilling and
sometimes unwitting, comic characters. The comedian sees the so-called
noble and superior person as subject to unwarranted vanity and something of a fool. And there is no fool like a great fool. At the same time,
comedy elevates those persons and conditions which, from the standpoint of nobility and superiority, are unworthy of attention or are worthy only of the attention of ridicule. What comedy proposes is to
challenge those very hierarchical valuations that follow from the distinction between noble and ignoble, superior and inferior, sublime and
ludicrous, beautiful and ugly. Comedy, by turning attention to all that
have been judged to be "beneath us," or beneath somebody somewhere,
discovers in these outcasts subjects of special interest and worth.

The comic achievement is quite remarkable. With little to work with
in the way of heroes and heroines, fine costuming, labyrinthine plot,
profound dialogue, elegant scenery, dramatic action, or casts of thousands, it manages to mesmerize us with life's pots and pans, street scenes,
and social rejects. Like so many family and situation comedies, it gets
along very well with the kinds of people, petty circumstances, and typical irritations that make up 99 percent of our lives. In fact, the very
difficulties and disturbances that in real life may weary us, make us
sick, throw us into a rage, drive us up the wall, or have us shouting or
crying or depressed, are transformed by comic ritual into occasions for
enjoyment, if not hysterical laughter.

What do we do when we get together with friends or have a party?
We tell stories. And often those stories consist of tales, told with great
relish, of the various terrible, stupid, embarrassing, or unfortunate things
that have happened to us—to the entertainment and conviviality of all.
This is the ultimate human transubstantiation, and the true test of the
alchemy of the human spirit. Comedy takes the most common table
items of our lives, like bread and wine—items that may also be sur-

rounded by real anguish and suffering—and transforms them into the body and blood of our salvation. The elements remain exactly the same in appearance, yet the inner meaning and outer effect is radically transmuted by a spiritual alchemy from lead into silver and gold.

The miracle of comedy is that what is the source of limitation and dismay to tragic inspiration becomes the source of amusement and celebration. Instead of banging defiantly on the bars of flesh or developing grand schemes of escape, the comedian finds special charm in all the sights, sounds, smells, tastes, and touchings within our immediate perception. It is as though in some sacred sense this world for all its inequalities and this body for all its frailties and this time for all its inconsequentia is where one ought to be. It is as though life were intrinsically holy, and that to fail to savor it, rejoice in it, and be humored by it would be a great sacrilege. It is as though we were created out of this dust, to be divided and united as one flesh, and surrounded by this incredible zoo of creatures, both animal and human, determined to venture forth in the belief that, in some larger sense, "God saw everything that he had made, and behold, it was very good" (Gen. 2:3 RSV).

The major task of the comic protagonist, as Nathan Scott insists, "is to remind us of how deeply rooted we are in all the tangible things of this world: he is not, like Shelley or the author of *To the Lighthouse*, a poet of 'unbodied joy.' The motions of comedy, to be sure, finally lead to joy, but it is a joy that we win only after we have consented to journey through this familiar, actual world of earth which is our home." Such is the peculiar but very real salvation that the comedian stoops to bring. It is the comedian who moves within the dustiness and density of the real world, unafraid to get hands dirty and feet muddy, without anxiety over losing face or tarnishing some polished image. "The comedian is not generally an aviator; he does not journey away from this familiar world of earth; he refuses the experiment of angelism; he will not forget that we are made out of dust."[3]

Comedy therefore does not encourage speaking about food and clothing and sex and material things in a hushed voice of apology for the lowly plight the spirit has gotten itself into. Comedy vents our many embarrassments and tensions, and our feelings of shame and guilt, in these areas. But the purpose is the opposite of attempting to liberate the spirit by disparaging any of the characteristics of human life and thus disabusing the spirit of further interest. Comic simplicity has nothing to do with a righteous beating of the body into numbed submission. Rather, it is an opening up of one's total capacity for wonder and delight, and just plain savoring, in the widest manner possible.

One may of course survey the transience of things that, despite their transiency, are so frantically desired, clutched, fought over, and even died for. And one may declare them to be nothing in comparison with eternity, or in their vanity unworthy of the wise person's attention. A considerable fool literature has argued the point. In Sebastian Brant's *Ship of Fools* (1494) this common sentiment was characteristically developed:

> All things have I recognized as vain, foolish, perishable, doomed soon to slip like water into the earth. Nothing is firm, solid, durable. This brief hour snatches away whatever you may for a short time possess.... [O world] I flee you, I leave you, and abandon you completely. And may the gods, and God himself help me, that I may rather prefer to worship you alone, Holy Father, and to follow you, gracious Christ.[4]

Yet time is only a sieve or a sinking ship or a prison if we *choose* to view it that way. Time, as one wit has put it, is simply nature's way of keeping everything from happening all at once.

One may also see in this, for all its apparent piety and sacrifice, a failure to celebrate that form of life given to humanity. In Brant's own religious terms, though life is transient, it is in its very transience holy by virtue of its createdness and givenness. While things may be perishable, it does not follow that they are necessarily vain or foolish. The type of expression represented by Brant has the look of offering creaturely praise and glory to the Creator in preferring "to worship you alone." But it is actually a lament against the Creator and creation. The world is piously despised as unworthy of human affection. It is as if to suggest that we had been cheated and betrayed by the ephemerality and imperfection of life. Surely we are much too noble for a world where things are constantly breaking, decaying, dying, and otherwise confounding and disappointing us.

A good deal of rebellion and complaint has been passed off in this manner as thanksgiving and devotion. And the confusion is considerably aided by doctrines of some original paradise, on earth or in the heavens, where matters were not so and from which we have fallen or been evicted. Ergo, the cultivation of whining or disgust is not only permissible, it is a religious virtue—or, in other mythological circles, a mark of existential authenticity, accompanied by litanies of alienation, anxiety, dread, nausea, and abandonment (e.g. Sartre).

Whether motivated by the religious quest for the purity of Heaven, or the rationalist quest for Pure Reason, or the idealist quest for Pure Spirit, or the existentialist quest for Pure Freedom, all have similar consequences in the end: they are illusory forms of transcendence that turn life into a clash between imagined perfection and a universal imperfection. As quests they are escapist; and as readings of human existence, they are tragic, for they define authentic existence as an agonized lamentation over the disparity between what is and the imagined purity of something or other. The comic inclination, by contrast, is to accept and celebrate the drama of life, in spite of its resistance to being molded by any of the idealisms proposed for it. Confronted by the density of matter and the vagaries of history, the comic response is more along the lines of Mark Twain's comment on *Webster's Dictionary*: "This is a very interesting and useful book...I have studied it often, but never could discover the plot!"

The evil is not in time and matter. The evil is in that very salvation that would measure time by eternity, matter by spirit, and history by syllogisms. The beauty of matter is that it is so material. The beauty of time is that it is just like time. The beauty of history is that it is so unpredictable. The beauty of change is that it is so changeable. Plum blossoms and cherry blossoms, as the Japanese have appreciated almost to the point of a national passion, are beautiful despite the fact, and in a sense because of the fact, that their beauty is so fragile and brief. Thus Kenko could write, "If man were never to fade away like the dews of Adashino, never to vanish like the smoke over Toribeyama, but lingered on forever in the world, how things would lose their power to move us! The most precious thing in life is its uncertainty."[5]

If one judges an old, cracked, misshapen tea bowl, with its irregular coloration and happenstance configurations, by the standards of finely detailed and lacquered porcelain, it may appear ugly. And yet it is highly prized; for that which is old and worn, that which is imperfect and unfinished, that which is off-center and asymmetrical and accidental, has a special beauty all its own. No image of its opposite can ever negate that beauty. If anything, it can only enhance it by comparison. The old, rough, irregular tea bowl is of great value precisely because it is *not* new, symmetrical, and finished to perfection.

Though nothing in this life is "firm, solid, durable," it does not follow that its elements are "vain, foolish, and doomed." What is vain is to imagine things to be otherwise, and to lament the fact that they are not. Fleeing from such a perishable and imperfect world is the very foolishness from which the comedian would save us. The idea of paradise is itself the fall. It is a falling away from an acceptance and celebration of the actualities of life.

Dusty Dignity

Comedy, however, does not point only to flesh and finiteness and dustiness. Since what comedy chooses to portray is usually what has been omitted, its content has some dependence upon whatever the omission of the day. This does not mean that comedy is parasitic, but rather that its task is one of counterbalancing and mediation. It is there to tame the beast or tie down the angel in us, whichever is parading at the moment. Comedy is a moderator of passions, both subhuman and superhuman. It is the restorer of unity and wholeness.

One thing that is so often missing, whether in the ritual arena or in everyday life, is the *spirit* which comedy represents: laughter, lightheartedness, playfulness, gaiety, frivolity. And that spirit it insists upon, whatever the subject matter or concern. But the *form* and *content* of comedy may differ considerably, depending on what has been omitted. Commonly what is missing is a full recognition of human limitations and hence a sense of perspective relative to those lofty portraits and painted pretensions with which we flatter ourselves. So comedy displays our finiteness, our foolish bunglings, our phallic fantasies, our lustings after power, our famished appetites, and our chamber pots.

But if the prevailing portrayal is reversed, and humanity and human relationships are in danger of reduction to the physical level or of being deluged by dirt and smut, comedy can recoil and parody this as well. The human animal who seems to be all muscle or all stomach or all sex organs can be just as comical as someone who seems to be all brain or all talk or all-important—as in the dynamic of the relationship in the T.V. comedy *Cheers* between the intellectual Diane Chambers and the physical Sam Malone. The monkey, the pig, the cock, the ass—these are stock figures in comedy which not only call attention to our kinship with the animal kingdom but also remind us that we are something more than monkeys, pigs, cocks, and asses. We are something more even in the act of trying to reduce ourselves to these dimensions.

Comedy is not, therefore, to be identified simply with earthiness, for in content it is not necessarily focused on sensuality any more than on spirituality, the realities of matter any more than those of mind. Obviously there are follies of the body as well as of the mind. The point that comedy succeeds in making emphatically is that human nature is *both*, intertwined. And in its insistence on both is its defense of the whole person, the fully human.

Implicit in this defense is thus a repudiation of the illusory separation of spirit from body in the first place, and all resulting "ghost-in-the-machine" dualisms. The body is not seen as inhabited by some fallen bird of paradise, trapped in a cage of matter and flesh from which it flees every chance it can get and perhaps hopes eventually to flee altogether. The distinction between spirit and body is seen as a deceptive distinction made possible by a periodic forgetfulness of the body, lost in thought or transported in imagination. Spirit and flesh, mind and body, are convenient fictions for pointing to aspects of what is fundamentally one person. The comic perception is that of a basic unity of "spirit" and "flesh" that become two by a process of mental abstraction from the whole person.

This perception is already announced in one of Aristophanes' early comedies, *The Acharnians* (425 B.C.):

> Here I contemplate, here I stretch my legs;
> I think and think—I don't know what to think.
> I draw conclusions and comparisons,
> I ponder, I reflect, I pick my nose,
> I make a stink, I make a metaphor,
> I fidget about, and yawn and scratch myself.[6]

While a more noble and heroic image of the species would wish to limit the list of human attributes and activities and extract pure thought or pure spirit from its distractions, in comedy all this is perceived as the activity of *one* person. Contemplating and stretching, thinking and yawning, making a metaphor and making a stink are not only intermingled but finally inseparable. In alluding to this, however, and making some sport of it, comedy is not ridiculing the life of the mind per se. Rather, it is ridiculing the presumption that the life of the mind exists apart from

and in abstraction from the totality of one's being. For all its iconoclasm, there is in comedy an underlying affirmation of the sacredness
and worth of the whole of life.

To this point there is an agreement with those mystical visions of
unity in which the human problem is seen as having something to do
with the separation and alienation of one thing from another. But comedy
is inclined to include among these divisive factors those very categories
that are so often used in trying to transcend the problem: spirit and flesh,
mind and matter, reason and irrationality, eternity and time, being and
becoming. Instead of proposing to resolve the difficulty by attempting
to turn attention increasingly away from the "imperfect" and fragmented
forms of matter to the "perfect" and unbroken forms of mind, a la Plato,
the comic solution is to transcend the distinctions themselves. As John
Dominic Crossan has argued, "the range of comic play extends from the
·scatological to the eschatological. I would even suspect that the greatest
comedy is that which fuses together 'low' and 'high' comedy, scatology
and eschatology, into a transcending unity."[7] Ancient Greek comedy
was often very scatological in word and deed. But this must be measured by the fact that it was to be performed in the temple of Dionysus,
whose symbol was the phallus, before a male audience, surrounded by
phalluses that had been brought in procession from local shrines.

From the comic perspective, the world of illusion and delusion from
which we are to be delivered is not this world of space, time, body,
history, and matter. It is the world that separates and estranges spirit
from body, mind from matter, sacred from profane and sets up a series
of gradations from one category to the other. Comedy does not encourage retreat into gross sensuality and pure animality, any more than it
encourages flight into some ethereal realm of pure ideas, ideal forms,
floating spirits, or mathematical relations. Despite its gleeful delight in
openly displaying the awkwardness of our being, comedy throws us
into the zaniest contradictions as a reminder of our many-sided complexity and as a mock prelude to uniting us again.

As William Lynch has put it, "to recall this incredible relation between mud and God is, in its own distant, adumbrating way, the function of comedy."[8] Did even Plato entertain this possibility in the end?
Perhaps, if Nietzsche's "happily preserved *petit fait*" is correct, "that
under the pillow of his deathbed there was found no 'Bible,' nor anything Egyptian, Pythagorean, or Platonic, but a volume of Aristophanes."[9]

The Mystical Cat

Religions are often credited with contributing to the problem by dazzling the minds of devotees with ecstatic experiences, promises of bliss in heaven or nirvana, images of lost paradises and paradises to come. And sometimes it is true that religions become supply houses for mythologies of disenchantment and rituals of disengagement. The problem is well illustrated from an incident in the life of the nineteenth-century Hindu *sadhu* Ramakrishna, who from childhood had manifested a tendency to pass into trances. The tendency was accentuated during his later priesthood to the point that he once went into *samadhi* for six months, kept alive only by the grace of an attendant who forced food and water into his mouth and cleaned up his body wastes. He eventually regained normal consciousness by virtue of contracting dysentery— which will bring down the spirit every time!

During one such state of trance, Ramakrishna was performing the prescribed morning ritual before the altar of the goddess Kali. As frequently would happen, partway into the chant he began to have visions. Everywhere he looked he saw Mother Kali: the stone image, the altar, the water vessels, the marble floor, the open doorway, a worldly passerby outside the temple. All became so many forms of the goddess. Just at that moment a stray cat wandered into the temple, meowing hungrily. Ramakrishna, hearing the cry as the voice of Kali calling to him, took the consecrated food from the altar and set it on the floor for the cat. At that moment the overseer of the temple had entered the sanctuary and, shocked by Ramakrishna's sacrilege, demanded an explanation for his conduct. Ramakrishna replied innocently that he had had a vision of the presence of the goddess in everything and that when he had heard the goddess meowingly imploring him to give her the food, he had done so.[10]

In one sense this is very much akin to a scene replayed again and again in the history of the comic tradition. Something holy is profaned (sacred food), and something profane is elevated and treated as holy (a common cat). Customary expectations are overturned, and established categories are jumbled or reversed. But the case of Ramakrishna's cat is only a partial success, and the reasons for this are quite revealing of the problem of ecstasy. Though the story is not lacking in humor, something is missing. And essentially what is missing is the *cat*.

The question immediately presents itself: Would Ramakrishna in a normal state of consciousness have given the offering to the cat? Would Ramakrishna have been willing to offer the food to the cat *as a cat*, in fact, the most profane form of cat (an alley cat), rather than as a form of the goddess? Would Ramakrishna have had compassion on the cat because the *cat*, inconsequential and lowly though it was, was hungry and begging for food? Or has not Ramakrishna, in the very act of endowing this common cat with the supreme value of being an embodiment of the goddess, emptied the cat of any intrinsic value it may have had by virtue of simply being a cat? It is as if being a cat is not enough to qualify for priestly attention or human compassion or sacred food.

What is now of value is not what the cat is in itself as a cat—in fact, in its own unique individuality as this particular cat—but as an empty vessel for some universal divine presence. And relative to this ultimate reality, this pathetic stray cat, already near the bottom of the scale of values and hopelessly profane, can now only appear as nothing, a hollow shell, an apparition in the illusory world of *maya*.

At this point the comic tradition parts company with those idealisms that place a premium on ecstatic oceans of bliss and transcendent unities of being, relative to which the spheres of ordinary consciousness, everyday concerns, and individual uniquenesses are downgraded as imperfect and unenlightened levels of perception. Like mysticism, comedy aims at overcoming dualities, breaking down walls that separate one thing from another. It juxtaposes opposites as a means of softening the opposition, establishing a sense of the feeling "We're all in this together." But it does so by challenging our hierarchies of value as well, which also separate one thing from another or deceptively unite things by reducing them to something else.

Comedy liberates us from those boxes in which we isolate and insulate ourselves, and from those grading systems in which we make ourselves out to be superior or inferior. But it does not then dissolve individual difference and separate worth in some ultimate oneness that alone, or even supremely, is holy, true, good, and beautiful. Comedy continues to wonder about cats.

6

Jester To The Kingdoms Of Earth—The Fool

Evil prevails where laughter is not known.

—Iglulik Eskimo saying[1]

At the court of King Alboin of Lombardy in the sixth century A.D. there suddenly appeared a creature named Bertoldo. Court records describe him as being ugly, dwarfed, and deformed, with carrot-colored hair. He marched directly to the throne, and brashly seated himself beside King Alboin. The king demanded to know who he was, where he came from, and by what authority he dared enter the king's court uninvited and sit beside the throne. Bertoldo replied: "I am a man. I was born the night my mother bore me. And the world is my country."[2]

One of the redeeming features of ancient and medieval monarchies was that they recognized that a king needs a court jester, not only to be the scapegoat for court jokes but also to play the role of the king in comic caricature. A part of the function of jesters was to make kings laugh and to offer themselves as objects of laughter, but it was also their function to make kings laugh at themselves and to permit others, indirectly, to laugh at them. To be sure, jesters, with their comical appearance and manner and speech, were engaged and retained as a form of entertainment. Yet in their entertaining way they represented a spirit and perspective that stood outside the laws and jurisdiction of any particular earthly kingdom. They provided a comic restraint to the inherently tragic possibilities of royal power and authority.

It was hardly an accident of history that kings permitted such deformed, dwarfed, and "demented" figures as Bertoldo to intrude on the royal presence. The elevation of the royal person and rule to a godlike station required the comic person and mock rule of the jester in order to preserve that delicate balance of power on either side of which were the pitfalls of tyranny and anarchy. If the king did not admit the jester to his court, the door was open to absolutism and despotism. If the jester's iconoclasm became too successful, the door was open to social disruption and political chaos.

The jester thus represented the humorous qualification of all human orders and enterprises. The kingdom was served by a comic king who stood outside the earthly authority of the monarchy and in tension with it. The jester was a creature without rank and power, from whom the king had, it would seem, nothing to fear. Yet as a fool, and because a fool, the jester was capable of playing a prophetic role and representing a larger spirit and higher wisdom.

Truth-teller

In Roman times it was the custom of returning conquerors or heroes to carry a slave in their chariot as a symbolic acknowledgment that they were human beings and not a threat to the power of the gods. It was the duty of this *servulus* to exhort warriors not to be overly proud of their victory, lest they be guilty of what the Greeks called *hubris*. They were to be honored by the populace as they rode to the capital, but abuses (*molestie*) in the form of taunts and jests were also permitted. In ancient Rome it was also the practice for a jester (*mimus*) to follow in the funeral procession of the emperor to provide diversion from the somberness of the occasion and even to mimic the dead emperor. Suetonius mentions a *mimus* named Faco who accompanied Vespasian's funeral procession dressed as the emperor, mimicking even such traits as his presumed miserliness by asking bystanders how much the funeral was costing him.[3]

Jesters were conventionally bald, dating back to the Greek mirthmakers (*gelatopoioi*) who were bald—at least up to Cardinal Wolsey's jester Saxon who went along with the wig craze. Lucian in his *Lapithae* describes the appearance of the Roman jester as having a shaved head, except at the top where a lock of hair was left to resemble a coxcomb. The cock was a favorite symbolic associate of jesters and fools because, while a rather stupid bird, he is nonetheless given to strutting proudly about, lording it over a clucking harem that largely ignores him, crowing loudly with a suggestion of authority and self-pronouncement, waking everyone at some ungodly hour for no good reason, God's gift to barnyards and hen-houses. Another common animal symbol was the ass, mule, burro, or donkey. Asses' ears came to be added to a "fool's cap" to which bells were attached. The bells announced the presence of the fool and were associated with celebration, merriment, festivals, and revelry. Asses, mules, burros, and donkeys were fitting associates as lowly beasts of burden, given to stubbornness, and noted for their toothy grins and whinnying "laughter." In other countries different animals were used, as in medieval Japan where the jester was likened to a monkey and the jester's songs were called "monkey-music" (*sarugaku*). An eleventh-century Japanese treatise on the subject, attributed to Akihira Fujiwara, defines their comic purpose as being "to twist the entrails and dislocate the jaws of spectators with foolish nonsense."

Records of jesters in the English monarchy go back to the court of Edmund Ironside (eleventh century), and for the French line to Hugh Capet (tenth century). Though introduced primarily as a diversion, in a later time jesters were often to become quite influential figures as advisers and confidants. Edward IV had his Scoggins; Henry VIII his Will Sommers and John Heywood; Queen Elizabeth her Richard Tarleton; Charles II his Tom Killegrew; Henry III (of France) his Chicot. Not all kings, it is true, had jesters. According to one account no jester of any consequence was known to have been retained by the court of William Rufus, "the king, indeed, hardly needing one; for he was accustomed not only to make his own jokes, but to laugh louder at them than any other person!"

In a sense, the jester provided the king with a comic alter ego, a less serious, more human, and more flexible self to step into. The jester was the king's symbolic twin—as is suggested in the belief registered by Rabelais in *Gargantua and Pantagruel* that "those who wear the crown and scepter were born under the same sign as those who wear the cap and bells." In the king-as-jester—or jester-as-king—there was a softening of the contradiction in the person of the king as both sacred ruler and mortal human being. In the form of the jester, the king was prevented from pretending to be what he was not and permitted to be what he really was: a human being like everyone else, who participated with all his subjects in the frailties and follies of the human condition. The freedom of the court jester to violate all the proprieties and taboos of royalty, to flaunt pomposity and decorum, was vicariously experienced by the king as his own freedom, his personal emancipation from the rigid confines of his role and the loftiness of his responsibility. He was able to step out from behind the mask and costume of his official self and station into his other self. What Wylie Sypher has said of the function of the carnival may be said of the role of the jester:

> Those in the thrall of carnival come out for a moment from behind the facade of their "serious" selves, the facade required by their vocation. When they emerge from this facade, they gain a new perspective upon their official selves and thus, when they again retire behind their usual *personae*, they are more conscious of the duplicity of their existence.[4]

Through jesters, kings preserved both their sanity and their humanity.

At the same time, the court and populace were provided with a relatively harmless—though not necessarily ineffectual—avenue for venting animosity and discontent. The behavior of the jester was an instance of what Max Gluckman has called "rituals of rebellion." "Every social system is a field of tension, full of ambivalence, of cooperation and contrasting struggle."[5] To act out these conflicts is a way of acknowledging that the conflicts exist and of permitting a certain amount of rebellion to exist. But because the antagonisms are *played* out, and especially when played out comically rather than tragically, they are prevented from being destructive of the order and authority within which they move. Yet they are capable of making a difference.

In certain African kingship systems, rather than a jester playing the role of king, the king was required annually to play the fool. The king, who by virtue of rank and power was elevated above all other members of the tribe, made this periodic descent from the highest to the lowest station, thus reversing and overturning his normal status. He dressed in rags, walked unescorted through the village, and begged for food. The members of the tribe, over which the king held sway through the rest of the year, were permitted to taunt and insult him. And the king was supposed to talk gibberish as if he were the village imbecile. In this way the social hierarchy was inverted for a season. The king moved from the top of the social order to the bottom, while his subjects were permitted to "lord" it over him. The sacred person and role of the king were thus ritually profaned, rendering the inequities and rigidities of the social system more tolerable. A similar custom prevailed at the Roman Saturnalia, when slaves took the role of their masters, and masters were to obey their slaves.

The symbolic kinship between king and jester is further evident in the fact that the jester was often the one member of the court who had the most immediate access to the king, requiring no special permission or announcement, as if the jester were the king's shadow. Though the jester was a shadow that could be beheaded, this eventuality was remarkably rare, considering the amount of freedom this peculiar station afforded. The jester was one through whom difficult news might be passed when no one else dared tell the king the truth—as in the case of the defeat of the French fleet of Philip by the English fleet of Edward III. When the task of informing Philip was given to his jester, the jester began pacing about muttering curses on the cowardly English sailors who were afraid to jump in the sea when so many brave French sailors did so so readily!

An important aspect of the jester's role was therefore that of truth-teller. The social distance between king and jester was so great—like that between adult and child—that the jester could stand closer to the king, and deal with him more directly and straightforwardly, than others who might constitute a more obvious threat to royal authority and power. This paradoxical classification gave the jester a kind of freedom and license that other humans did not have, not even the king who was still bound by the dignity and expectation of his role. Thus in a court full of flattery, elegant manners, elaborate protocol, and pretty speeches, the jester was the one capable of the greatest directness, honesty, and candor.

One may cite the case of the Chinese emperor responsible for completing the Great Wall, Ch'in Shih Huang Ti, who had a court jester named Yu Sze. After the 1,500 miles of wall had been constructed at great expense and with considerable hardship for the tens of thousands of laborers, the emperor decided to have it painted. All knew this would mean an even greater expenditure of resources and lives, yet none of the court advisers had the courage to question the emperor's wishes—except for Yu Sze, who so successfully ridiculed the proposal that the emperor abandoned it.

Jesters were notoriously bold in their ridicule, criticism, and advocacy. Even though their remarks and insinuations might be dismissed as "fool's license," they had the potential for wielding considerable political and social power. As one early commentator, John Fuller, said of Elizabeth's Richard Tarleton: "He told the Queen more of her faults than most of her chaplains." Jesters, because of their social marginality and their wit and humor were the ones most able to say or do what for anyone else might result in imprisonment or execution. When Henry VIII and his court were celebrating the conferral of the dubious title "Defender of the Faith," the king's jester shook his head in mocking disapproval and said, "Let thou and I defend one another, and let faith alone to defend itself."[6]

Jesters served, therefore, what might be called a prophetic function. They did not necessarily claim any divine message or mission, but they moved in and out of the social and political orders of the day as if representing some higher order. Like the prophet Nathan before a King David who had schemed to get Bathsheba by having her husband Uriah sent to the front lines where he would be most likely to be killed in battle (and was), the jester was able to enter the inner sanctum of the palace and tell the king an innocent story, the punch line of which was "Thou art the man."

In the Muslim world the paramount example is Nasr-ed-Din of the fourteenth century. Diminutive in stature and wearing a huge turban, he appeared at the court of the ruthless conqueror Timur (Tamurlane), seeking employment. Timur said he would give him a job if he could answer a list of questions; if not, he would be executed. Nasr-ed-Din's responses so amused the emperor that he accepted him into the court. Like all court jesters, he tended to be very bold in his speech, always walking the thin line between employment and execution. One day Timur saw his aging face in a barber's mirror and began to wail at the sight. The court politely wailed with him, including Nasr-ed-Din. After the emperor regained his composure, Nasr-ed-Din continued his loud lamentations. When Timur asked why he carried on so, Nasr-ed-Din sobbed, "You wept over just one glimpse of yourself. But I have to look at you all day!"

It is difficult for us to imagine at this point in time the degree to which fools were highly visible and almost commonplace individuals in ancient, medieval, and renaissance societies. They were found not only in king's castles but also at the tables of nobility, in the houses and bedchambers of the wealthy, and even at the side of popes, cardinals, bishops, and lesser prelates. A fool was part of the normal entourage of almost anyone of stature, a member of the household in a manner similar to a servant, yet in a world apart. Dwarfs and midgets in particular sometimes acted as companions to children in the combined role of playmate and servant. Fools were also found in traveling shows and festivals, processions and country fairs, taverns and brothels. Even university professors could get part-time positions entertaining as palace fools! This prevalence of folly made the fool a familiar figure in the art, literature, drama, and moral treatises of the period.

Yet by the nineteenth century fools and jesters had become increasingly out of fashion in the royal courts and among the aristocracy, being less suited to reformed, educated, and enlightened tastes. The domain of folly was reduced to the performing stage, traveling show, and country fair, where kindred spirits had always been. The more grotesque "freaks" were hidden away, to reemerge in nineteenth-century sideshows. Dwarfs could await the coming of the circus and the cinema. The demented and the retarded began to be cared for in the new social fashion of cloistering them in institutions.

Today individuals who formerly might have found employment as jesters and fools, and who give us some surviving link to the tradition of folly, are now comic actors, comedians, clowns, mimes, cartoonists, poets and artists, circus performers, sideshow attractions, or residents of state asylums. There was a time, however—and it was a long time—when fools in one or another form had an important niche in society and played a significant social role. The fool was therefore a considerably more immediate and powerful symbol than today, when the remembrance of so tangible a figure belongs only to renaissance plays and history books.

What happens when governmental leaders no longer have jesters? It is a chilling observation to note that Adolf Hitler and Joseph Stalin had no court fools. In democratic countries the role of court fool sometimes seems to be filled by cartoonists, comedians, and political satirists—though without the same direct access and influence. Søren Kierkegaard, who saw himself as jester to Denmark in the mid-19th century—"gadfly" as he called it, after the model of Socrates as the "gadfly of Athens"—offered the following description of the ideal king in the absence of a jester. The advice was offered in person to the king of Denmark.

> In the first place, he very well could be ugly. In the next place he should be deaf and blind, or at least pretend to be, for it simplifies many difficulties.... Finally a king must not say much but have an aphorism he uses on every occasion and which consequently says nothing.... And one thing more, a king must see to it that he is sick occasionally so that he arouses sympathy.[7]

The Religious Fool

Historically the jester has stood in a mocking relationship to spiritual as well as political kingdoms. Here too we find a bold iconoclasm, in this case mediating between the tyrannies of dogmatism and authoritarianism and the chaos of a skeptical pluralism in which "every man does that which is right in his own eyes" (Judges 17:6 RSV). In modern Haiti the Guede jesters offer a good-natured ridicule of religious matters in a mock ritual called "the catechism of the Guede," in which Roman Catholic devotees, catechetical instructions, and ecclesiastical functionaries are parodied. At the end of a ceremony in honor of ancestral spirits (the Guede), the participants are commanded by the leader to form a line and are given a mock catechetical examination, the answers to which are facetiously or ludicrously phrased. Each answer qualifies the "catechumen" for some prestigious ecclesiastical, political, or military title. At the culmination of the examination the most unlikely candidate—perhaps a fat girl of jolly spirits—is acclaimed "Pope."[8] Such burlesque may seem to border on sacrilege, except that it is performed in a buoyant rather than malicious spirit for the common sport of all.

Of similar order were the three medieval festivals following Christmas: Holy Innocents Day, the Feast of Fools, the Feast of Asses. On Holy Innocents Day (*festum puerorum*) the gravity and grandeur of the holy office of bishop was suspended in the appointment of a boy bishop. For one day the awesome authority and responsibility of the church was returned to the playful innocence of childhood, with the boy bishop officiating at a service in which the ecclesiastical positions and functions were assumed by children, concluding later with his bestowal of the episcopal blessing from the residence of the archbishop.

The Feast of Fools (*festum stultorum*) had less of the aura of innocence about it. In a period of reveling following Christmas, the inferior clergy burlesqued the offices and roles of their superiors. In many cases a "lord of misrule" was elected to supplant the holder of the *baculus* (wand of office), the installation occurring at Vespers during that portion of the Magnificat beginning "He has put down the mighty from their thrones, and exalted those of low degree" (Luke 1:52 RSV). In some instances this theme was elaborated to include also a "fool's pope." The Feast of Asses (*festum asinorum*) became yet another vehicle for comic qualification. As a festival commemorating Mary's flight into

Egypt, an ass was ridden into the sanctuary by a young girl carrying an infant boy. With the ass and its riders standing beside the altar, a mass was sung in dog-Latin rhyme, with priest and congregation braying the refrain: "Haw, Sir Ass, he-haw."[9]

Donkeys and burros have been ridden or accompanied by comic figures from early Greek miming to modern clowning. In Greek processions one might have seen mimes riding in or following the donkey cart of comedy. In the Middle Ages, fools were depicted with asses' ears—an association drawn upon in Erasmus' *Praise of Folly*. The English clown Grimaldi sang one of his most popular songs, "Me and My Neddy," astride a hobbyhorse. The fact that Jesus was represented as riding into Jerusalem on an ass, as well as being similarly transported in the flight to Egypt, provided an early symbolic association between Jesus and the fool/ass tradition. Even in triumphal entry into Jerusalem, Jesus came more as a fool's king than as a victorious hero. He rode not in a steed-drawn chariot of power and glory but on a lowly beast of burden, as if belonging to a mock procession among a conquered people. The early church was not long in making the further connection between the crucifixion of this mock "King of the Jews" and the suggestion of a cross on the donkey's back. Jesus was a fool's Messiah, a donkey-deliverer, a jester to the political and ecclesiastical kingdoms of earth.

Religious associations with the fool also moved in yet another direction in the holy fool tradition, which appeared as early as the sixth century in the Greek Orthodox church and reached its fullest development in the Russian Orthodox church between the fourteenth and the seventeenth centuries.[10] A number of individuals were sainted as holy fools. Drawing upon the Pauline idea of the foolishness of Christian preaching, of the cross, and of God (1 Cor. 1:18–31), and of Christian disciples as "fools for Christ's sake" (1 Cor. 4:10), a type of sainthood developed in which the expression of piety was that of publicly making a fool of oneself. The monk or priest manifested his sincerity not by projecting an atmosphere of intense seriousness and sanctity, but by playing the part of the buffoon. Self-effacement was indicated by being ridiculous in appearance and manner and thus becoming the object of mockery. He became, in effect, a jester to the church. Through a holy madness, feigned or real, analogous to that often found among court fools, he abased himself in a renunciation of spiritual pride and a revelation of the folly of the people. He humbled himself, as it were, in a comic identification with the humility and humiliation of Jesus—not the exalted Jesus of ecclesiastical pomp and pageantry, but the peasant Jesus who rode into Jerusalem on an ass as a scapegoat savior. Like the early Franciscans, who also called themselves "the world's fools" (*mundi moriones*), the holy fool withdrew from the riches and power and splendor of the church, as well as from elaborate scholastic theological disquisitions, to follow in the footsteps of a penniless itinerant who was hailed as king by being given mock robes and a crown of thorns and a cross for a throne.

The dangers of such associations with the fool tradition degenerating into outright sacrilege are evident in the many ecclesiastical attempts at suppression. And yet fools and their foolishness point to the necessity of permitting the periodic overturning of human hierarchies, of confounding human reason and its assured verities, of profaning the sacred altars of all earthly principalities and church authorities. Such functions have, of course, been performed in all cultures, quite aside from comic figures and seasonal festivities, in the less formalized and more spontaneous indulgence in humor and nonsense. Whether in the repertoire of the "professional"—fool, jester, clown, humorist, comedian—or in the momentary remark of the "lay person," a perennial profusion of puns, anecdotes, and witticisms has always existed alongside sacred places, persons, beliefs, acts, and objects. They represent an inevitable, essential, and irrepressible human response to anything or anyone that is exalted to sacred status. Some are completely innocent, others quite risqué: some a profaning of holy things only in the sense of interspersing seriousness with humor, others more substantively in an overt caricature of religious concerns. Jokes and jests are constantly being evoked by those matters that we otherwise take with great seriousness, and all attempts at suppressing them are not only ineffectual but also misguided. It has been the characteristic concern of despots and dogmatists alike to safeguard dictates and doctrines from comic disturbances. Yet laughter at most is only driven underground.

Ship of Fools

A common theme in the fool tradition is that all human beings are fools in their various ways, the stage fool and the social fool being only exemplars of a universal phenomenon. As the chant of a sixteenth-century fool's society concluded its roll call of fools: "Fool here, fool there,

fool everywhere." Moralistic fool literatures attempted to map out major types of human folly, but usually not in a way that included everyone.

The most brilliant literary exploration of the fool tradition was that of
Erasmus in his eulogy of folly, *Moriae Encomium* (1509). The approach
of the *Encomium* is decidedly unlike many another medieval and renaissance treatise on the subject, such as Brant's *Narren-Schiff*, published fifteen years earlier, with its 112 garden varieties of fools. In such
moral treaties there was a clean division between those who were judged
wise and those who were deemed foolish, with simplistic recommenda-
tions accordingly. Erasmus saw the human drama, the sweep of history,
and the categories of wise and foolish in a more ambiguous light. He
went further even than his Flemish friend, Badius Ascensius, who felt
that what was lacking in Brant's "Ship of Fools" was that it did not have
enough women on board—a "failing" that Ascensius amply remedied
by producing an enlarged edition that charitably provided six additional
ships for female fools!

Rather than building more ships, Erasmus reinterpreted folly in a more
subtle manner that generously included everybody, including Ascensius
and himself. To add to the ambiguities, Erasmus boldly offered his work
in *praise* of folly, when outside the specific social roles of fool and
jester folly was understood in a univocal sense. Folly was to be shunned
as leading to evil and disaster. "A fool and his money are soon parted."
Or, "the fool says in his heart, 'There is no God'" (Ps. 14:1 RSV). Or, "a
foolish man builds his house upon the sand" (Matt. 7:26, RSV). A book
of folly was expected to be a moral and religious treatise with very direct warnings concerning various sorts of what were judged to be foolish
behavior. Erasmus, however, confounded the categories, finding foolishness in wisdom and wisdom in foolishness and comedy in the whole.

Erasmus credits Plutus, earth-god and god of the underworld, with
being the progenitor of humankind. Dame Folly herself is mother of us
all. The mythological equivalent to Prometheus is his distant Egyptian
cousin, the moon-god and baboon-god Thoth. Thoth was the patron deity
of scribes and learning, giver of letters, numbers, and geometry which
"that evil genius of the human race excogitated for the hurt of man, and
which are so far from furthering his happiness that they actually hinder
it."[11] The assessment here is at considerable distance from that offered
by the Prometheus of Greek myth and tragedy! Folly continues: "First
the arts were discovered—by evil spirits.... Then the superstitions of

the Chaldeans and the frivolous curiosity of the Greeks added hundreds more: all vexations of the spirit."[12]

Special words of praise are reserved for "that rooster Pythagorus" who in his various reincarnations had been many things: "a philosopher, a man, a woman, a king, a subject, a fish, a horse, a frog, I think even a sponge." On the basis of these various transmigrations he had come to the conclusion that "no creature is more miserable than man; for all others are satisfied with their natural limitations, but man alone strives to go beyond the bounds proper to his station."[13]

These inclusions in folly are particularly remarkable in view of the expansive intellectual mood of the time, a mood that Erasmus himself shared as a leading humanist and scholar. The Renaissance was vigorously celebrating a new age and new spirit. There was a revitalized confidence in the possibilities of reason, imagination, and creativity. Inspiration was being sought and found in the classical civilizations of Greece and Rome. Fresh currents of thought, bold explorations, striking discoveries, and ingenious inventions were turning attentions expectantly toward new frontiers. Only seven years before the *Encomium* Columbus had appeared in the court of Ferdinand and Isabella, bringing cocoa beans from America. Nevertheless Erasmus persisted in including the whole of the human enterprise under the term "folly." And there is certainly a strong warning throughout of the tragic possibilities of human claims and ventures apart from a sense of their ambiguities and follies.

For Erasmus the donkey cart of human history was driven by none other than Dame Folly, holding her carrot stick just beyond reach, with enough of a nibble now and then to entice the donkeys onward. "One burns with zeal for revolutions; another is toiling upon his Grand Scheme. This man leaves wife and children at home and sets out on a pilgrimage to Jerusalem, Rome, or the shrine of St. James, where he has no particular business.... What commotions and what tragedies this animalcule, little as he is and soon to perish, sets agoing.... You would never believe what sport and entertainment your mortal mannikins provide daily for the gods.... There is no show like it."[14]

The universality of folly is a theme subsequently picked up in a sixteenth century French farce in which the Mother of Folly is asked who she is and where she comes from. "I come from France, Flanders, Picardy, Normandy, England, Rome, Italy, Spain, Germany. I am at home in the courts of princes, among ecclesiastics and women, with students, beggars and lawyers. And I understand both astrology and theology."[15] In fact, rather than excluding science (astrology) or theology as representing some firm and unquestionable point of reference from which folly was to be seen and interpreted, the fool tradition has tended to take the position that all participate in a common folly (the comic equivalent of finitude and original sin). Within this common folly there is no higher folly than religious folly, precisely because religion claims to represent the highest authorities and to be dealing with the most ultimate questions of meaning and value.

A sixteenth-century comedy, *Des cris de Paris*, offered this description of "subtle fools":

> They find such profundities in their minds
> That if you were to believe their writings
> You would think they were God's first cousins.[16]

Relative to the subtle fools, who are so confident in their genius and correctness of understanding, the fool tradition places the "simple fools," who readily believe anything anyone tells them, like the Yiddish Gimpel for whom everything was possible. When people would come to him and say, "Gimpel, there is a carnival in heaven" or "Gimpel, the rabbi has given birth to a calf" or "Gimpel, a cow flew over the roof and laid brass eggs," Gimpel believed them without question. If the subtle fool confuses faith with dogmatism and self-righteousness, the simple fool confuses faith with credulity.

Like all comic figures, the jester reminds us of the essential awkwardness of the human condition—an awkwardness that is only intensified in the religious situation. The awkwardness that is portrayed on a more trivial plane in the endless pratfalls of the clown, the predicaments of the comic hero, or the confusions of the fool reaches its climax as we attempt to deal with matters of ultimate concern and with the most fundamental questions of "reality." It is an awkwardness the comic side of which has never been adequately summarized in traditional philosophical or theological categories.

Absolute conviction and self-assured dogmatism belong, if anywhere, not at the level of the profoundest and most encompassing issues with which we have wrestled—and over which we have endlessly disagreed. If defensible at all, such postures belong at the superficial level of experience and importance, as in the counting of tables and chairs or chickens and sheep, where there is a realistic chance of confidence and general agreement. The most fundamental and important issues—the great mysteries of being and nonbeing, of source and destiny, of value and morality, of the nature of knowledge and the mind—are the very regions most needing to be approached with a keen sense of rushing in where angels fear to tred and walking gingerly on cosmic eggs. Where a sense of folly and comedy is least required and of least consequence is in relation to the more peripheral and insignificant matters that concern us. Yet conventional wisdom has advocated just the opposite: humor belongs at the circumference of our lives, not at the center. Such wisdom is a perennial source of folly.

Take the case of the theologian whose office it is to articulate the implications of the faith and life of a particular religious community, the theologian who now, say, at the ripe age of thirty-five undertakes to give considered thought to the most encompassing issues of all, who ventures in fact systematically to explore the nature of God in relation to the world, to develop a methodology appropriate to its divine object, perhaps even to engage in a respectable little "science of God." Whether acknowledged or not, the theologian is in the clumsiest of possible positions. The importance of the office notwithstanding, the very ultimacy of the object of inquiry makes of theology the highest form of foolishness—with philosophy running a close second: the king and queen of folly!

The words of Yahweh to Job are instructive. Job is in the midst of earnest reflection on the most tortuous of human problems, having sought with fellow theologians over the space of thirty-seven chapters to interpret the relationship of the ways of God to the fortunes of humankind. God interrupts with a question that well expresses the humorousness as well as the pathos of the religious situation: "Where were you when I laid the foundation of the earth?" (Job 38:4 RSV). It is as if a celebrated theologian of the church had just completed the final declarations of a one, two-, three-, or perhaps twelve-volume systematic on "nature, man and God," expecting to hear the words "Well done, thou good and faithful servant," only to hear instead, "Where were you when I laid the foundation of the earth?" That question is the beginning and the end of all theology.

Karl Barth, in his twelve-volume (and at that unfinished) *Church Dogmatics*, gave a scant two pages to humor—and in doing so exceeded the attentions of most theologians. Nevertheless, in his later years he remarked concerning these prodigious theological efforts,

> The angels laugh at old Karl. They laugh at him because he tries to grasp the truth about God in a book of Dogmatics. They laugh at the fact that volume follows volume and each is thicker than the previous ones. As they laugh, they say to one another, "Look! Here he comes now with his little pushcart full of volumes of the *Dogmatics!*"[17]

In this manner the great corpus of his theological investigations is finally placed within the parentheses of the comic perspective in a simple confession of the humanity of all theology. The books fit nicely in a small wheelbarrow.

Humor carries us beyond all our theisms, and our atheisms as well, for humor corresponds to both the awkwardness of religious and philosophical inquiry and the inexhaustible mystery of the object of that inquiry. Every Holy of Holies and every metaphysical claim—or disclaimer of the metaphysical—points ultimately to the Mystery of Mysteries. In Gerardus van der Leeuw's words,

> The religious significance of things...is that one which no wider or deeper meaning can follow. It is the meaning of the whole: it is the last word. But this meaning is never understood, this last word is never spoken: always they remain superior, the ultimate meaning being a secret which reveals itself repeatedly, only nevertheless to remain eternally concealed. It implies an advance to the farthest boundary, where only one sole fact is understood: that all comprehension is "beyond."[18]

Before this Mystery all participate in a common foolishness, and the subtle fool may be no closer to the truth of things than the simple fool. All of our affirmations and denials, all our concepts and arguments—even the wisest and profoundest and holiest by one human standard or another—are finally dissolved into silence. All words philosophical and poetic, all words theological and mystical, all words psychological or sociological or sociobiological, with which the grand issues of our existence are addressed are—to use an old Indian simile—like fingers pointing at the moon. No matter how straight or long, no matter how firmly supported or well manicured, the pointing fingers never quite reach the moon!

Faith and Foolishness

It is most unfortunate that patristic and medieval Christianity did not include humor and humorlessness in its moral glossaries of the seven cardinal virtues and the seven deadly sins. Humility includes the ability to laugh at oneself and the refusal to take oneself too seriously. Laughter may open the way to moderation and charity, for in laughter hostilities are softened, allowing even former enemies to laugh together.

That little religious attention has been devoted to the relationship between the sacred and the comic, or faith and humor, is itself a reflection of the taboo mechanisms that commonly surround holy things. Laughter and humor, at first sight, seem quite out of place, and their object seems simply that of profaning the sacred or dissolving faith. Especially when the sacred is defined as the sphere of ultimate concerns and fundamental values, any introduction of the comic appears to be reducible to a failure to take sacred matters seriously, if not an outright rejection of their sacrality. The comic mood gives the initial impression of standing in contradiction both to the sacredness of the sacred and to the pious emotions and beliefs it should evoke. That which is sacred is only to be approached in fear and trembling, in awful solemnity, in lowly obeisance and humble adoration, nor in levity and gaiety. If so, humor, as Reinhold Niebuhr argued, is acceptable in the outer courts of the temple, and its echo may be heard in the sanctuary, but only faith, and not laughter, is appropriate in the Holy of Holies.[19] If there is "a time to laugh" and "a time to dance" (Eccles. 3:4), it is not around the altar but in the streets. And as the church has often insisted, there is a certain pagan aura that clings to fool's feasts, a sinful rebellion in profaning holy things, if not a bit of the old rogue Satan in the devilish gleam in the eyes of the jester.

This type of attitude has been paid compliment by Harold Watts as "a by-product of that modesty which kept the comic writer strolling in the public square and which forbade him to have traffic with holy places, be they temples or churches, synagogues or chapels."[20] Yet something is missing in this view, apart from which faith is easy prey to fanaticism, sacred images and forms become idols, and promised salvation becomes spiritual bondage. While religious faiths and holy places have served as bases of human unity, they have served just as successfully as bases of human disunity. Religion, which has elevated the human spirit with visions of common bonds, self-sacrifice, harmony, and compassion, has also proved to be one of the greatest single sources of segregation, pride, prejudice, antipathy, destruction, and bloodshed. Religious history is littered with reminders of the tragic possibilities of faith without humor and the sacred without the comic.

Religious expression at its best functions within a delicate dialectic between faith and laughter. On the one side is the peril of idolatry—the elevation of any finite form or understanding to an absolute, divine status. On the other side is the peril of a relativism for which nothing is sacred. Faith without laughter leads to dogmatism and self-righteousness. Laughter without faith leads to cynicism and despair. This is not to say what Reinhold Niebuhr has said—that humor represents a "no-man's-land" between faith and despair. There is a more intimate relationship between humor and faith than this. Humor does not stand midway between *faith* and despair but between *fideism* and despair, just as in the sociopolitical realm the jester stands midway between tyranny and anarchy. There is always the danger that humor without faith will fall into a cynicism concerning all meaning and value, where everything is doubted and nothing is holy any longer. But there is also the danger that faith without humor will fall into dogmatism and absolutism. Thus the melodramatic "Saviors of Gotham City," Batman and Robin, when in costume as the "Caped Crusaders," never cracked a smile, even in the midst of uttering the most pious banalities, while their adversaries— Joker, Riddler, Penguin, Iceman, Catwoman, and company—never stopped laughing, and turned even crime into a parlor game.

If skepticism is the occupational hazard of clowns, jesters, and fools, self-righteousness is the perennial temptation of prophets and priests. Whether formally acknowledged or not, this realization is intuitively sensed and irrepressibly expressed in a variety of informal ways in every age. As William Austin Smith observed in the iconography of Gothic architecture: "How one loves those laughing, indecorous imps one spies in Gothic cathedrals, safety valves of the comic perception of those bohemian journey-man builders, signaling to posterity their conviction that piety at high Gothic tension needs always the vigilant eye of the Comic Muse."[21]

The humorous remark or comic gesture is the footnote attached to every pious act and statement of belief that reminds us of our humanity, our mortality, our finiteness and fallibility, our foolishness. It is the parentheses placed around even our most serious and sacred moments that qualifies them as human moments, and the seriousness as human seriousness. To take oneself seriously *as a human being* is to laugh, for that which is taken in all sincerity and good faith as being ultimate is taken as such by human beings inhabiting this or that culture in this or that moment of time. Even the interpretation of faith as an ultimate and unconditional concern (e.g., Paul Tillich)[22] has an aura of ultimate and unconditional seriousness about it that human beings cannot give to their concerns without absolutizing their experiences and perceptions. Faith does not exclude humor any more than it excludes doubt, for faith is always being returned to the ultimate mysteries to which faith has responded and out of which faith has come. The opposite is equally true: skepticism does not exclude humor any more than it excludes faith; for skepticism, too, is returned to the ultimate mysteries of being and nonbeing.

Though the various forms of humor in relation to ultimate questions may appear blasphemous, true blasphemy is to be found not in humor as such but in the *absence* of humor, for at the heart of the comic spirit and perspective is an acceptance of the prophetic warning against idolatry, and against that greatest blasphemy of all, the claim to understand or to be as God. Erasmus chided the scholastic theology of his time which, equipped with the most learned "definitions, arguments, corollaries, implicit and explicit propositions...abounding in newly-invented terms and prodigious vocables," undertook to divine the "most arcane matters, such as by what measure, and how long the perfect Christ was in the Virgin's womb, and how accidents subsist in the Eucharist without their subject," or whether an omnipotent God "could have taken upon Himself the likeness of a woman? Of a devil? Of an ass? Of a gourd?"[23] Had Erasmus lived long enough, he might also have offered similar wisdom for other disciplines in like manner equipped with the most learned "definitions, arguments, corollaries, newly-invented terms, and prodigious vocables."

Myth arises out of a profound sense of the mystery of existence—the mystery of existence as such and the mystery of every existing thing. Yet though an attempt may be made to respond to this mystery by offering interpretations of life that somehow "reveal" this mystery, the mystery is never exhausted or overcome. No amount of philosophical reasoning or scientific investigation or theological argument can net it and capture it and add it to the informational zoo of human knowledge. We are not confronted with mystery in the sense of a problem to be solved, a puzzle to be put together, or a detective story that discloses the culprit on the final page. This mystery stands at the beginning and the end of all thought. It represents the limit, the final reaches, of every reason and system. Insofar as myths offer themselves as the ultimate answer and truth, it is properly so in the sense that they function on the last horizon of human understanding, where all understanding proceeds from and is returned to the *mysterium* out of which it has come.

Such a sense of mystery is, however, not darkness but light, not a burden but a joy, for one is freed from the awesome responsibility of having the last word, the final say, and therefore delivered from the necessity of defending this unquestionable truth against all detractors, or from the impulse to play God relative to the universe. One is free to be fully and simply human. In that freedom, nothing is ever completely closed off, finished, wrapped up, sealed. The adventure always remains, the search continues unending, the truth is inexhaustible. One is truly free to laugh before that Mystery of Mysteries that forever eludes and surprises us and that can overwhelm us even in the most obvious, taken-for-granted, and therefore presumably well-known regions of our experience. Here even a mouse, as Walt Whitman put it, "is miracle enough to stagger sextillions of infidels" (*Leaves of Grass*). Or as Santayana phrased it, existence is comic inherently, the oddest of possibilities masquerading momentarily as fact.[24]

The jester's function is humorously to profane the categories and hierarchies with which we would capture the ultimate truth about things, domesticate it, and add it to the electronic data bank. From the standpoint of the jester, who refuses to take any human pretensions or demarcations with absolute seriousness, the moat that defines and protects the king's castle is also the moat that imprisons the king. Hence, the neat patterns of rationality and value and order with which we organize and solidify our experience are confused and garbled. Sense is turned into nonsense, order into disarray, the unquestionable into the doubtful. The jester does not fit into, indeed refuses to fit into, the established conventions and hallowed structures of this or that human sphere. The jester is always about to bow the knee to earthly kingdoms, but never quite manages to go through with the motion. Instead, everything comes out wrong: the speech, the logic, the gestures, the decorum. Yet in this wrongness is a rightness of another sort. In this foolishness is another level of wisdom.

7

Putting Humpty-Dumpty Together Again—
The Clown

*Here is a man like himself, only more pathetic and
miserable, with ludicrously impossible clothes—in
every sense a social misfit and failure.... [Yet] he
has a protective air of mock dignity, takes the most
outrageous liberties with people, and wears
adversity as though it was a bouquet.*

—Charles Chaplin[1]

Clowns require no announcement or introduction. When they appear
they are immediately recognizable by everyone, regardless of their location, costuming, or behavior. Whether bursting in upon a tribal ritual,
ancient comedy, festival parade, circus ring, or modern cinema, their
presence is unmistakable. There are clowns who are silent and clowns
who are subtle, but there are no incognito clowns. Clowns refuse to be
missed or ignored. The clown suddenly materializes within the worka-
day world or the sacred arena like some imagined visitor from outer
space, a roaring monster from a funhouse grotto come to life in graceful, jerky motion, a brightly colored child's toy wound up for a noisy
moment. At times the clown seems like some harmless escapee from an
asylum for the insane, come to sweep away neatness and stir up the
settled dust of our lives. At other times the clown resembles a ghostly
apparition from the spirit world, paradoxically seeking with grinning
death-mask to renew life and revive our slumping spirits.

Yet despite their antiquity and their clamorous familiarity, clowns
present an enigmatic image. And this lack of clear definition turns out
to be the secret of their challenge to the rigid identities and absolute
assurances of the tragic mentality. Clowns offer such a jumble of iden-

tities and loose ends as to prevent simple definition. From Indian rituals to modern circuses, they stand there with great ringed eyes and mouths upon gaily painted faces, outlandish in gesture and attire, perhaps with wild hair or a bald spot or a little of both, grinning and leapfrogging about in defiance of easy description and common understanding—and defying a great many other things as well. One may bounce along like a polka-dotted balloon, while another strides about like a long stick on stilts. There may be a friendly giant out of a child's fairyland, or a mischievous dwarf from a leprechaun legend. Clowns are, as a Navaho term for them translates, "delight-makers" (*Koshare*). But they are also, as the police officers in many a Chaplin or Keaton film would have phrased it, "disturbers of the peace." And while they seem to epitomize the grossness and density of matter and flesh, they persist in floating around in a freedom of spirit that is at least six inches off the ground.

Clowns are so childlike, yet so adult; so human, yet so nonhuman; so vivid, yet so unreal; so oversexed, yet so asexual; so bold, yet so easily scared away. They can be devilishly knowing in their winks, yet bear such an innocent look on their faces. They are permitted considerable license in their behavior, but not without being chased and punished for their offenses. At their best they are hilarious, but with a touch of sadness and perhaps wearing a tear or a frown. Clowns move somewhere between order and disorder, life and death, hope and despair. To the very small child, especially up close and all-of-a-sudden, they are often ugly and frightening, like ogres with a grotesquely terrifying presence. But they are actually both ugly and beautiful, terrible and funny. And their relationship to society is equally ambiguous, as among the Yaqui Indians, where clowns both profane Holy Week and its liturgies and act as police officers who restrain others from getting out of line.

The High Priest of Fun and Laughter

While it is impossible, therefore, to give any simple definition to the clown, one element is always there. And through that element the disparate pieces of our existence are joined in a kind of madcap shotgun wedding. The clown is laughter incarnate. But the clown is not fun and funny only in a momentary and miscellaneous manner in which we laugh and have done with it. We are touched at the center of our existence. The clown dares to sport in the inner sanctum of our being, for this is the joke about *ourselves*, suddenly realized. The clown is the multiplicity without us and within us openly and humorously displayed: the whole—otherwise tragic—range of conflicting human emotions and aspirations clapped together in one great ovation of applause.

The clown is the personification of much else besides laughter, sometimes even of pathos and sorrow and death. But the center of gravity is in laughter, and in all those other uniquely human capacities that are associated with a comic sensibility and that separate us from both animals and computers. If we are "laughing animals" (*homo risens*), with the lifelong ability to play with our existence, to imagine other possibilities and impossibilities too, to take words and things and circumstances in multiple senses, to stand back and joke about anything and everything—then the clown is zany proof that we are human and not monkeys or machines.

Even in the form of the poker-faced Keaton who never smiled, or the sad-faced Emmett Kelly who had little to smile about, clowns are laughable and lovable. They are still the agents of laughter, officiants in a special ritual of mirth and foolishness. When Kelly the ragged bum is incapable of performing the simplest of tasks—like sweeping the floor—correctly and without mishap, or when a deft Buster Keaton stares in blank resignation at the collapsed house to which he has just given a final hammerblow, we laugh. We are called to laughter. And we laugh not only because analogous misfortunes have happened to us, leaving us feeling similarly inadequate and helpless, but also because we are capable of taking even the darkest and most painful situations in more than one way. We are not limited to one-possibility responses. We are not eternally confined to taking things straight and univocally. In laughter we transcend not only the animals but also ourselves and our circumstances. We transcend disappointment and suffering. We transcend the jumbled contradictions of our lives. We transcend even the self-imposed requirement that life always make sense, conform to a plan, work out, give us our due, or be equitable and just.

The best modern example of these comic capacities is still Chaplin's tramp figure. Chaplin as a child had known what it meant to be poor and a nobody. He had known what it meant to wear cast-off and mismatched clothing, to eat cheap herbs and stale bread and doubtful eggs, to walk slum streets and live in one room, to have creditors come to carry off whatever few possessions one had, to be taken to workhouses and orphanages. And he never forgot this in his films. Most of his films started out from the remembrance of what it meant to be hungry and cold and jobless and penniless and alone. Charlie was never the clown who simply enters the arena in the midst of festivity and gala celebration to bring laughter to tables that are already sumptuously laden with holiday feasts, and everyone is already singing and dancing in their finest attire. Charlie entered the world of his films in the lowest and darkest hour, where there was poverty and suffering, where despair was easy and hope was hard and joy almost impossible. The little tramp came like a character out of the London slums of Dickens' *Oliver Twist* or *A Christmas Carol*, yet miraculously transformed into a figure that was as comic as it was pathetic. He refused to allow personal tragedies or overpowering tragic forces to crush the human spirit.

In *City Lights*, Charlie is homeless and jobless, sleeping where he can. In *Life* he is in a flophouse. In *Police* he is an ex-convict with nowhere to go. In *The Vagabond* he is a vagabond. In *The Circus* he is left alone in an empty, littered field when the circus has moved on. In *The Kid* he rescues a boy being taken away to an orphanage, and he eludes the law with an orphan girl in *Modern Times*. In *The Gold Rush* he is so hungry that he boils his leather shoe for dinner. In *The Champion* he shares his last sausage with a bulldog.

Yet in the midst of all this misery and deprivation the little clown came, with his antics and his human tenderness and his magical transformations. He came with a plucky spirit that refused to be dismissed or ignored or overcome. He came with a sense of individual worth and personal pride for the lowliest of the low—for who could be lower than Charlie? He came with a measure of hope that might give in to tears but would not give in to despair. He didn't stop to philosophize. He didn't offer tragic soliloquies. He didn't stand there waiting for Godot. He didn't stand there waiting for anybody. And we saw in him what stout and resilient people we were or could be. As Chaplin said of the Charlie he had created,

> I am always aware that Charlie is playing with Death. He plays with it, mocks it, thumbs his nose at it, but it's always there. He is aware of death at every moment of his existence, and he is terribly aware of being alive. . . . And he is bringing more life. That is his only excuse, his only purpose.[2]

This meaning of the clown is not peculiar to the modern West. In the mythological recounting of the history of the Jemez Indians, for example, it is this role as agent of transcendence that is credited to the clown. When the Jemez emerged from a hole in the earth to the far north, they found food to be scarce and the weather inhospitable. So they began a long, arduous journey to the south. As they migrated they had difficulty finding food along the way, their blankets wore out, and many died of cold and hunger. The survivors attempted to be courageous, but as their numbers were continuously being depleted, they too prayed to die—whereupon the Moon Mother entreated the Sun Father to come to their aid. So the Sun Father created the clown.

> The Sun took one of the survivors of our people, painted his body in transverse black and white bands, decorated his hair with corn husks, and suspended eagle feathers behind each ear. As soon as he was thus painted and decorated, this man became a "funny man," and began to dance, cut capers, and make grimaces. So interested did the people become in his performing that they forgot their sorrows and became glad. They then resumed their journey...which they continued till they reached the Rio Grande.[3]

It is interesting that the Sun Father does not rescue the Jemez from the problems of cold and hunger and death, but rather provides a vehicle for coping with these hardships and misfortunes that are a normal part of life. It is also interesting that the "funny man" enters not at the point where there is health and plenty to celebrate but at the lowest and darkest hour. He invites laughter and gladness, despite the fact that there is little to celebrate. He is the renewer of courage and hope and the will to live.

The myth-teller continues by recounting how, when the Jemez reached the warm lands of the south, they were attacked by other tribes who drove them into caves. But they kept their spirit, and a hero was sent who dispelled the enemies of the Jemez and taught the Jemez how to build villages, hunt, and perform the proper religious rites. "And he made the clown-dancers [*Koshare*] the sprouters of grain (the spring-summer clowns). He made the funny men [*Kurena*] the maturers of grain and of everything that lives and grows upon the earth (the fall-winter clowns)." The hero also gave them the power to represent the people before the gods.

Similarly, among the Laguna and Kere Pueblos, the Corn Mother is said to have wished to have someone to make her laugh and to make people laugh. So she rubbed her skin and rolled a piece of her skin into a ball, covering it with a blanket. From underneath the blanket came the clown (*Koshare*) "to make fun, and to make people forget their troubles." The Corn Mother then created the rainbow for the clown to climb up and down on.[4]

The Pueblo clown, as the high priest of fun and laughter, is given a rainbow as a ladder, and the power to represent others before the gods. With this rainbow, and the clown's own "rainbowishness," the clown restores color to life, combines the various hues of our being, and offers a sign of hope. While there is no promise of a pot of gold at the end of the rainbow, nor any guarantee against future hardship or catastrophe, the clown does point to a means of bringing light out of human mud and limitation. And we are enabled to laugh once more.

The Catholicity of the Clown

The Pueblo clown displays another common trait of clowning—that of being a mediator, a go-between, a *doppelganger* as the Germans put it. The mediation takes place by means of the clown's own special form of the *axis mundi*—the sacred pole at the center of the world—the rainbow ladder. The clown climbs up and down, brightly and garishly, between sky and earth, the divine and the human, the human and the animal, one person and another, and the various zones of our individual being. No one plane or zone can define or hold the clown, who moves, leaps, slips, and stumbles back and forth among them all. Through the rainbow ladder and the clown's own coat of many colors are reconnected the many fragmented shades of our existence, if only by tossing them laughingly side by side and calling their ephemeral combination a link between the heavens and the earth.

One reason clowning is so difficult to define is that clowns take upon themselves the human diversity, encompassing in their grab-bag generosity the most varied examples of the species and its behavior. In so doing, clowns also encompass those areas of tension and conflict within a given society or within human nature as such. Here we observe the clown's peculiar manner of dealing with what might otherwise become areas of tragic alienation, as in the nursery rhyme "Humpty-Dumpty."

> Humpty-Dumpty sat on a wall;
> Humpty-Dumpty had a great fall;
> And all the king's horses and all the king's men
> Couldn't put Humpty-Dumpty together again.

What all the king's horses and men cannot do, the clown proposes to do. In a kaleidoscopic identity the clown is many people and many moods, formed and reformed out of the same disparate pieces of humanity. Thus clowns come in all sizes and shapes, in all colors and wrappings. They may be tall or short, thin or fat, with a coat of many colors or covered with mud and feathers. The European harlequin was as brilliant as a peacock, while among the Jicarilla Apache the clown was known as "striped excrement." Clowns dramatize the fragmented and alienated character of our individual and social existence, yet at the same time offer a kind of resolution of it. They propose to put the Humpty-Dumpty of our tragic humanity back together again.

Basically there are two ways in which this ritual brokenness and reunion is carried out in clowning. One is by means of a comic duo that embraces certain extremes of the human spectrum. Oliver Hardy was plump and domineering; Stan Laurel was skinny and browbeaten. Harpo Marx never spoke a word; Groucho Marx never stopped talking. Mae West was the seductively aloof beauty cooing, "Come on up and see me some time"; W. C. Fields was the puffed and puffing scalawag who had difficulty climbing the stairs. Dean Martin was the handsome, urbane, crooning ladies' man; Jerry Lewis was the awkward, bungling, daffy, squeaky-voiced kid whom only a stray mutt could love. Abbott was the straight man and wit, Costello was the fool and butt of every joke.

Among the Pueblo, clowning involved a marked contrast between the restrained bearing and colorful striping of the *Koshare*, and the grossness of the *Koyemshi* smeared with mud, and the *Ne'wekwe* who drank urine.[5] In the European circus and stage, clowns have often appeared in the antithetical forms of the elegant white-face and the shabby Augusto. The white-face clown performs acts of skill and grace, uses plain white makeup with accented beauty lines, wears splendid hats and costuming and shoes, and parades with the poise and comeliness of a fashion model. The Augusto, by contrast, uses bizarre makeup, displays jarring colors and lines, and wears tattered and mismatched clothes, funny hats, and outrageous shoes. The Augusto is anything but august: a dunce, a bungler, a mess, a disaster area.

In this manner, two opposite kinds of comic figures are set in dialectical motion. Our whole being is put joltingly together by the simple device of slapping opposites against one another. The other, more complex and ambitious type is the solo clown, who manages to contain such polarities within a single figure. From tribal to circus clowning, one finds figures who in their body paint or costuming stripe themselves black and white or yellow and green, or wear a ragtag jumble of colors, or the harlequin's coat of many colors. If they wear oversized shoes, they will like as not wear an undersized hat. If they give themselves a gaudy smile, they will probably also add a tear. If they are graceful one moment, they will likely be jerky the next. They may tiptoe like a ballerina on a case of eggs, then race through a vegetable market like a crazed bull. They will walk ever so carefully, then trip most clumsily. Or they will take precisely measured aim with a large wooden hammer and then smash the thumb carelessly left holding the peg. In this form the clown is the bearer of Walt Whitman's self-affirmation in *Leaves of Grass*:

> Do I contradict myself? Very well.
> I contradict myself; I am large,
> I contain multitudes.[6]

Buster Keaton capitalized on an expressionless and seemingly inert "stone face" in contrast to great agility and an almost frantic movement of the body. He could run, dart, climb, catapult, leap, and paddle himself out of the most inescapable dangers! Yet to the many kinds of crises in which he found himself, Keaton turned the same immovable stare. Face and body, and face and situation, seemed to have nothing to do with each other, as if belonging to separate stories. Even those circumstances that might normally precipitate intense emotional expression—fear, anger, hatred, dismay, elation, passion, laughter—were taken with a passivity that would be the envy of both gods and Zen masters. The human extremes of serenity and frenzy, aloofness and involvement, innocence and knowledgeability, were hilariously united like clashing cymbals.

Claude Levi-Strauss developed the thesis—previously applied by Hegel to tragedy—that the function of myth is that of reconciling points of conflict and tension within a given human context. The logic of myth is that of mediating contraries. Thus, the oppositions between life and death, fertility and killing, agriculture and hunting, may be mythically represented by herbivorous and carnivorous animals that are reconciled in the narrative by the figure of an omnivorous animal.[7] The clown in these terms shares in the same mythic functions. The clown as "Everyman" is the representative of the many-sidedness of our existence and the tensions between sides—not any one side or set of characteristics. The clown is omnivorously human.

Chaplin was the most successful in this role of any of the early film clowns, and perhaps in the whole history of clowning. It started with the playful donning of Fatty Arbuckle's ample trousers and Chester Conklin's tight-fitting coat. To this were added shoes too large and a hat too small and a flexible cane that was itself a functional contradiction. Then Chaplin added the laborious, shuffling, penguin-walk of an old cabdriver he had seen hobbling along in London to what was otherwise a youthful, light-footed, acrobatic figure. The paradoxes that such combinations produced and made possible were so many and so profound that even to Chaplin the resulting figure was a mysterious being that seemed to have been revealed to him and that he would have to spend much of the rest of his career exploring. He said later, "For me he was fixed, complete, the moment I looked in the mirror and saw him for the first time; yet even now I don't know all the things there are to be known about him."[8]

Chaplin knew very well, however, the extremes that were surfacing out of his own experience and uniting themselves in the unusual form of Charlie. He was beginning to earn good money at the same time, and he was soon to become the highest-paid actor in the world. But he had come from a broken home in a poor section of London, his father an alcoholic, his mother destitute and in ill health admitted to a poor house and later taken to a mental institution, with young Charles and his stepbrother placed in an orphanage from which they eventually ran away to live in the streets. In Charlie the clown, Chaplin was putting the Humpty-Dumpty of himself and his world together again. The elements were partly happenstance. But he had taken, in effect, the fastidious bowler hat, dress coat, white shirt, black tie, and walking stick of an English gentleman and combined them with the baggy pants, floppy shoes, and unkeptness of the poor and the homeless. The top and the bottom of the social order were thus thrown together in one person. The oppositions between rich and poor were simultaneously intensified and softened. Chaplin was henceforth *both* gentleman and tramp, and *neither* gentleman nor tramp. The most extreme ends of the social spectrum were contained, united, and transcended in one slender individual. Chaplin recalled his first interpretation of the clown character to Mack Sennett in 1914:

> This fellow is many-sided, a tramp, a gentleman, a poet, a dreamer, a lonely fellow, always hopeful of romance and adventure. He would have you believe he is a

scientist, a musician, a duke, a polo player. However, he is not above picking up cigarette butts or robbing a baby of its candy.[9]

Human beings, after all, from lofty to lowly are both meticulous and sloppy, polite and crude, graceful and awkward, rational and irrational. The aristocrat in fine clothes and suave sophistication was revealed as being something of a bum underneath. And the bum, despite a crumpled appearance and bad manners, was revealed as having a certain dignity and grace. Charlie as an aristocrat and Charlie as a bum were equally delightful and equally ludicrous and equally incomplete. And their union affirmed a common humanity that lay beneath all those distinctions and separations to which we ordinarily grant such importance.

Given this paradoxical being, Chaplin would often play in sudden turn the gentleman and the hobo, the bully and the coward, the tyrant and the impotent, the tenderhearted sentimentalist and the devilish little trickster. In *Life*, Chaplin, finding himself in a flophouse, puts fellow tramps to sleep in the most direct manner by striking them on the head with a wooden mallet, then dutifully and motheringly kissing them goodnight. Or he carefully disposes of his cigar ash in the open mouth of a snoring drunk, in preparation for kneeling beside his cot to pray. In *Easy Street* he good-heartedly aids in the distribution of food to children in a local orphanage, but he does so as if he were scattering birdseed to pigeons. In *The Tramp* he thoughtfully helps another farmhand off with his boots, but when one boot does not slip off easily he kicks him in the face to get leverage to dislodge it. Or he "helps" his partner carry feed sacks by prodding him in the rear with a pitchfork as if it were a cattle prod.

In these terms Chaplin approximated the total clown in a way in which few clowns have ever succeeded. This, no doubt, is one reason he had such universal and enduring appeal. He was nobody in particular, yet everybody all at once. No one could stand outside the parentheses of his bowler hat and floppy shoes. He was, as Robert Payne said of him, "the whole human comedy wrapped in a single frail envelope of flesh."

When Aristotle defined the ludicrous as a species of the ugly, he missed the extent to which comic characters can be both inferior and superior, ugly and beautiful, simultaneously. Chaplin as the tramp had the beauty and grace of the white-faced clown, yet all the awkward and slovenly character of the Augusto. There was certainly a handsome, polished, lovable side to Charlie, no matter how disheveled and dirty and uncouth the little tramp might be. But, unlike the mighty hero or the celebrated film idol, his was not an unblemished beauty or dashing heroism. He could order people about and stand proudly with an air of complete mastery and assurance. He could become terribly self-important, as occasion might permit. Yet in a twinkling he could become equally subservient and cowering. Now and then he would make some heroic attempt at saving maidens in distress, but defending maidens was usually mixed with hiding behind them. His heroism involved a strong aversion to pain and a distinct preference for running. It was always abundantly clear that he participated in the total human condition.

In his trampishness, Charlie was very close to the level of sheer animal survival much of the time, where elegance is irrelevant and where one easily disposes of most of the niceties and pleasantries of polite society. Yet even as a tramp, and therefore at the bottom of the bottom of the human kingdom, he restored a sense of worth and pride to the lowliest, most forlorn individual. In his very tatters and tumbles he was still endearing and still very human.

The genius of Chaplin was that in the figure of the tramp he embraced a common humanness. He expressed what we all are: both beauty and beast, domesticated and uncivilized, clothed and naked. In biblical terms he was both the noble creature of Genesis 1, created in the image and likeness of God, and the clay figurine of Genesis 2, into whom is breathed the "breath of life," fashioned like the rest of the animals from the dust of the earth, and with a considerable dustiness clinging to him. As the tramp Charlie was clearly enough close to the earth most of the time. But if he was down, he was never out. He had style and deftness and bravado, and an unconquerable sense of his own importance. Yet if he put on too many airs, as circumstances might permit, he was quickly dumped back in the dirt again—if he did not suddenly leap there himself.

In an episode in *City Lights*, Charlie is driving a Rolls-Royce convertible that belongs to a rich man who has befriended him. For a moment Charlie's trampishness gives way to the opposite, which is already prefigured in his bowler hat, coattails, vest, and cane: aristocratic snobbishness. He drives the Rolls around the city streets with his head cocked back in an air of superiority and self-importance and with all the dignity of a gentleman—or at least the *chauffeur* of a gentleman. But as he turns a corner, he spies a cigar butt on the sidewalk. He spies it in fact at the same time that another tramp, busily patrolling the gutters, has spotted it. Charlie's *other self* makes no hesitation in returning. He brings the Rolls to an abrupt stop, leaps out, and just as the gutterbum is lean- ing over to pick up the cigar butt, Charlie kicks him aside, grabs the prize, jumps back into the limousine, and speeds off—to the utter aston- ishment and bewilderment of the hapless bum.

The clown insists on putting side-by-side many of those things that we spend considerable time keeping in separate pockets or separate rooms or separate drawers of the mind: altruism and selfishness, ratio- nality and impulse, religion and sex, kings and commoners, Rolls-Royces and cigar butts. The clown identifies our tensions and our ambivalences, running and leaping to and from the other side of the tracks. Then sud- denly we find ourselves put back together again in a hilarious slam- bang fashion. This is the clown's peculiar form of salvation: a comic ritual of redemption for the human race. What is otherwise experienced as a tragic contradiction, collision, or alienation is here experienced as a playful catharsis of paradoxical richness.

The Lord of Ambiguity

What we are reluctant to acknowledge, but what the clown fixes on, is that we are composed of and dream of contraries. We fantasize about complete freedom and complete security, rugged individualism and so- cial harmony, amorous adventures and marital bliss, higher wages and lower prices, something worth fighting for...and peace and tranquil- lity. We project utopias where material goods abound cheaply and plen- tifully for all, and Edenic gardens free of trash and litter and tourists and nuclear dumping grounds. We imagine a world in which things are im- perishable and a world in which everything is easily discarded and bio- degradable; so we develop indestructible plastics and disposable diapers.

"Self-contradiction," as Wolfgang Zucker has argued, "is the clown's most significant feature. Whatever predicate we use to describe him, the opposite can also be said, and with equal right."[10] Yet the self-con- tradictions and incongruities that the clown incarnates are held together happily and delightfully in a single, mysteriously particularized human being. The clown seems schizophrenic and clearly displays our indi- vidual and collective schizophrenias, yet without coming completely unglued or flying apart at the seams. The clown seems awkwardly uni- fied at the same time—like the awkwardnesses of sexual union—which

is one reason the awkwardness can be so funny. What we all are is expressed to some degree or other, but in a way that does not leave us torn
and broken. In this odd figure the complexities of our being and the
cross-purposes of our lives are patched and pinned loosely and playfully together. We are judged and accepted, humbled and healed, divided and united—all in the same comic ritual.

The clown has commonly been referred to, along with the fool, as the
"lord of disorder" and "lord of misrule," and suspected of having some
sort of unholy alliance with the devil. True, the Greek god Momus, lord of
pleasantry and patron of clowns (mummers), was the son of Nox (nox-
ious) and grandson of Chaos, while Discord, Death, and the Furies were
his brethren. And certainly the clown introduces a large element of chaos
and confusion into every situation and has a special talent for profaning
holy things. But this is hardly the full sum of the function involved.

The key to the paradox of the clown's person and performance is a
disturbing yet liberating ambiguity. The clown is now this and now that,
and neither this nor that. Whether the relationship is to order or disorder, rationality or irrationality, sacred or profane, that relationship is
ambiguous. Ordinary canons of dress and decorum do not apply. Colors
and accessories, sizes and styles, sense and nonsense are mixed together
in the most mad and marvelous manner. The rules of etiquette or social
distinction or sexual propriety are not carefully followed or kept. Like
John Gardner's Sunshine Man, the clown does not subscribe to the laws
of the state or of reason—and sometimes not even to the laws of gravity.

But this does not mean that clowning is simply anarchic or antisocial, or cynical with respect to reason and truth. Clowns are not "simply" anything. Thus no specific sacred or moral order can contain them.
No social rule or standard can measure them. No logical or aesthetic
category can exhaust them. Whatever the understanding of the holy or
definition of truth, beauty, and goodness, they do not fit. They are blurred
and relativized. The clown breaks through all the boxes and badges with
which we package and label our lives or attempt to confine others.

In *The Pilgrim*, for example, Chaplin played the dual role of an escaped convict who had disguised himself in the only available clothing
on hand at the time: the garb of a clergyman who was swimming in a
nearby river. The two social poles of convict and minister are thus suddenly united in a single person who now becomes, quite ambiguously
both. In his flight from the law, Charlie takes a train out west with the

cash he finds in the clergyman's clothes. But when he alights from the train in a small southwestern frontier town, he is greeted by a congregation that is eagerly awaiting the arrival of their new pastor. They insist on a church service immediately. Charlie makes a valiant effort at preaching and otherwise playing the role. He recalls some Bible stories from his youth and renders them in the style of a theatrical evangelist. But he has certain bad habits that betray another identity. During the morning offering he has nothing to do, so he sits down, crosses his legs, and lights up a cigarette!

Once the convict/minister double identity is discovered, we are introduced to the larger ambiguities of law and lawlessness. Rather than face a return to prison, Charlie is mercifully escorted by the town sheriff to the Mexican border to freedom/exile. Yet no sooner does he cross the border than he finds himself in the middle of a shoot-out between Mexican bandits. The film ends with Charlie running along the border, hopping back and forth from one side of the line to the other, then waddling off with one foot in Mexican "lawlessness" and one foot in American "law and order," carrying the ambiguity of his situation through to the very end.

The clown is not the lord of disorder per se. A more appropriate designation would be the lord of ambiguity and relativity. The clown is lord of that no-man's-land between contending forces, moving back and forth along all those human lines drawn (not without arbitrariness) between law and order, social and antisocial, reason and irrationality, friend and foe, fashionable and unfashionable, important and unimportant. The clown is now on one side, now on the other, and ultimately both and neither. Clowns thus often look like mottled figments of our dreams, hovering between nightmares and visions of sugarplums. They are so many pieces of fantasy and reality sewn haphazardly together and precariously held in place by strings and pins and suspenders—as all of us are, even in our relative normality. They are the multiplicity of human emotions and tendencies, broken apart and reassembled in a surprising, sometimes shocking, but still comical, manner.

Dreams are what clowns are made of, as much as dreams are what myths are made of. There are good dreams and bad dreams; glimpses of greatness and realizations of weakness; hopes and fears; recollections of childhood and anticipations of old age; the dance of life and the dance macabre; joy and sadness. And the unreal reality of dreams is there too in a strange assortment of shapes and colors and movements. The clown comes to us as a denizen of this world of myth and dream where sense and nonsense are mixed, a flood of apparently disconnected images thrown up from the subconscious and united in surrealistic combinations.

The curious result of all this is not, as one might expect, a dark and disconcerting awareness of the labyrinthine tangle of human life. One is not left with the sinking feeling that the way has been lost, a light has failed, or former verities have been called into question. Life does not seemly suddenly dislocated or disoriented. There is no pausing over a tragic impasse or suffering *agon*. The result, in fact, is a renewed sense of freedom, a liberation of the spirit. One finds new faith in the elasticity of the species, a larger vision of humanity, a more inclusive acceptance of the manyness of the self and other selves. The world does not seem as inflexible and confining as it had been before, if only because someone has taken a smoke in front of the altar during the morning offering.

Among the Hopi and Zuni tribes, the Koyemshi (Mudhead) clowns find mythological justification for their ambiguous character by tracing their ancestry to the twelve Koyemshi born of an incestuous relationship between a primal brother and sister. The twelve offspring are said to have been afflicted with one or another of the twelve human imperfections: gloominess, cowardice, fear, ugliness, pride, and so on. The Koyemshi clowns, therefore, take upon themselves the imperfections of the people and offer themselves as objects of laughter. Yet they are privy to a special knowledge and power. "Silly were they, yet wise as the gods and high priests...the oracles of all olden sayings and deep meanings."[11]

The scatological practices among some of the clown societies of the Pueblo Indians, particularly the Zuni, are notorious examples of this clownish capacity for pointing to and containing the total human condition. One is initiated into the Zuni Ne'wekwe order by a ritual of filth-eating—a strange sort of Eucharist indeed. Mud and excrement are smeared on the body for the clown performance, and parts of the performance may consist of sporting with excreta, smearing and daubing it, or drinking urine and pouring it on one another. Among the Hopi, a group of males known as "singers" play about with vulva-shaped sticks during initiation ceremonies, singing taunting and obscene songs to the women and running after them to "bless them" with filth. The women, in turn, being well-prepared, douse the singers with foul water or urine.[12]

This may not be one of the more palatable aspects of clown symbol-ism. And relative to it more "civilized" clowning may seem tame. Yet it is there, and in some cultural contexts very much there—just as it is universally present in all societies in coarse language, jokes, and pranks. The clown, through comical associations with these aspects of our existence, returns us to the preformal, and to the dust from which we have emerged to breathe the breath of life. This is not only a comedown from the more splendid images we have of ourselves, but also a reaffirmation of the total human condition. Our muddiness is not to be dismissed as impure and profane and shameful. It is fundamentally good.

The clown reduces life to its basics. Hence the common association of clowning with food, sex, and evacuation in exaggerated proportions (gluttony, obscenity, and scatological play). For all our pious creeds and momentous concerns, the basic requirements of our lives are relatively simple: a good meal and restful sleep, freedom from anxiety and freedom from constipation, the enjoyment of sex and the laughter of children, the satisfaction of work and the pleasure of play, the conviviality of friends and a moment's peace. Among the contexts for clowning, therefore, have always been the carnival season and the springtime and harvest rituals, where the *joi de vivre* is paramount and the renewal of life through food and fertility is celebrated. Without life, after all, there is no reason, no morality, no religion. And without fertility and food and the elimination of bodily wastes, there is no life. Life and the sources of life are primary. We cannot live by spirit alone.

Thus the Koyemshi clown of the Zuni and Hopi Indians comes forth with body smeared in the red-brown mud from around the sacred springs of the tribe, as did the first Koyemshi. He is mud and spirit combined. If he profanes sacred matters, he comes from the sacred springs themselves. If he disrupts the Kachina dancers, he combines the primordial powers of earth and water which make possible the dance. He wears the six primary colors, which represent the four directions, the zenith and the nadir of Pueblo cosmology. He is a comic/cosmic symbol of the total context of life. And he encompasses the whole of the human microcosm as well—in William Lynch's words—"down to the last inch of the little beastie."

The clown is more than an iconoclast or a satirist. There is more here than an invasion of sacred precincts or a puncturing of high-flying balloons or a kicking of pompous asses. There is also an element of celebration of this common humanity of ours, a fundamental yea-saying to the curious business of being mortal creatures of the earth. Being "all too human" is not seen as necessarily a great weight that drags us down or a curse that has been placed upon us, but something potentially delightful, as clowns are delightful. For the proud and pretentious this may not be so delightful, or for those who require clean lines, precise calculations, absolute points of reference, and clear and distinct ideas, clownish revelations may not be so amusing. But for those who are not pretenders to thrones that are not theirs or to a divinity they have not attained, or even to some superior form of humanity, the clown enables us to embrace ourselves and each other as the luminous lumps that we are.

In the form of the clown we feel, as Nathan Scott once wrote of Charlie the tramp, "that here is the real human thing itself—clothed not in the unearthly magnificence of tragic heroism, but in the awkward innocence of an essential humanity."[13]

Profaning Sacred Things

What is most surprising about clown behavior is the degree which the clown is permitted to profane things most sacred to the culture: taboos, beliefs, persons, objects, rituals. Behavior that normally would be prohibited, and perhaps considered sacrilegious, and certainly not to be tolerated without penalty, is tolerated in the clown. All those things which are not only taken seriously, but seem to be unquestionable, absolute, and inviolable, are questioned, relativized, and violated.

Among the Navaho, for example, in the Night Chant ceremony— essentially a serious religious ritual—the Water God (*to ninili*) is impersonated in the sacred dance by a clown, dressed in inferior clothing, perhaps rags, wearing a fox tail, and playing the buffoon. While the other masked dancers, also personifying various Navaho deities, are intently and meticulously pursuing the intricate rhythms and patterns of the ceremony, his function in relation to the rest is to mimic the entire proceeding. He dances out of step with the others, staggers, trips, and falls to the delight of the audience. He presents comic exaggerations of their gestures and movements, sometimes stumbling or leaping out of the prescribed arena. He gets in the way of the other dancers, or gives signals for various movements of the dance at the wrong time. He loses his fox tail, then pretends to search diligently for it around the ritual arena when it is in the plain sight of all. He tires of the dance, sits on the ground, rocking stupidly back and forth, or peering foolishly at various onlookers. Now and then he dashes into the crowd, teasing children, taunting adults, playing pranks, stealing objects. He accosts women and makes mock love to them (the water and fertility connection). When a sacred dance is completed, he continues the dance as if oblivious to its termination, then discovering that the other dancers have exited, he races after them.[14]

This is a surprising kind of religious ritual. Far from being performed to one side in the shadows, or in a more profane time and space, the clown's ritual—and version of the sacred ritual—is performed simultaneously with and incorporated within the sacred festival itself. The dialectic of seriousness and laughter, sacred and profane, absolute and relative, taboo and violation, faith and doubt, is openly enacted. Both sides of the dialectic are represented, acknowledged, and expressed. The clown thus brings into focus the ambiguities of our nature and of nature itself, as well as the ambivalences in our attitudes, which reflect these ambiguities. Human beings are not only like the nine masked dancers, perfectly and reverently executing the prescribed religious forms in stately manner. They are also like the tenth dancer. The whole person, as it were, dances before the gods.

Among the Mayo Indians of the Sonora region of Mexico, the primary function of the clowns (*capakobam*), performing during the Lenten Season and Holy Week, is to profane the central and most sacred aspects of Mayo culture: religion, marriage, sexuality, social relationships, food, curing, tribal etiquette, and funeral rites. At a time of heightened gravity and piety, there is also a heightened qualification of that gravity and piety. One set of emotions and demonstrations is counterbalanced by another.

In the Lenten procession, while the *fiesteros* are solemnly making the stations of the cross, the *fariseos* (Pharisees) appear, wearing grotesque masks and clownish costumes, and begin to mimic the devout and play around the procession. They burlesque the movements of the *fiesteros*, tease one another, roll in the dust, trip over dogs, and display mock fear before children or animals. They may set a doll on the ground and venerate it as a saint, while showing disrespect for sacred images. Ritual acts are reversed, such as crossing themselves with their left hands, or circumambulating crosses and churches to the left rather than the right. They pull down house crucifixes and even pretend to defecate on the cross. During Holy Week they impersonate the enemies of Christ, capturing an old man from the crowd and symbolically crucifying him. They offer substitute rituals of their own, lampooning the ceremonial leaders and their chants, interrupting church services with the clatter of their wooden swords, the beat of their drums, and the unpleasant music of their flutes.

Interwoven with these acts are profanations of other fundamentals of Mayo Indian life. A mock marriage takes place in the church with exag-·gerated pomp, much horseplay, and a hint of the real union itself. Similarly, the rites associated with illness and curing are pantomimed in clownish fashion, as are the sacred dances of the hunt. Both the act of dying and the funeral ritual are parodied. Food taboos are violated in the extreme by pretending to catch manure from a horse or burro and to eat it with relish. The social order, too, which in this case is fairly egalitarian, is ridiculed and replaced by an opposite structure, in this case hierarchical.[15]

Such rituals legitimize the "other side" of human attitudes toward whatever the normative standards may be in whatever the area of human life. They are not only directed at sacred acts, persons, and beliefs; they are directed at anything that is otherwise taken very seriously as the definition of proper behavior or objects of sober interest. A part of the motivation behind the clowning in such sacred times and places may be an expression of the tensions between traditional Indian culture and Spanish/Christian culture, a form of ritualized hostility and rejection. But the clowning is also directed toward other features of Mayo society that are not specifically derived or imposed from outside. The clowns are legitimating the "other side" of human attitudes, generally, toward persons and things said to be extremely important or sacred or inviolable. Instead of suppressing or repressing these attitudes, they are ritualized, given a place to be, and channeled in a positive direction.

Such clown behavior, however, is not the last word either. The extremes in which they indulge are also qualified in various ways. They are, after all, "Pharisees" and therefore to some extent may be discounted. Also in addition to parodying the solemn processions, they patrol the processions, helping to keep others in line—if not always themselves. Though mockers of the religious practices, they are referred to paradoxically as "the Protectors of Customs." The same wooden swords with which they interrupt services and processions, and with which symbolically they kill the Christ, are the swords with which they maintain crowd order and guard the altar, the image of Christ, and his special servitors. The clowns, too, make sure that everyone attends church services and they prevent people from departing before the ceremonies are concluded. If a fight breaks out between spectators, the clowns appear on the scene to intervene, or begin fighting with their wooden swords in a hilarious manner, defusing the situation.

Some of the Mayo interpret the sacrilegious aspects of clown behavior as a re-enactment and confession of sin on behalf of the people. The men doing the clowning may also be muttering prayers and carrying crucifixes, so as to avoid any negative consequences that might be imagined to come from their profanity. During the period of clowning, too, they are to abstain from alcohol and sex and maintain ritual purity.[16]

Often clown performances are concluded by running the clowns out of the ritual arena, a practice which continues into the modern circus. Clowns are permitted, enjoyed, applauded, then chased off the stage. Just as the clowns themselves incarnate opposites, and give vent to opposite feelings and values, so the attitudes toward such ambiguous figures are ambivalent. What has been welcomed so clamorously, must also be put to flight somewhat ingloriously. The clowns who have indulged us vicariously, must also vicariously pay a price for their profanities. The scapegrace becomes the scapegoat.

In Pueblo clown rituals accompanying the Kachina dances, the Chuku clowns are given four warnings by the Owl Kachina during the ceremonies, with each warning to behave delivered from the four sides of the dance arena—that is, from the four directions and thus numerologically a *complete* warning. Each time the clowns totally ignore the warnings, returning to their mockery of the Kachina dancers, their humorous antics, their sexual sporting, their gorging of themselves, their mudslinging. Near the end of the dances, however, the Owl Kachina reappears for the fifth time, accompanied by a number of other figures, each carrying a whip made of willow branches. The clowns are chased down, given a whipping, stripped of their clown costuming and paraphernalia, then dowsed with buckets of water until they are cleansed of the mud with which they have covered themselves—and perhaps also cleansed of their sins.[17]

While on the one hand this serves to "bring down the curtain" on clownish foolishness and profanity, it also serves to return life to normalcy—which is somewhere in between the ritual extremes of great solemnity and formality and equally great frivolity and tomfoolery. The totality has been embraced, immoderately and now in moderation. And, since one of the reasons for the sacred dances was to bring the fertilizing rain, not only is rain brought by the Kachina dancers but also by the Chuku clowns: by the mud with which they have been smeared and the water with which they have been cleansed.

After the whipping and dousing, the clowns are permitted to return by singing their way back. The Kachina punishers form two lines, and the clowns process between them, one by one, singing an entertaining song. Then food is distributed among the spectators in a general atmosphere of good will and celebration. Our double, yet single identity as both Kachina and Chuku is established and affirmed. The clown is, indeed, a *doppleganger*.

The Celebration of the Commonplace

Harvey Cox in his *Feast of Fools* has argued that the appropriateness of the fool as a religious symbol is as the "personification of festivity and fantasy." And Cox has identified as the essential ingredients of this feast of fools "conscious excess," "celebrative affirmation," and "juxtaposition" (i.e., that which is "noticeably different from everyday life").[18] While this is partially correct, it does not necessarily direct us to the right fools or the whole "feast." In fact, one of the peculiarities of a fool's feast is that by the usual standards it often appears to be no feast at all, but rather a feast *for* fools. We are escorted, as it were, into an elegant dining hall gaily decorated for merrymaking, only to discover that beneath the lid of the silver serving platter are the crisp remains of a common sparrow!

Though clowns and fools in their frivolity and garish attire are certainly party to, and even officiants in, festivity and fantasy, one must be careful to note the unusual character of their revelry. They are, after all, most ambiguous figures. They may appear to be from another planet, but they are authentically this-worldly. Not only do they stand outside and over against the sphere of ordinary existence, merrily transporting their audience into some Land of Enchantment. They also revalue life by standing, at the same time, most deeply and humanly within it. Clowns and fools move between fantasy and reality, profundity and nonsense, the sublime and the commonplace. That is a part of their mediation, their dialectic, their salvation.

Take the world of the circus clown. It is not just a secondary word of fantasy that soars away from our world on balloons and kite strings and butterfly dreams. And it is not always "noticeably different from every-day life." In many respects it is noticeably *like* everyday life. The props and tricks of clowning are usually nothing spectacular at all. The clown will pull from baggy trousers a lollipop or a string of sausages, perhaps a paper geranium or a whistle, and act as though it were wonderful to do so. Though there is a suggestion of eating sumptuously, the actual diet is likely to consist of long chains of hot dogs and great bunches of ba-nanas. In costuming and accoutrement, the clown often appears to have visited a strange other world of fantasy indeed, namely grandma's attic, a third-hand clothing dispensary, a dime store, and a junkyard! And with these patches and mismatches, this riotous combination of colors and prize collection of trinkets and trash, our attention is noisily solicited, as if something noteworthy were about to take place. It isn't.

The clown will propose to engage in any number of marvelous ma-neuvers: walk a low-strung tightrope, dive into a bucket, swallow a lighted firecracker, tear a lion limb from limb. But the actual result is little more than a small child could do. And what we find ourselves enjoying about this peculiar fantasy is that the clown has really done nothing fantastic at all. That is the trick, the joke. The clown has abruptly brought us back down from the electrifying world of the high-flying trapeze and the swaying tightrope and the cage of snarling lions to the world of familiar objects, simple accomplishments, and common bumblings. And in this world we discover again a child's delight in life's little bits and pieces.

There are clowns who have used magic, and clowns who have dis-played fine musical ability or acrobatic and juggling skill. Bill Rice, the great American clown of the nineteenth century, was especially noted for his spellbinding singing of ballads and ditties. The famed English clown Joseph Grimaldi not only sang entertainingly but leaped and somersaulted as few had ever done. And there are many clowns, such as Buster Keaton, who have exercised considerable artistry in falling, running, jumping, climbing, and catapulting. Such nimble and scintillating clowns may move for a time in the direction of pure hero-ics and artistic genius, but this is always combined with or accompanied by the clown who is a nobody doing nothing special, who makes such a fuss over baubles, the clown who is skilled, if anything, in appearing dense and awkward and clumsy without suffering all the ill effects of such.

The master European clown Grock was such a figure. Though an accomplished musician, he once remarked that the secret of being a good musical clown was that one had to be capable of hitting exactly the wrong note at exactly the right time—a technique elaborated to full effect by Victor Borge. In his autobiography, *Life's a Lark*, Grock defined the special genius of his occupation as that of "transforming the little, everyday annoyances; not only overcoming, but actually *transforming* them into something strange and terrific." It is "the power to extract mirth for millions out of nothing and less than nothing: a wig, a stick of grease paint, a child's fiddle, a chair without a seat."[19] This is the clown's peculiar form of "festivity and fantasy," the real "feast of fools." And the clown's ability to discover some magical transformation in such objects and events presupposes that there is already something strange and terrific about them which we, for all our sophistication, have missed or forgotten.

In Mark Twain's "Which Was the Dream" the narrator of the story has been reading a tale to two children and has suddenly been interrupted. "For ten minutes I had been wandering with these two in a land far from this world; in the golden land of Romance, where all things are beautiful, and existence is a splendid dream, and care cannot come. Then came that bray of brazen horns, and the vision vanished away; we were prisoners in this dull planet again."[20]

But is this intrinsically a "dull planet" in which we are, as it were, imprisoned and from which we must see ourselves as driven to effect an escape—whether into some fantasy of the mind and its creation, or paradise of the imagination, or blissful heaven, or utopian project, or timeless nirvana? Or is this dullness itself a matter of the mode of perception, the dulled art of seeing and savoring? Is not this, in fact, an art that is often dulled by the wandering visions, golden lands of romance, and splendid dreams themselves? Is it not like increasing the amounts of spice added to rice to the point that the rice itself has no taste at all? Or like intensifying the brightness and boldness of colors so much that the subtle differences between muted shadings go unnoticed and become instead so many variants of drabness?

When Chaplin in *The Immigrant*, just off the boat and penniless, manages by a stroke of luck to obtain a plate of plain beans, we are given a lesson in the categories of drabness and dullness. After peering hungrily in the window of a restaurant and emptying his pockets in vain, Charlie discovers a coin on the sidewalk. Though later it turns out to be counterfeit, he joyfully scurries into the restaurant to buy what the coin would buy: a plate of beans. With utmost care he begins by taking each bean, one by one, savoring each tiny morsel, as if it were filet mignon—which to a poor and hungry immigrant is what it was. Similarly, and on another scale, Chaplin in *Modern Times* was able to restore the magic thrill of the most timid kiss or hesitant touch of the hand in befriending an orphan girl, which even the grossest sensualism is incapable of achieving.

> ...We have seen
> The moon in lonely alleys make
> A grail of laughter of an empty ash-can,
> And through all sound of gaiety and quest
> Have heard a kitten in the wilderness.
>
> Hart Crane, *Chaplinesque*[21]

While clowns and fools may indulge in the same flights and fantasies as other mortals, exemplifying them and vicariously taking them to ridiculous extremes, impulsively they insist on returning to a defense of the ordinary. And the vicarious extremes are themselves a part of that return. The clown slaps opposite ends of the scale of value together—like serving caviar on paper plates—while the fool confuses the categories and garbles distinctions—like mistaking dried peas for pearls. In this manner, attention is called to that perennial human problem in which we become so caught up and imprisoned by our valuational pyramids of important and trivial, brilliant and dullish, beautiful and ugly—in fact a whole thesaurus of antonyms, and gradations between—that much of our experience is turned into a surrounding desert sand. By perceiving things comparatively, even competitively, we develop the habit of looking down upon and dismissing vast areas of potential experience. Instead of savoring beans as beans, we compare them with filet mignon, or at least with jelly beans. We compare them with other beans eaten on some more memorable occasion, or with some fantasy we have of what beans ought to taste like under more ideal conditions, or with those magical beans available only in "Jack and the Beanstalk."

But there is another way of viewing the matter. Maturity—which is what the seeming immaturity of the clown and fool represents—does not come in an escalation of this process until one collapses in the arms of God, or in the arms of an ambulance attendant. It comes in a reversal of the process, a de-escalation. Instead of terminating in a kind of cynicism or despair over life, as if caught in a speeded-up merry-go-round from which one yearns to get off, one is reawakened to a new zest for life. Or instead of the world's being scorned in favor of some spiritual region judged to be eternally satisfying, the world is reopened in its fullness. It is a recovery, at a higher level, of the child's sense of wonder and worth relative to the whole of life, even the slightest particular. One can smell flowers and notice trees, feel water and taste beans, and hear the sound of growing grass once more.

This is the sort of perspective on life that some, like Nikos Kazantzakis' Zorba the Greek, seem never to have lost.

> I felt, as I listened to Zorba, that the world was recovering its pristine freshness. All the dulled daily things regained the brightness they had in the beginning, when we came out of the hands of God. Water, women, the stars, bread, returned to their mysterious primitive origin, and the divine whirlwind burst once more upon the air.... Everything seems miraculous to him, and each morning when he opens his eyes, he sees trees, sea, stones and birds, and is amazed.[22]

8

A Happy Ending Of Sorts—The Underdog

(i who have died am alive again today,
and this is the sun's birthday;this is the birth
day of life and of love and wings:and of the gay
great happening illimitably earth)

—e. e. cummings[1]

The happy ending has commonly been seen as one of the identifying marks of comedy. By contrast, an ending containing unresolved conflicts, self-destruction, or mutual destruction, along with a kind of relentless march of events toward such an end, has been seen as one of the identifying marks of tragedy. Tragedies terminate in death and dissolution, comedies in life and reunion. In tragedies things fall apart or are destroyed by conflicting forces; in comedies things are put back together, and this happy result is often signified by a marriage, a feast, and a general mood of celebration. Tragedies produce funerals and disasters; comedies produce weddings and happily-ever-afters. But is this really the case? And does this really describe the flesh and blood of comedy?

Several decades ago F. M. Cornford advanced the intriguing thesis that the origins of both Greek comedy and tragedy were to be found in the religious drama enacted during the seasonal spring rites. Theatrical tragedy arose out of the first half of the ritual: the dying of the old year, the death and dismemberment of the fertility god, the symbolic demise of the king, the return to chaos, and the resultant mood of lamentation. Comedy arose out of the second half of the ritual: the birth of a new year and a new order, the resurrection of the god, and the reenthronement of the king, or the crowning of a new king. Comedy in particular picked up on the culminating movements of the spring rites: the marriage of the king and queen, the union of the fertility god and goddess, triumphal

157

marches and wedding processions, feasting and revelry (*komodia*, the revel song). The *agon* (conflict) was over and the agony became the ecstasy. Life was again victorious over death, cosmos over chaos, sexual union over disharmony, fertility over barrenness, spring over winter, laughter over lamentation.[2]

The argument is appealing in its simplicity. Structurally and thematically many tragedies and comedies do fit the two respective phases of the festival ritual. Sophoclean and Shakespearean tragedies follow an unmistakable pattern of descent into dismay, dissolution, darkness, death and decay. But Aristophanes' *Birds* or Shakespeare's *Comedy of Errors* or Molière's *Miser* swirl upward lightly into the sunshine of good fortune, unlikely resolution, and united lovers, having won through by means of sundry mysterious forces and providential happenstances. *Hamlet* achieves multiple funerals; *As You Like It* culminates in a quadruple wedding. *Othello* begins with his wedding to Desdemona, but ends with Othello murdering her and then killing himself. To tragedy belongs guilt and judgment; to comedy, love and grace.

Certainly Dante understood matters in this way and followed the conventional happy ending popularized in the second century B.C.E. by the Roman Terence. In Dante's *Epistolae* (X.10) he explains the reasoning behind his unusual choice of the title *Commedia* for a cosmic drama with such grand themes as hell, purgatory, and heaven. "It is clear why the present work is called a comedy. For if we examine the theme, in the beginning it is frightening and foul, because it is hell; at the end, fortunate, desirable, and joyful, because it is paradise."

Comic Eschatology

If so, comedy is properly "the mythos of spring" (Northrop Frye).[3] It is "an art form that arises naturally wherever people are gathered to celebrate life, in spring festivals, triumphs, birthdays, weddings, or initiations" (Susanne Langer).[4] By extension, one might see a special affinity between later Christian themes of resurrection, ascension, and paradise and kindred themes of comic art—themselves derived from earlier Easter rites. All the movements of such a tragicomic structure are there in early Christian symbolism: death and dismemberment of the god/king, end of the old order, descent into hell, resurrection, new kingdom, new heavens and earth, marriage of Christ and his bride (the

Church), nuptial/victory feast (Eucharist), and ascent into heaven. In these terms, tragic symbolism moves into comic symbolism and is incomplete apart from the comic conclusion. Thus Wylie Sypher can argue,."Tragic action runs through only one arc of the full cycle of the drama.... Consequently the range of comedy is wider than the tragic range.... The comic cycle is the only fulfilled and redemptive action." One might then conclude that "the drama of the struggle, death and rising—Gethsemane, Calvary and Easter—actually belongs in the comic rather than the tragic domain."[5]

In further support of this, one might point to the early Christian imagery of Jesus as the bait used to trap the devil. Or one might note that the early church did not reenact the Last Supper in a funereal atmosphere, but rather as a love feast, a sacred banquet, celebrated in the spirit of victory and rejoicing. Or one might cite the ancient custom in Greek Orthodox circles of setting aside the day after Easter as a day of merriment, a day in which games and dances were held in the churchyard and joking and jesting were considered appropriate within the sanctuary because of the "big joke" God pulled on Satan in the resurrection. Tragedy issues in sorrow and death, salvation belongs with comedy. Comedies effect redemption, restoration, renewal, reunion.

Such associations continue to be made in more recent studies of biblical literature. There are those, for example, who have attempted to classify stories in the Hebrew Bible as tragedies or comedies according to plot lines which either swing upward (comedy) or downward (tragedy) in the end. Thus Cheryl Exum and William Whedbee, in *Tragedy and Comedy in the Bible* see the stories of Isaac and Job as comedies, while Saul and Samson are tragedies, as measured by the principle that "tragedy may grant its protagonist a moment of glory, but then descends into darkness.... Comedy, on the other hand, ultimately ascends from any momentary darkness and concludes with celebration, joy, and new life."[6] Similarly, Dan O. Via, Jr. in *Kerygma and Comedy in the New Testament* draws upon the same standard characterizations of tragic and comic action. A tragic plot involves "a downward movement toward catastrophe and the isolation of the protagonist," while that of comedy "moves upward toward the well-being of the protagonist and his inclusion in a desirable society."[7] On this basis, Jesus' teachings are divided into tragic parables (e.g., the unforgiving servant) and comic ones (e.g., the prodigal son). By adding the parables to the death-burial-resurrection scenario, one is led to conclude that "the full Christian story is a comedy, but a comedy in which tragedy is included and overcome, as we see in the Prodigal Son."[8]

An immediate problem in this thesis is that—as Crossan has noted—"the world of resurrection is itself divided into Hell and Heaven, which means that tragedy and comedy are simply relocated elsewhere and frozen into everlasting and unchanging actualities."[9] Via has, in effect, granted the same point by dividing Jesus' parables into tragic and comic types, since those with "tragic" conclusions remain unredeemed. Unless one takes the universalistic position of Origen or Karl Barth, there is no "overcoming" of the tragic—as in the parable of the ten virgins, five of whom were ready and admitted to the marriage feast and five of whom arrived late and were shut out. If one is to speak of biblical stories as comic, this would seem to have less to do with endings—the way the plot turned out—and more to do with the manner with which life, from beginning to end, is perceived and received. Religion, like comedy, is primarily a matter of spirit, not form.

As has already been indicated, too, the design of early tragedy was to carry the action through to a reconciliation. Once the seemingly irreconcilable positions were mediated, the parties to the compromise having, as it were, shaken hands, could now celebrate—and comedy was one of the forms of that celebration. Later, when tragedians left the tragic *agon* in a largely unmitigated agony, some comedians brought matters to a happy conclusion in their own terms, debunked tragic extremism and recalcitrance, and proposed feasts—including the feast of laughter—to which all were invited. At this point we may say that such comedies came into being as a result of the failure of tragedy—the failure to come to a happier and more hopeful conclusion. In its most developed form in antiquity in the comedies of Terence the earliest tragic structure was elaborated into a five-act movement which began with areas of tension (Act 1); leading to conflict (2); reaching an impasse (3); then moving to resolution (4); and finally to reconciliation, union, and celebration (5).

Comedy, however, is no more tied to the happy ending than tragedy is to an unhappy one. If, in fact, comedy manages a happy ending, it is in some measure in jest. As in the many ingeniously contrived conclusions of Molière's plays, where suddenly and miraculously everything works out beyond anyone's wildest imaginations, the final harmony of forces and integration of loose ends is just too good to be true. And that is half the point and the basis for laughter in comedy. We may be permitted to indulge our fantasies, to symbolize our dreams and desires, and to ritualize the most ambitious finale. But all this is accompanied, as if there were persistent crickets in the woodwork, by a retinue of built-in comic signals that retain or restore a sense of reality. Walter Kerr's description of a Molière ending does him—and comedy in general—perfect justice: "So many long-lost children restored to their parents, so many friends who have not met in twenty years meeting now, so many people who have been meeting daily without recognizing one another suddenly blinking twice and gasping 'You!', so many secret documents so opportunely revealed."[10] The ending is so complete that we laugh out of sheer delight and sheer incredulity over such an impossible network of happy coincidences so cleverly made possible on the ritual stage.

When the down-and-out Chaplin in *Easy Street* is converted in a Bowery mission (that is, he falls in love with the organist), he vows to go straight and make something of himself. He becomes a police officer. His first assignment, without any training and without even knowing the front of his police hat from the back, is to the worst beat in the city, Easy Street. Despite the odds, he succeeds in defeating the local Goliath through a series of tricks and bluffs. By the end of the film the underdog has gained such an upper hand that the absolute chaos of Easy Street is turned into absolute order, and everything is love and peace and flowers.

In viewing such pleasant preposterousness relative to city toughs and street gangs and thieves and related varieties of urban ills, one laughs—joyfully, to be sure—over the symbolic triumph of David over Goliath and the Philistines. The spirit is uplifted at this sudden realization of the Kingdom of God on earth, the New Jerusalem in the New York Bowery. But one also laughs just as heartily because that isn't the *way* things happen and that isn't *what* happens. In fact, at the end of the film, when the local thugs and scoundrels, including Goliath himself, are all dressed up in Sunday suits, politely escorting their wives and girlfriends to the new mission established on Easy Street itself, one laughs over the spotlessness of the finale in a newfound nostalgia. Remarkably enough, it is not the "nostalgia for paradise"—which has just been vented—but the nostalgia for a little realistic chaos here and there! The ending is so clean and orderly that we laugh in an amused sense of its absurdity and in a realization that it is so finished that the action and drama is now over forever. We begin wishing to see just one more brawl in the middle of Easy Street, one more difficulty to test us. Secretly we pray, May the Lord of Disorder revisit us!

While comedy may end as paradisally as a romance or a fairy tale, with hero and heroine married and living happily ever after, it does so with a knowing wink and a mischievous grin. We know that that is not the way life is, has been, or is ever likely to be. But we are permitted the beatific vision and the momentary enjoyment of utopian circumstances, while at the same time being alerted by the comic muse not to get too lost in sentimental idylls—like Feste the clown at the end of *Twelfth Night* who reminds the audience of "the wind and the rain." This alerting, however, comes not out of sarcasm or cynicism but out of a humor that lies between fideism and despair. And it does not come as a cold slap in the face. It is administered through that very different sort of jolt—the joke, the comic twist, the humorous aside, the wry remark, or simply the preposterous finish.

When Aristophanes in *The Birds* has Hopeful, accompanied by his friend Plausible, soaring by play's end to the top of the highest heaven as king of the universe, we know that our feathers are being pulled. The comic climax is hope*lessly* *im*plausible. Or when Molière masterminds one of his elaborately contrived endings, where all the pieces suddenly move into place and perfect love and justice prevail, we shake our heads in disbelief. We know that it is a clever trick, an ingenious farce, and we laugh. Our wildest dreams have been simultaneously indulged and debunked.

In *The Navigator*, Buster Keaton and his love are surrounded by cannibals. They are about to escape in an outrigger but instead fall in the water. With their arms around each other, they begin to disappear beneath the surface, destined to drown in a lover's embrace. Then suddenly they begin to ascend. At that precise moment a submarine happens to be surfacing, and they reappear from their water grave, standing on what turns out to be the ship's hatch. *Deus ex machina.*

In a sense, it does not matter whether the comic victory is ever achieved in the real world, whether good finally conquers evil, or justice everlastingly prevails over ruthless power, or the meek at last and invincibly inherit the earth. Such is the peculiar mythological requirement of linear views of history that can only justify the meanderings of history as leading to perpetual progress or some final bliss. In the fantasy of comedy, the human dream has already been achieved, and is achieved, in every comic ritual—*symbolically.* Yet it is not achieved in such a way as to freeze life and its ongoing dramas. It permits the game to be played again and again. Its mission is not to annul history or conquer death or obviate suffering but to renew and celebrate life. While in the real world, hope is often defeated and evil often triumphant, in the world of the spirit, hope eternal is nevertheless preserved. In the comic rite all the emotions and satisfactions of a real victory are there, to be repeated like the Easter liturgy itself, in all subsequent symbolic victories. And this is the redemptive catharsis of comedy. As Cedric Whitman has argued with respect to Aristophanic comedy,

> The world as it is perhaps cannot be transcended; but the comic hero is not stopped by that. He invents his own world and then subdues it.... This is, indeed, madness, but it is poetic madness; and it is neither directly moral or immoral. It is an heroic absurdity, the absurdity of the helpless little self out-absurding the incorrigible world.[11]

The same self-consciousness that presents the problem of suffering and evil to human reflection—animals do not worry over it—is the self-consciousness that is capable of transcending the problem in comic myth and ritual itself. In the world of the spirit, the dragons may always be slain and the villains properly vilified. Only among those who insist, as a prerequisite of celebration, upon literal historical victories now or forthcoming does prosaic fact triumph over poetic license and comic absurdity. Then we are left with either a stubborn clinging to utopian dreams or a disenchanted cynicism and despair.

The Not-So-Happy Ending

But comedies by no means always have a happy ending. The comic ending may be at the furthest remove from a fantastically or even moderately successful conclusion. Perhaps nothing works out, the project is a failure, everything goes wrong, and the final scene is anything but blissful. Now where are we? Buster Keaton in *Cops* goes to great lengths to make something of himself in order to win the affections of the mayor's daughter. But when, after heroic efforts to become a success and after being successful at least in eluding the police through much of the film, she still spurns him, he throws himself to the mob of angry police officers. The last image: a tombstone with Keaton's hat atop.

In between the riches or rags endings for comedies are those comedies that settle for smaller successes or eventuate in more limited failures. The hero doesn't get the girl, but he does get the horse. And perhaps, he decides philosophically, the horse will prove to be a more reliable and less costly companion anyway. So he kisses the horse and rides off. Or he gets the girl, but not the one he had his heart set on. Though she is not the ravishing creature that had set him swooning in the first place, that difference may not be so noticeable with the lights out. He accepts the realities of his fate with a toss of the head and a *c'est la vie*. He may blurt out a quip or a curse or two to express his disappointment, but also in a refusal to be destroyed by it.

In Keaton's frontier classic *Go West*, the plot is much like that of most Westerns, before and since. The hero (Keaton, after a fashion) vanquishes the bad guys (after a fashion) and rescues the damsel in distress (also after a fashion). She happens to be the daughter of a wealthy old rancher, so that a just and equitable finale naturally suggests itself. The hero will be receiving the girl and some financial blessing as a reward. All circumstances seem to be leading in that very direction. The old rancher congratulates Keaton, and the daughter winsomely flutters her eyelashes. But Keaton doesn't know quite what to do with girls, or money. The final scene is unsurpassed. Keaton is being driven off in the rancher's touring car. In the front seat are the father and his daughter. In the back seat, Keaton and a cow!

In another of Keaton's comedies he is putting the finishing touches on a little wooden bungalow. He stands back to survey his handiwork, and decides to give a nail one final hammerblow for good measure. It brings the whole structure collapsing around him. But the stone-faced Keaton is nonplused. When the front wall of the house fell toward him he was standing in the spot framed by the open doorway, and he emerges unscathed. One must be thankful for life's little blessings.

There are also those comedies that end ambiguously, like *City Lights*, where we shall never know if Charlie and the girl he had rescued from blindness ever got together. We are left in the final scene with that unforgettably ambivalent face: Charlie, with a hesitant-hopeful-fearful smile, rose between his teeth, wistfully happy, yet shy, embarrassed, wondering—as we are left wondering. A whole gamut of opposite possibilities and emotions are captured in that one final enigmatic moment. And that is precisely what is enjoyable about the ending: its unresolved and unspoiled ambiguity.

To this we must add all those comedies that show us at first a completely successful ending. The perfect caper has been consummated. As in *The Lavender Hill Mob*, the unrobbable bank has been robbed after years of meticulous research and brilliant scheming carried out with clockwork precision. But the latch on the suitcase in the rumble seat of the getaway car was carelessly closed, and the wind scatters a trail of bills behind the speeding vehicle. One tiny bit of fallibility brings the whole escapade to nought.

Or, a romance is properly culminated in an idyllic wedding, and the swooning lovers are off to Niagara Falls and honeymoon bliss. But one final scene cannot be resisted. It is captioned "And They Lived Happily Ever After." The wife is in curls and disheveled bathrobe; the baby is screaming; the mother-in-law is busily berating; and the husband is slouched, undershirted, unshaven, and grumpy. The last shot shows the husband back at the scene of the honeymoon, standing on an observation deck beside the falls, contemplating suicide. Finis.

Why such treatments of the ending, whether sublime, disastrous, or any of several shadings in between? Because comedy impulsively returns to the real world, real people, real situations, real possibilities, real pasts, presents, and futures. Yet it is not just any real world. Comedy returns to the real world with a special flourish of its own. The real world, after all, can be harsh, cruel, malicious, boring, depressing, hateful, violent, tragic, destructive. So it is the real world, seen in a special way, infused with a special spirit, offering a special grace. It is not paradise. But it is also not the ordinary world as ordinarily perceived. It is a world in which all the winnings and losings, dreams and dreadings, are appropriated comically. It is a world in which comedy has the last word and the last laugh. Implicit in its vision is the intimation of a world that—though not quite one or another of the usually contradictory paradises we have imagined—could be better if that vision were more pervasive. As James Sully has suggested, "While satire, sarcasm and their kind seem to be trying to push things away, or at least to alter them, humor, curiously enough, looks as if it were tenderly holding to the very world which entertains it."[12]

There is a further reason for the multiplicity of comic endings. Comedy does not *need* any particular ending at all. The comic hero may be victor or victim, trickster or tricked, or just a vagabond wandering in and out of fortune and misfortune. Stan Laurel could end an escapade in a daffy grin or a woeful sob or a squeal of mischievous delight. His pal

Oliver easily slid back and forth between proudly and pompously wiping his hands over a momentary triumph, theatrical outrage over the latest bit of bungling, and quivering like a frightened child caught with his hands in the cookie jar. Where it all ended was arbitrary, as all storied endings are arbitrary, as life itself is arbitrary. But whatever the ending, one could be assured that comedy was going to play with it, turn it over and around and even upside down.

Freud argued that humor is the capacity for transferring energy from unpleasurable circumstances and feelings to pleasurable ones. And that is certainly part of the secret. As in the tale of the Lithuanian Yiddish fool, Khabad, whose house caught fire, when the house was going up in flames, instead of running about in a panic as his neighbors were doing, he began to laugh. "At last," he exclaimed, "I have my revenge on the cockroaches!"[13] But the reverse of Freud's thesis is also true: Comedy takes pleasurable circumstances and reminds us of unpleasurable ones. Comedy insists on a "reality principle." In this case, if it happened to be some villain's house burning, the cockroaches might well be shown transferring themselves to the house of an overly gleeful underdog.

The comic spirit seems capable of standing apart from and adjusting to whatever the circumstances, with a shrug or a wink inserted somewhere or other. It takes on both plenitude and famine, weddings and funerals, triumphs and defeats. This, in fact, is an expression of one of the most saving attributes of human nature: the capacity for freedom and transcendence that enables us to laugh and joke and see the humor in things great and small. It is a resilience of spirit which can reassert itself when life is coming up daffodils or coming up dandelions or coming up with nothing at all. Even Emmett Kelly's "forlorn and melancholy little hobo who always got the short end of the stick and never had any good luck at all...never lost hope and just kept on trying."[14] The comic is like the child's toy that is weighted at the bottom and painted with the face of a clown or some humorous character which, however struck down or laid to rest, bobs straight up again.

The "sense of regain," as Harold Watts called it, is central to comedy—though not in the niggardly way he used the phrase: "A sense of regaining what the more cowardly part of our natures had feared might be gone forever...a universe compact of familiar objects and painless ideas." Nor is it an unheroic "retreat from the precipices where one stands to talk to the gods," offering us instead a place "to be cradled, to forego mental and spiritual growth in favor of a lively jounce." Nor is it merely the regain of "a commonplace set of values," a "mediocre kind of sanity," and the comfort of "current platitudes."[15] What is regained is a sense of perspective and balance relative to the self, its circumstances, and its world. Whether the focus of the moment is on the sublime or the commonplace, the exceptional or the mediocre, the profound or the platitudinous, comedy bobs straight up again.

If comedy is "the mythos of spring" (Frye), it is not that it belongs only to aspects of life associated with spring: birth, fecundity, marriage, feasting, festival. Comedy also belongs to summer, autumn, and winter. It is the mythos of spring in that larger sense in which it brings the refreshing breath of springtime to any season and situation.

Tragic visions may point grandly at human courage and tenacity, and dig in for heroic confrontations and a Custer's last stand, but it is in comedy that we prove to be fully free to laugh at and take on the world. And this requires no small courage and size of soul. If the book of Job may be said to approach the comic domain, it is not in the final verses in which Job receives back everything that has been taken from him, but rather at the point when everything is lost and he nevertheless affirms, "The Lord gave, and the Lord has taken away; blessed be the name of the Lord" (Job 1:21 RSV).

The Comic Transformation

There is a scene at the end of one of Chaplin's early shorts, *The Tramp* (1915), which in a single moment captures the heart of comic courage and freedom. It was Chaplin's first full-fledged use of the tramp figure and exploitation of its ambiguous possibilities. The film begins with the tramp walking down a dusty road, being twice knocked to the ground by a passing car and twice getting up to dust himself off with the whisk broom he seems to carry for such purposes. He then chances on a farmer's daughter on her way into town for shopping who is being set upon by three thieves. Although he rescues the maiden and her money, and although she escorts the hero back to her home and introduces him to her father, he does not get the girl or her father's financial blessing. For a reward he is offered *work*. An affair of the heart seems for a time to be in the making, but the tramp is soon disappointed, for what he thought was love proves to be only pity and girlish flirtation. When her dapper boyfriend drives up from the city in his roadster and bursts on the scene, backslapping the father and embracing the daughter, the little tramp is quickly forgotten. Instead of the fairy tale beast being released from his lowly estate and transformed by a maiden's kiss into a handsome, dashing prince, a different transformation occurs. It is a *comic* transformation.

The final frames of the film show the tramp at first sadly scribbling her a note and dejectedly leaving the farmhouse. He says an awkward good-bye to the girl, who is busily chatting with her boyfriend. The boy has gotten the girl, but it is the wrong boy. The tramp is offered money by the jovial boyfriend, but he refuses it. Forlornly he trudges back down the dusty road on which he came into the picture. Then suddenly it happens. In the final seconds of the film the tramp straightens up, kicks up his heels, and walks briskly, even jauntily, away. *That* is the courage and the transformation. The tramp discovers, and the viewer discovers, that the truly human figure was there all along, truly free in spirit, risen above the ups and downs of life. In a sense there was no need for miraculous transformation into a prince, no need to be snuggled into this or that human order, no need for the fine garments and castles (or farmhouses) and happily-ever-afters. The tramp was fully human and fully free, just as he was. Here was a humanity, an uncorrupted and uncompromised genuineness, that no amount of cultivated city-slickness could match and no amount of job satisfaction or marital bliss could purchase. Dirt and all, and all in all, *this* was the prince.

If comedy may be said to have an eschatology at all, it is a very "realized" eschatology. "Paradise" is to be experienced *now*, in the midst of the turbulence of life. In Chaplin's last tramp film, *Modern Times*, produced in the depression years and released in 1936, the homeless tramp and a homeless orphan girl (Paulette Goddard) find a place to live. Both are ecstatic over it. We are then shown the object of their enthusiasm: a flimsy, abandoned shack along the waterfront. As Charlie enters, a ceiling beam falls on his head. The mirage of a table collapses when he leans on it. The chair he sits on drops through the floorboards. When he nonchalantly relaxes against the wall, he falls through into the water outside. "It's a paradise!" she exclaims. And so it is, a comic paradise.

Shortly, however, they have to leave their paradise to escape the police, the orphan girl accused of stealing bananas and the tramp of stealing a loaf of broad. By film's end they have nothing but each other and are walking hand in hand down a country road, as the soundtrack plays "Smile"—a tune Chaplin had written for the film.

> Smile when your heart is aching,
>   Smile even though it's breaking,
> When there are clouds in the sky
>   You'll get by
> If you smile through your fears and sorrow,
>   Smile and maybe tomorrow
> You'll see the sun come shining through for you.
> Light up your face with gladness,
>   Hide every trace of sadness,
> Although a tear may be ever so near,
>   That's the time you must keep on trying.
> Smile, what's the use of crying,
>   You'll find that life is still worthwhile
> If you'll just smile.

Yes, there are comedies with perfect endings, even all-too-perfect endings. The difference is that they are, after all, *comedies*. We know, or should know, that what has been given with one hand is to be taken away with the other. Or, better, it is both given and taken away in the same dramatic motion. Paradisaical episodes and happily-ever-afters are presented humorously and as fantasies, and therefore in such a way as not to lose sight of or devalue the actualities of everyday life. Comic eschatology returns life to the present moment and its circumstances, be they ever so humble. The game is not suspended, even in triumph. The game itself is celebrated, not just an occasional victory. The game is always allowed to begin again, in some new form perhaps or in the same old form. "Comic eschatology," as Crossan has argued, "restores the world *sub specie ludi*." Comedy is "the epiphany of play."[16]

In all this comic play, a fundamental yes is said to the world, despite its problems and tensions and incongruities. The result is not a low view of life as irredeemably absurd—though comedy does employ its share of absurdities. One is not tormented by the failure of life to live up to all the plots and plans and purposes laid out for it. Comedy does not proceed from or lead to a sense of futility, alienation, or despair over the mysterious meanderings of our lives. It is true that certain playwrights—Chekhov, Beckett, Ionesco, Pirandello, Pinter, Albee, and kindred spirits—have used the comic to show that life is absurd. Their "comedies" are thus bittersweet at best, a "comic grimace," as Pirandello called them, leaving one not knowing quite whether to laugh or cry. There are humorous lines and comic situations, yet the overall effect is not comic. The result is not a celebration of life or a call for justice or a renewal of faith and hope, but a void in the pit of the stomach, a void that reaches out to engulf the universe.

Satire, to be sure, uses the comic to prove that certain actions or beliefs are absurd. And irony uses the comic to clarify the absurdity in our incongruities and self-contradictions. But comedy as such uses the absurd to prove that life is comical. And it finds some basis, somehow, somewhere, for enjoying the humor in it. Absurdity is not the meaning of comedy but the method. If matters were otherwise, then, as G. K. Chesterton insisted, "in a world where everything is ridiculous, nothing can be ridiculed.... If life is really so formless that you cannot make head nor tail of it, you cannot pull its tail; and you certainly cannot make it stand on its head."[17] Comedy presupposes some frame of reference, some article of faith, some vision of hope, some aura of mystery that has not been reduced to an absurdist credo.

The world of comedy is not the world of Robbe-Grillet's *Jealousy*, where nothing significant happens because there is no longer any standard of significance, or of Sartre's *Nausea*, where in the absence of a meaning for life Roquentin is left with contemplation of suicide in disgust over the dirty hodgepodge of chaotic phenomena around him. It is not the world of Beckett's plotless "sequence" of rambling incidents, where, as in *Waiting for Godot*, it hurts Vladimir to laugh, or Henry in *Embers* can only muster a "long horrible laugh," or Arsene in *Watt* offers but the dregs of the cup of laughter, "the bitter, the hollow, and the mirthless." Nor is it the world of Ionesco, "in which all human behavior tells of absurdity and all history of absolute futility...so what possible reaction is there left, when everything has ceased to matter, but to laugh at it all?"[18] This mirthless laughter, which Beckett crowns as "the *risus purus*," the "laugh of laughs," is not comedy but the death rattle of comedy.

Comedy expresses, not the disillusionment that can often be found in irony and satire, or the scornful scoffing of a skepticism which makes mockery of everything but itself. For all the doubts and contradictions and absurdities which comedy entertains, there remains as its center of gravity the joy of life and a gratitude for the gift of life. As in Camus' treatment of *The Myth of Sisyphus*, the endless rolling of the stone up the mountainside, only to have it come crashing down again, does not issue in a sense of meaninglessness or futility or self-pitying condemnation, but surprisingly in a smile born of an eternal playfulness. So does Camus conclude that "the struggle itself toward the heights is enough to fill a man's heart. One must imagine Sisyphus happy."[19]

The laughter of comedy is not the hollow laughter of cynicism or the anguished laughter of tragic despair, masking bitter disappointment underneath and making obscene gestures to the sky. The effect is not that of some fond dream shattered, some belief disillusioned, some abyss opened up. Even in those comedies that end ambiguously or in defeat, one is left with a distinct sense of faith renewed and hope rekindled. A stubborn affirmation of life wells up irresistibly in the comic vision, a heroic "courage to be" (Tillich) that refuses to be daunted or destroyed. Comedy, as Christopher Fry has insisted, is an escape, to be sure, yet "not from truth but from despair; a narrow escape into faith. It says, in effect, that, groaning as we may be, we move in the figure of a dance, and, so moving, we trace the outline of the mystery."[20]

9

Wandering Within The Great Food-Chain Of Being—The Trickster

The reason he did these things was that
mortals might always laugh,
whenever his story is told,
as long as there is an earth.

—Menomini storyteller

The arbitrariness in the fortunes and misfortunes of life is a universal human experience. No matter how egalitarian or advanced a society, there are still the advantaged and disadvantaged, intelligent and retarded, attractive and unattractive, nimble and lame, long-lived and short-lived, and every other gradation to which mind and body are heir. Individual life as well, no matter how privileged on any scale of value, is a mixed array of successes and failures, just and unjust deserts, happy and unhappy coincidences.

In the comic tradition, these elements of randomness and happenstance that swirl through much of our lives are made the special focus of attention. They are elements that we often downplay, or attribute to sinister forces, in favor of an emphasis on natural laws, divine plans, historical patterns, and fated inevitabilities. Philosophers from Plato and Aristotle to Hegel and Whitehead, and scientists from Bacon and Newton to Einstein, have assumed the fundamental rationality of the universe as essential to knowledge and the possibility of science. Einstein put the credo simply by affirming that "God doesn't play dice with the Universe." Laplace much earlier had articulated the grand dream of scientific inquiry, writing in the exuberance of the Enlightenment. He imagined an intelligence which, if in possession of all relevant information, "would be able to embrace in a single formula the movements of the largest bodies in the universe and those of the lightest atoms; for it nothing would be uncertain; the future and the past would be equally present to its eyes."[1] This might sound like a definition of divine omniscience or, at least, an IBM supercomputer. But, no, it is the common faith and hope in the basic orderliness and rationality of the "laws" of nature which, given enough time, research, and federal money, could be discovered. The happy result would be a life that was increasingly intelligible, controllable, and predictable. Noted theoretical physicist Stephen Hawking continues the dream when he affirms that "the eventual goal of science is to provide a single theory that describes the whole universe.... nothing less than a complete description of the world we live in."[2]

Cosmos and Chaos

This trust in rationality, law, and order is a sure prescription for tragic despair. For, despite our most concerted efforts at shaping things into a rational, meaningful whole, life is not notably orderly, intelligible, predictable, or just. The "principles" of uncertainty and indeterminacy (Heisenberg) seem also hard at play. And *play*, with its suggestion of spontaneity and impulsiveness and freedom, seems to be a more fitting metaphor than *work*, which suggests a process that is planned, methodical, predetermined, plodding, and as free as possible of surprises. Perhaps the Western preference for the imagery of the work of creation needs to be counterbalanced by the Indian sense of the divine play (*lila*).

A recent development in the natural sciences, in fact, is that of *chaos theory*, which acknowledges "the irregular side of nature, the discontinuous and erratic side," with a new appreciation for "randomness and complexity, for jagged edges and sudden leaps," as James Gleick puts it.[3] While classical science stressed order, stability, equilibrium and uniformity, the new science calls attention to the importance of systems that are open, rather than closed, and therefore open to disorder, instability, fluctuation, and diversity. The new scientific vocabulary speaks boldly of anomalies, singularities, unpredictabilities, and tentative orders arising out of turbulences and disturbances. In short, chaos.[4] We have been a little more willing to admit to this side of nature in the social sciences, inasmuch as we are dealing with human nature. But now a more fluid and dynamic view of all processes is

compelling greater attention in the natural sciences. Even in mathematics we have had to develop a new geometry—that would have
been quite disturbing to Pythagorus, Euclid, and Plato—a geometry
which more accurately reflects a universe that is "rough, not rounded,
scabrous, not smooth…a geometry of the pitted, pocked, and broken up, the twisted, tangled, and intertwined."[5]

As lightheaded, as well as lighthearted, as comedy is supposed to be,
it is remarkable that comedy is the one arena of human invention and
action in which this other side of life has been consistently recognized
and given its due—not in scientific or philosophical terms, of course,
but in its own inimitable way. Comedy has always supported a chaos
theory of the universe—not over against order, but as a qualification of
order and a reminder of the presence and importance of these aspects of
our experience which we are not always eager to allow. Hence the comic
delight in playfulness, spontaneity, immediacy, irrationality, confusion,
and absurdity. Hence all those quirks of fate, meandering plots, curious
surprises, playful messes, petty interruptions, and odd circumstances
that proliferate themselves in comedy.

The comic toleration for, and even enjoyment of, phenomena that are
so frustrating to purists, perfectionists, idealists, rationalists, determin-
ists, legalists, tragedians, and weather forecasters, derives from several
sources. It arises, in part, out of the association of laughter with pleasurable surprises from early infancy; in part, out of the employment of absurdity in jokes and jests; in part, out of the development of the comic sense
from a playfulness toward life; and in part, out of the realization, implicit
in the comic spirit, that an existence which was totally ordered, determined, and determinable would be totally boring. Comedy readily comes
to terms with the arbitrariness of life, and with the muddiness of experience, without any quick sweep under the rug or profusion of excuses—in
fact, by accepting this state of affairs as essential to the adventure itself.
Apart from this side of things, there would be no sense of adventure, no
risk, no challenge, no surprises, no drama. Absolute order, equality, and
predictability would guarantee absolute monotony. The universe imagined by Laplace would be nice for about ten minutes. If in the beginning
God created order out of chaos (Genesis 1:2), God also created chaos.
Chaos is the other side, perhaps the underside, of order.

The ancient symbol of this perception of existence is the trickster—
ancestor to all clowns, fools, rogues, and comic heroes. The trickster

has been known in many cultures under many names and forms, both animal and human. In a majority of tales the trickster is identified with an animal suggesting clever and wily traits: coyote, wolf, fox, raven, raccoon, badger, spider, jay. He is almost always "he"—perhaps in part because the trickster is a vagabond, and vagabondage has been much more of a male possibility and occupation than a female one. The trickster is an individualist and a wanderer, a "lone wolf" who survives by his own cunning and prowess. He is a master of camouflage and disguise. Sometimes he is literally a shapeshifter, with the capacity to turn himself into a variety of forms—like Hermes who escaped detection by slipping through the keyhole as a mist.

Yet for all the trickster's bagful of tricks, he is also noted for his ignorance and foolishness. Sometimes he outwits others, sometimes he is outwitted, sometimes he outwits himself, and sometimes an unforeseen turn of events outwits everybody. Yet clever or foolish, the trickster manages to survive to pick up either the spoil or the pieces. In areas where the coyote is common, the coyote is the most popular animal trickster. The coyote possesses the ideal combination of traits, such as intelligence, persistence, stealth, and modest size—all important to the survival of a hunter or scavenger in harsh conditions. The coyote is also fooled easily, yet not easily defeated. In the mythology of many American Indian tribes the character of the coyote combines cleverness and seeming indestructibility with vainglory, ignorance, gluttony, and sexuality in comical proportions. In ritual appearances, the coyote is similar to the figure of the clown in the modern circus. His very presence is a signal for amusement and laughter.

The Trick as Existential Metaphor

In the trickster we may be seeing, as some scholars have speculated, one of the oldest figures in all mythology.[6] If so, he is one of the earliest images of human existence. Yet he is not just a relic from the prehistoric past. We find him in the Greek Prometheus who tricks the Olympian gods into eating bones concealed in fat as a sacrifice, or in the biblical serpent who tempts Eve to eat the forbidden fruit. He is very much at home in the literature of the rogue or *picaro*. He is quite familiar in the Negro tales of Bre'r Rabbit or the boyish forms of Tom Sawyer and Huckleberry Finn. We have known him in Chaplin's tramp, in the huckster and the flimflam man. The world of the trickster is, in fact, most alive and well in the legion of modern film cartoons, some of which consist almost entirely of tricks and shapeshifting, from the intrepid Bugs Bunny, who always gets the best of every situation, to the give-and-take of endless cat-and-mouse and cat-and-bird episodes, to the hapless coyote in *Roadrunner,* whose every trick, no matter how ingenious, results in personal disaster.

Trickster themes are common throughout the history of clowning and comedy in the use of pranks, practical jokes, sleight of hand, or some quirk of fate as stock comic devices. The joke itself is a trick played on our reason and expectation. Everything proceeds in good order up to a certain point. Then comes the comic twist that introduces a wild exaggeration or understatement, a contradiction, or an absurdity. And we are, strangely, amused.

In the tales of the trickster, the trick is the basic metaphor through which life is perceived. The choice of metaphor is a primitive, yet remarkably profound one. Tricking and being tricked are inevitable features of the struggle of creatures to survive. This is the nature of life as we know it and experience it. The world is "full of tricks," life "plays tricks on us," and the business of living is itself a "tricky business." The phrases and images are as modern as they are ancient. The image of the trickster and the metaphor of the trick may no longer be a self-conscious part of our symbolic repertoire. And in their original form they no doubt belonged to the earliest cultural strata of food-gathering, hunting, and fishing, where the caprices of nature's food supply, the lack of control over animals and the environment, and human techniques of stalking, baiting, and trapping, easily suggested trickery as a fundamental element of life. Yet they still open up dimensions that more characteristic modern images and metaphors, with their heavily rational bias and their implicit faith in scientific and technological ordering, do not.

The majority of trickster myths present a hero of sorts, a "character" to be more accurate, who wanders from one adventure and misadventure to another. This itinerant hero has neither a clear place in the "scheme of things" nor a clearly defined social identity. In his nomadic meanderings he is involved in a miscellaneous series of episodes that have little logical or dramatic connection, except that they are usually concerned with survival and with getting in and out of tight spots. The trickster seems always to be hungry and in the process of trying to obtain food, eating it in large quantities as if it were his last meal, or having it stolen or conned away by other creatures.

One can easily see in the trickster the archaic ancestor to the Chaplin of *Behind the Screen* (1915) on a lunch break with fellow stagehands—but without a lunch. One stagehand has spread out great stacks of sandwiches before him, another has unwrapped the remains of a leg of beef, while another has brought a large bunch of green onions. In the mist of this cornucopia, poor Charlie sits wistfully with but two empty slices of bread, trying to determine the best way to snitch a bite of beef from the end of the bone or to steal a sandwich from the pile, while avoiding the onions. The symbolic—and existential—distance between an ancient trickster and a twentieth-century film tramp is not very great after all. Nor for that matter is he very far removed from any of us. The trickster is life reduced to its rudiments: the arbitrary fortunes of life, the uncertainties of life, the struggle of life, life feeding upon life, life in defense of life, the fundamental nakedness of our life.

For all his prowess, not without cause is the trickster called, and does he call himself, "the foolish one." In a number of tales told about him, he is bungling, hoodwinked, teased, distracted, or taken advantage of. In many Indian tribes of the Southwest, the coyote was represented at ritual dances as a clownish figure, clever, to be sure, but whose antics, mistakes, confusions, and howling set the spectators "howling" with delight. Among the Algonquins, the trickster falls into a hollow tree and only manages to escape by throwing himself out, piece by piece, from a small hole in the side of the tree. In Winnebago tales, the trickster gets his arm caught in a tree fork while trying to stop the tree from squeaking in the wind, and as a result some passing wolves help themselves to a free meal of raccoon which the trickster has just trapped and prepared. Later he gets his head stuck in an elk's skull and has to trick people into thinking he is a spirit that will do wonderful things for them if they will break open the skull and let him out.

One of the trickier aspects of human existence is sexuality, and also one of the prime arenas where we experience awkwardness, foolishness, embarrassment, and endless tensions and problems. So it is no surprise to find sex organs, sexual desire, and efforts to organize sexual behavior as themes in trickster mythology. Sexuality is a perennial source of being "bewitched, bothered and bewildered," as a song of the forties expressed it. One of the members of the Navaho pantheon is Be'gocidi who functions part-time as a divine trickster. Despite his divinity, he is the subject of many humorous episodes, mostly having to do with sex. His name, in fact, derives from the Navaho word for breast (*be'go*) and he is reputed to render himself invisible in order to make sport with young women's breasts, or to disguise himself as a hunter in order to sneak up on the men, grabbing their testicles as they take aim!

The trickster, whether divine or human or animal, is usually over-sexed, and therefore possessive of a superabundance of life and fertility. With exaggerated sex organs he is capable of remarkable sexual feats. In the Winnebago cycle, trickster's penis has a kind of independent existence (as sex organs seem at times to have among human beings generally). He has, in fact, such a long penis that he keeps it coiled up in a box which he carries over his shoulder; then at the appropriate (or inappropriate) time he "lets it out." In one episode—commonly told in the coyote cycles as well—he desired the chief's daughter. Though she was on the other side of the river, he had no difficulty in sending his "little brother" swimming across the river to impregnate the maiden. But alas! He was once using it to probe after a chipmunk in a hollow log, and it was chewed down to its present size!

Another episode in the Winnebago cycle accounts for the discovery of a certain herbal laxative in use in the tribe. Trickster was walking through a field one day when he heard a little voice repeatedly saying, "He who eats me will defecate." After much searching about for the source of the voice, he finally realized that it was a tiny bulb on a bush doing the talking. Being such a small bulb, however, trickster discounted its potential powers on someone as large and strong as he. He even bragged a little about how it would take more than a tiny bulb like that to phase him. So he ate the bulb. Soon he began to break wind in a crescendo of increasingly louder explosions, culminating in a thunderous sonic boom that felled trees all around. Then trickster is hit with a series of convulsions and defecations that have him climbing a tree to escape the mounting pile. He is forced to climb higher and higher, till he comes to the treetop. The climax comes when a branch breaks and he falls into the mountain of excrement. Most unheroically, he has to dig his way out.[7] Pride indeed comes before a fall.

The trickster is much like an overgrown child, orphaned and wandering in the wilderness, trying to learn how to cope with his environment, fending for himself in a world of competing forces and creatures, with no foreknowledge of how best to proceed. As the fox says to the trickster in the Winnebago cycle, "the world is going to be a difficult place to live in." The trickster does not doubt it for a minute. He has, as it were, been thrown into existence—as are we all. He awakens to find himself existing and sees no obvious niche for himself or any obvious plan of action, but he is nevertheless determined to make the best of it. He lays claim to no special revelations, neither does he complain that he has not been provided with any. In the absence of a ready-made blueprint for his existence, he learns through trial and much error. Yet he shows no particular resentment over these circumstances, or any inclination to speculate on how things might or should have been. He conveys no sense of being cast out of some primordial paradise, or condemned to ignorance, earth, flesh, thorns and thistles—or "condemned to freedom" (Sartre). Life is taken as it comes, and with gusto he throws himself into existence.

Even when the trickster acts stupidly or is outsmarted, he is not entirely defeated and dispirited but possesses a childlike resiliency that enables him to get back up and be back at it again, without grudge or malice, a little bruised or hungry perhaps, but also a little wilier and wiser. He would hardly agree with Camus' proposition in *The Myth of Sisyphus*—assuming that he would read Camus—that "there is but one truly serious philosophical problem, and that is suicide." Trickster is too busy surviving to have the luxury of decadent contemplation. Rather than being weighed down by his misfortunes and limitations or the apparent inequities and injustices of life, he takes life as a challenge and makes a game of it. All the while, the setting of his adventures, winning or losing, is a decidedly comic one. It leads to laughter as well as tears and dismay.

Throughout these materials is a very candid yet good-humored acknowledgment of the actual conditions of human life. Though one might point to a certain givenness to existence and its possibilities, the knowledge and power necessary for survival have to be wrested from nature, and in some degree from one another. And this the trickster sets out to do, groping and grasping his way along. For him the most basic elements of food and shelter are not freely given, as by an indulgent parent, or in the largess of some idyllic garden where all things needful grow in spontaneous abundance. Nor does he lament their absence and invent instead his own utopia. He must forcibly pluck the fruit and contend with a variety of competing forces in so doing. Pipe dreams aside, the necessities of life must in some degree be taken and defended by trickery of sorts.

This trickery is not vicious or malicious in character, but marked by playfulness. A Tlingit myth tells how Raven came upon a group of boys who were tossing chunks of meat back and forth as a game. Raven was hungry; so he began throwing pieces of excrement at the boys. This led them to throw their pieces of meat at him, which he promptly devoured. In another Raven story, when his wives and relatives were about to go deer hunting, Raven pretended to be not only too ill to hunt, but dying, so as to stay home with the meat of the previous day's kill. His family dutifully sang mourning songs over him, and extolled his soon-to-be-lost hunting prowess. Raven became so carried away by all the attention and eulogizing that, at the risk of revealing his deception, he "rallied" from his death-bed long enough to sing a few songs about himself. His songs, in fact, were more flattering than those of his family! Then he "collapsed" and "died"—convincingly enough that the family concluded there was nothing more to be done for him, and went on the hunt. As soon as they were gone, Raven jumped out of bed and ate all the meat.

In a similar Chinhook tale, Coyote conspires with Skunk to feign illness, and when various animals come to sing cures over him, Skunk gasses them! Coyote and Skunk share in the catch. The "virtues" of the trickster—beyond playfulness—are slyness, stealth, cunning, and deception—all traits that are helpful both in real life and in the world of the game, whether in stealing food or stealing second base. Correspondingly, the theft motif is especially widespread in trickster tales. Both of the trickster figures in Greek mythology are associated with theft, as is the biblical snake in the garden. Hermes is called "the thief" and Prometheus is most noted for his theft of fire. The Chinese trickster, the Monkey King, steals the secrets of metallurgy from the Dragon of the Sea and the peaches of immortality from the Garden of the Gods. This identification of the trickster with thievery is not necessarily an ethical judgment against his behavior. Rather it is a primal recognition that life is taken as well as given, that it is sustained in part by taking, and that in a sense we are all thieves. What, actually, belongs to anyone that, in some sense, has not been taken in the great struggle of creatures to survive?

Life preying upon life—as life has been doing for a billion years or so—is a series of tricks. The hunter uses a disguise in order to trick the hunted. The hunted disguises itself in order to trick the hunter. And in the great food "chain of being" the hunter in turn may well become the hunted. As Mark Twain put it in *Roughing It*, "All things have their uses and their part and proper place in Nature's economy: the ducks eat the flies; the flies eat the worms; the Indians eat all three; and thus all things are lovely."[8]

> And God said:
> Let there be sprats to gobble the gnats,
> So that the sprats may nourish the rats,
> Making them fat, fine food for the cats.
>
> —Leonard Bernstein, *Mass*

The Game of Life

The trickster is probably the oldest mythological figure to represent life in terms of a game or sport. This is not in denial of the real possibilities of injury, failure, suffering, and death, as if life were a gentle romp through the idylls of the Elysian Fields. Despite all the dangers, difficulties, and disappointments life is approached enthusiastically as a challenge and adventure, and played as a game or sporting proposition.

This association of the trickster with the spirit of gaming is quite instructive of the vision of life that the figure embodies. One of the results of human imagination has been the invention of a seemingly endless proliferation of games. In creating games, we create microcosms organized according to our own principles and rules and given certain purposes and goals. Games are worlds that we imagine for ourselves and superimpose on the world at large. Into these fantasy worlds we step periodically, presumably to provide some respite from work and everyday affairs.

Now, we are able to create these microcosms very much as we please. Yet what do we do, given free rein and few constraints? We make these imaginary worlds remarkably similar in character to the world in which we live. We give them many of the same possibilities for surprise and even failure as generally obtain in the real world. In some games there is in fact a far greater proportion of disappointed losers than delighted winners, as in golf matches or state lotteries.

With some types of games we build in a high degree of chance and arbitrariness, as in dice, cards, and roulette. We place players in competition, if not open conflict, with a mission to defeat the opponent. We permit trickery and deception as proper tactics, as in baseball pitching. We even develop games with a much higher than normal risk of pain and injury, such as football and boxing, and with the distinct character of a tragic collision. We do not eliminate hazards but devise sports with considerable risk of danger and even death, such as skydiving or car racing or bullfighting. The risks are said to be part of the fun of it, providing an enjoyment and thrill that one could not obtain from a leisurely stroll in the park or a Sunday drive in the country.

The truth is that, given the opportunity to create worlds of our own choosing that we would consider it worth our time, money, and energy to play, we recreate *this* world. We even recreate it with greater amounts of chance, challenge, and jeopardy, requiring a higher degree of effort, training, intensity, and gamble than ordinary life on an average day. This we call play, game, sport, adventure, excitement, and pleasure. We say, in fact, that to reduce these elements would "take the fun out of it," empty the game of meaning and purpose, and make it not worth playing. All of those things that we complain about in everyday life, and in our wildest fantasies imagine to be missing from past or future paradises, we insist on having as essential ingredients of our play worlds.

Indeed, all of those things that skeptics, from Epicurus to Hume, have argued do not belong in a world attributed to a wise, powerful, and benevolent deity are the very things that we, with all the wisdom, power, and good intentions at our disposal, demand of the game worlds we create. In fact, so successful are we at making our game worlds correspond to real life and elicit the same emotional highs and lows that it is difficult to distinguish between the effects of a game world and those of the real world. One may be just as elated over winning a pennant as over receiving a promotion. In some games one also may be just as injured or bankrupt or even dead as in "real life."

Like the real world, the game world includes elements of both order and disorder. From one standpoint games appear to be logical and orderly arrangements of things. They structure space and time in certain ways, with time clocks and playing fields, courts, rings, and boards. They organize behavior according to strict rules, and add referees to ensure adherence to the rules. Yet the rules themselves, and the space and time allotted, are largely arbitrary. And the games have to introduce or permit some element of chance, disorder, or deception, otherwise the result might be completely predetermined. A properly programmed computer could calculate the outcome of a given contest, and it would not even need to take place. In fact, there would be no point whatsoever in playing the game.

To the degree that the elements of unpredictability and potential defeat are diminished, the enjoyment of any sport is diminished and it becomes no contest at all. If there were no possibility for a bad bounce or a lucky break, no chance for underdogs and long shots to win, no way of beating the odds or likelihood of losing, we would not consider it to be a game or sport at all. In football, for example, the peculiar shape of the ball alone adds a large measure of unpredictability in kicking, catching, and carrying it. Without such elements of interdeterminacy, the game would become that much more calculable, and the Dallas Cowboys would always win the Super Bowl. That is to say, the game would cease to have value or interest, and it would be meaningless to unfold the sequences of such a nonevent.

It is remarkable, then, that in most theological, philosophical, and scientific discussion of cosmos and chaos, historically, the predominant assumption has been that order, rationality, and natural laws are positive features of experience, while disorder, irrationality, and random occurrences are negative. Yet, as has been observed in the game analogy, orderliness and predictability alone would eliminate a wide range of alternate values: freedom, novelty, creativity, flexibility, drama, suspense, and—in its fullest sense—history. Perfect order, therefore, would be imperfect. The game would not be worth playing or observing.

In myth, ritual, and symbol such perceptions of life as gamelike, and of games as lifelike, belong to the province of the trickster. The trickster comes introducing both order and disorder, with a zest for playing in the game of life, absent assurances and guarantees, and with a capacity to pick himself up and play again.

Life Betwixt and Between

In this game of life the trickster is governed by a simple set of "principles." If he is hungry and sees something edible, he wants it. If he spots an attractive maiden, he desires her. Like a small child, he is not inhibited or repressed. His desires are simple and "honest" ones. He is the indomitable, irrepressible will to live and abandon to living. As such he requires no particular plot or plan or purpose. His life is rambling, his story episodic. He loves life, lives it with a passion, as if life itself is the "point" and goal of life.

Yet despite a fluidity of being and a meandering existence, in the course of his adventures he becomes responsible for the discovery or invention or establishment of various features of the world, of human beings, and of customary behavior. Out of the formless comes form; out of disorder comes a certain order of things. Out of his existence come the vague outlines of a human essence. Through his explorations and tribulations, he also reveals something of what is and is not to be done.

In searching for an identity and station, the trickster moves on two frontiers: the border between animals and humans, and the border between humans and higher beings. In many tales told of him the trickster is envious of the special powers that other animals have: the power to fly like the eagle, or see like the owl, or leap like the cougar, or run like the rabbit, or eject musk like a skunk. The same logic lies behind the *totem* animal, an identification with which may give one the special powers associated with that animal—a logic that has continued into the twentieth century with highly financed and paid professional teams identifying with the bears, lions, seahawks, broncos, tigers, bulls, or dolphins.

In many trickster tales, however, instead of acquiring such powers— as totemists and tribal shamans might claim to do—he usually fails in his efforts and is made to look foolish for trying. In this way, too, he defines the human condition, along with a comic means of coming to terms with our aspirations and limitations. Humor is derived from his parodies of the attempt to transcend the human condition, and both the false claims and failures of such attempts. When he tries to fly he falls in a lump; when he leaps, he tumbles; when he pretends to see at night he runs into a tree; when he asks the skunk for some musk, he gets three shots in the face!

In a pretechnological perception of the world, whatever the human attributes, some animal can be pointed to which is superior to humans in nearly every respect. In addition, human beings are inferior in their nakedness, while all other creatures are provided with "clothing." Therefore, the first order of business for many tricksters is the acquisition of *fire*. In primitive societies, the most visible, tangible thing that human beings may be said to possess that animals do not is fire. While we would point to more abstract attributes, such as reason, conscience, creativity, language, or self-awareness as defining humanity, peoples with limited technology thought in terms of knowledge of fire.

Since human beings do not have fire as a natural part of their endowment, the mythological suggestion most commonly given was that fire had been stolen from some animal, spirit, or god—as in the fire-theft of Prometheus. Mac Ricketts, in his study of the North American trickster, has argued that the fire-theft story is the oldest and most widespread myth of the trickster type.[9] Fire also leads, not only to warmth, cooking, and protection, but to many of the advances in metallurgy, technology, and scientific knowledge. For the Greeks fire was the source and symbol of all that separated the citizen of the *polis* from barbarity and savagery, and ultimately bestial existence—in short, *civilitas*.

The fire-theft motif is of the same sort as, if not the pattern for, thefts of various other things seen as needful for human existence: water, game, fish, nuts, grain, fruit, and so on. But the trick/theft is not without cost, and usually results in some injury, loss, or newfound evil: flooding, disease, labor, death. A price is paid; a pound of flesh exacted. The advantages realized are qualified by disadvantages that come through a counter-trick or retaliation—as in the gift of Pandora with her curiosity, "tricky disposition" and jar of plagues with which the gods neutralized the human acquisition of fire. When the Hebrew serpent-trickster enticed Adam and Eve to eat the forbidden fruit from the Tree of Knowledge, while they gained power and wisdom and a knowledge of good and evil, they lost access to the Tree of Life, were expelled from the garden of their innocence, and were introduced to nakedness, pain, toil, and death. Similarly, when the Coyote-trickster of Upper Colombian mythology broke the dam with which Frog was hoarding all the water and fish in a private lake, the water and fish were released, but a flood, and all subsequent potential for flooding, came along with the destruction of the dam. In such ways *the cosmic balance of power is restored.*

The trickster, then, is a type of culture hero. Yet he is not such in the more idealized and sanitized sense. He is what we later know him as: a comic hero. Karl Kerenyi has characterized the trickster—in this case in the person of Prometheus—as "the archetypal image of the human." If so, he is the archetypal image of humanity and the human situation more or less *as is.* The trickster is a more frank and accurate, if not well-manicured and altogether flattering, representation of the human condition. In a comical and entertaining way he mirrors that peculiarly human combination of wisdom and folly, cunning and ignorance, creativity and clumsiness, success and failure, that we all are. He is thus an archetypal image of the human in a realistic rather than paradigmatic sense. We identify with him more totally than with those heroes that are beyond us.

The archetypal realism of the trickster offers an important counterweight to the archetypal idealism of those heroes or superhuman persons that we usually associate with myth and ritual. The trickster still has dirt behind his ears and between his toes. His antics and escapades also give humorous allusion to other culture heroes, and to shamans and priests, the tribal chieftain, clan mythology, puberty rituals, male/female relationships, and various customs and taboos. A fair amount of humor turns, too, upon the trickster himself for the extremes and improprieties of his eating, fighting, hunting, sexuality, and tomfoolery.

The myth and ritual is evenhanded. The life and order of the tribe is reaffirmed in comical violation: trickster gives a "free home demonstration" of what not to do. Through him vicarious expression is granted to contrary impulses and desires, in this way permitted. Those things that are sacred to the tribe are simultaneously reinforced and qualified. Though trickster myths may not have the same exalted status as the stories of the gods, heroes, and first ancestors, the meanings and functions of trickster myths are equally important. The storyteller entrusted with his tales is a priest in his own right. As Ricketts has suggested, "the telling of his tales is a kind of liturgy, and the laughter of the people is a sort of ritual response. They laugh at him until they are laughing at themselves...and in the end he saves them, through their laughter."[10]

Theodicy

When more systematic mythologies came to insist on impeccable creators who created more agreeable and intelligible worlds, or developed idealized culture heroes from whom weaknesses and fumblings had been culled away, the appeal of the trickster was diminished. He tended either to be refashioned in these terms as a more orderly fellow, or turned into a more devilish individual. If the former—as among the Pomo and Yuki tribes of California—he became a straight and stereotyped figure (high god, divine assistant, or great hero), gaining in reverence and predictability but losing in color and complexity. If the latter—as among the Maidu of California—he became the spoiler who had played a variety of mean tricks on the world, and thus introduced evil and disorder. The same may be said of the Christian reinterpretation of the snake in the Garden of Eden as the Satan of the New Testament.

Sometimes the trickster was split into two opposing figures, a good, benevolent creator and a malevolent or foolish one—as among the Iroquois and the Klamath. Sometimes his stories were simply pushed aside as secular tales, tolerated by priests and shamans "for entertainment only" but not to be taken seriously, and certainly not credited with mythological validity (Southwestern Plains tribes).

Clearly, the trickster was becoming a problem to societies which had a greater emphasis upon order, and a greater stake in orderliness. The increased development of agriculture itself involved an attempt at gaining control over the food supply and the vegetative cycle, as well as at getting in harmony with the orderly rhythms of nature. Since agriculture required a more sedentary, localized existence, farming peoples had close ties to the fortunes of the particular land being cultivated. They could not just pick up their tents and move as shepherds, hunters, and foodgatherers could do. As towns became cities, with larger concentrations of people, cities were combined into states, and states into empires, greater and greater emphasis was placed on order, predictability, and control. The myths, cosmologies, and rituals of sedentary peoples— and even more so of cultures centered in cities and capitals—have placed supreme value on these features, and by extension on organization, law, logic, rationality, symmetry, and systematization. Chaos is judged to be a great threat to such a cosmos, the sinister enemy of order, lurking in the underworld or at the edges of the world.

Recorded history is largely the story of peoples involved in cultivation and urbanization, with their increasing development of technology, mathematics, and science. The presumption through much of this history has been that life ought to be intelligible, conform to certain patterns, and harmonize itself with some all-encompassing cosmic order. Out of this understanding came visions—as for Pythagorus and Plato— of the heavens inhabited by ideal forms: bodies that were spherical, moving in precise circular motion. In such a realm irregularity, rough edges, and wobbling were not known, except as chaotic intrusions. The ideal architecture, likewise, as a reflection of the idealized cosmos, was the perfectly proportional and symmetrically appointed structure, set forth in circles, triangles, squares, and rectangles. The ideal garden was also laid out in geometrical tidiness, with trees and shrubs selected for, or given, proper geometrical shape—as in the French formal garden. The ideal city was platted in orderly fashion, reflecting the proportions and regularities of the cosmos, oriented toward the four directions, and in alignment with the heavens. In other words, a properly designed city was not a haphazard jumble like Pittsburgh, San Francisco, or London!

By contrast, shepherding, hunting, fishing, and foodgathering cultures had greater mobility and were less dependent upon the orderliness and predictability of nature. The caprices of the climate or the hunt or the search for food were more a normal, anticipated part of life, to which one adjusted and with which one flowed, rather than aspects of a threatening and destructive chaos. If the weather was too dry, one searched for greener pastures; if it flooded, one moved to higher ground; if it was too cold, one migrated to warmer areas; if the earth quaked, there was little to come tumbling down. In fact, there was always the gambler's chance that one would have extraordinarily *good* fortune in finding food, catching fish, baiting and trapping animals, taking deer by surprise, and avoiding lions and bears.

Thus we find that, among American Indians, the unadulterated tales of the trickster belonged primarily to the hunting, fishing, and gathering societies where the metaphor of the trick was a fitting expression for the way in which life was experienced and lived. A more positive value attached to that other side of life which is irregular, happenstance, capricious, and unpredictable. On the other hand, it was among the more sedentary and agriculturally dependent peoples, such as the Indians of the Southeast and Southwest, that the importance of the trickster was often diminished. If he was not whitewashed, he tended to become more unambiguously foolish, profane, mischievous, or malevolent. The randomness and amorphousness associated with the trickster and his world were features easily construed as the enemy of an order whose mission it was to overcome him and his disturbing kingdom.

Yet in any of these developments, however elevated or elevating their motives, some important perceptions came to be lost. The earlier trickster had not been the symbolic product of efforts to overcome the basic conditions of life, or lament them, or rail against them, or despair over them, or even to rationalize them—that is, try to make sense out of them and render them reasonable and just. While scholars such as Mircea Eliade have attempted to argue for the universality of the "nostalgia for paradise" and of the belief in a "fallen" humanity and cosmos,[11] the primary mythology of the trickster did not participate in this vision. The trickster did not imagine or propose perfect, model worlds, as if being thankful for some world *other* than the immediate one—in the past, the heavens, or the future—were somehow the appropriate manner of registering gratitude for life and its opportunities. He was a figure through whom life was accepted in all its resistance to being as predictable and equitable and orderly as we think we might have preferred. He came, like Kazantzakis' Zorba the Greek, with a

> savage bubbling laugh from a deep, deep well-spring deeper than the bowels of man, a laugh which at critical moments spurted and was able to demolish (did demolish) all the barriers—morality, religion, homeland—which that wretched poltroon, man, had erected around him in order to hobble with full security through his miserable smidgen of life."[12]

Noble efforts at theodicy have been made relative to individual fortunes, the fates of nations, and the vagaries of history. Various formulations have been offered in an effort to lend a semblance of justice or rationality to the inequities of life: sin and judgment, providence and predestination, karma and reincarnation, the fates and the stars. But the arbitrariness of life, which in Greco-Roman mythology is expressed in the theme of the "arbitrariness of the gods," and in the biblical context in the theme of "the will of God," is not easily reduced by offering apologetic rationales. "I have chosen whom I have chosen" admits of no higher court of appeal in Reason and its reasons. Perhaps Schopenhauer was right: Will and not Reason is the ultimate category.

Our respective lots in life do resemble the casting of lots, except in the most general sense that all suffer and die or that God "makes his sun rise on the evil and on the good, and sends rain on the just and on the unjust" (Matt. 5:45 RSV)—which to the just may well seem unjust. There is always, therefore, in any organization of experience—however well organized—a point at which reasons are finally exhausted, answers raise as many questions as they solve, and arguments begin to appeal to paradox, the limitations of reason, inscrutability, mystery, miracle, or having faith.

It is some such point as this from which, more directly and with less torture of mind, the tales of the trickster proceed, without any offer of some well-hidden cosmic plan, or elaborate attempts to justify the ways of God to the ways of humankind, or reports on the existential absurdity of life, but with a comic sense of playing in the rough and tumble of the game of life.

The trickster may seem an archaic figure from a savage past that higher civilizations have moved beyond. Yet human progress has not made the trickster obsolete. If anything, our scientific and technological successes—for all their rationality—have shifted the experience of capriciousness into a wide variety of new contexts: the stock market, state lotteries, quiz shows, sporting events, IRS audits, traffic lights, music fads, doctors' fees, clothing fashions. The potential sphere of the unpredictable and accidental has been enlarged enormously: power blackouts, oil spills, computer quirks, nuclear wastes, plane crashes, auto mishaps, chemical poisoning, lung cancer. Human progress, while attempting to bring things "under control" and give life greater predictability and security, has also succeeded in greatly increasing the number of arenas in which to encounter the arbitrary and the chaotic.

This is the ironic ambiguity that is already sensed in the figure of the trickster. Thus his fortunes are unpredictable, and his thefts commonly have ambiguous results. No matter how much structure and order we give our lives, no matter how much meaning and purpose and direction we see or think we see, no matter how successful we believe ourselves to be in making sense out of life or in making progress in some area or other, our lives and our histories still manage to move in mysterious and unforeseen ways. Every advance in the use of fire and every eating of the fruit of knowledge brings with it new problems and inexplicabilities.

So, like our most primitive forebears, we try in various ways to outwit evil forces, encourage good fortune, and obtain guidance by a miscellany of techniques. We cross our fingers, buy dashboard saints, play slot machines, kiss dice, and build apartment houses without a thirteenth floor. We carry trinket charms, wear lucky hats, hire astrologers, and cross ourselves before taking a turn at bat. We look for signs and omens, pray for special favors, and diligently consult the daily horoscope. "If I hadn't carried an umbrella today, it would have rained." Or, "If I hadn't been carrying this Testament in the shirt pocket of my fatigues, the bullet would have gotten me." In such ways, we fancy ourselves to be capable of beating the odds, tricking the weather or the Grim Reaper, and otherwise gaining some mysterious control over the stray happenings of our lives.

Even those of us who have lost all remembrance of the ancient trickster and are instead the proud inheritors of vast efforts to bring existence under the orderly procession of scientific knowledge and technological control, are as much of a mystery and problem to ourselves as before. Perhaps we have become *more* of a mystery and problem to ourselves than before, while life seems to insist on being as arbitrary and accidental as ever. There are still the rich and the poor, winners and losers, geniuses and imbeciles, the sane and the insane, beauty queens and ugly ducklings, the gluttonous and the starving, the healthy and the sickly, athletes and paraplegics, those who live a full life and those who die in youth or infancy.

"Who sinned, this man or his parents?" (John 9:2) is a question that is probably as old as human consciousness in its effort at comprehending the uneven fortunes of life. If we do not, perhaps cannot, answer in the simple terms of sin and judgment or karmic consequences or the determinations of the stars, we respond with the images of arbitrariness: "What have we done to deserve this?" "My number came up." "The deck was stacked against me." "Some people are just born lucky." "I'm a born loser." "You win some and you lose some." "Somebody up there likes me." "Somebody up there has it in for me." "I'm having a lucky streak." "I've been down on my lucky lately." "That's the breaks."

If we make a special effort to speak more scientifically, we talk of probabilities or percentages. The arbitrariness of a given case is by no means reduced in this fashion, but we are comforted when we express the matter in rational, orderly terms. "The National Safety Council predicts a traffic death toll of 450 over the holiday weekend." Or, "There is a 70 percent chance of rain tomorrow." By developing statistical surveys of the data and a calculus of probabilities, we are able to create the impression of having made sense out of the whole. We have provided a structure of likelihood and unlikelihood. "One out of every three people will die of heart disease." It does not tell us which people, but we feel better already.

Life, as we continue to remark in the most everyday experience, is "just one thing after another," with all its twists and turns, inequities and imponderables, surprises and incongruities. We may abstract slender threads of some pattern and design out of the miscellaneous patches of our existence, but these abstractions still leave the majority of our experiences in a kind of grab-bag pile of scraps and loose ends. Bravely arranged and stitched as the pieces may be, in the resulting patchwork of our lives may yet be seen the silhouetted forms of tricksters and shapeshifters.

Divine Arbitrariness

Life has probably always suggested itself as being in some measure the result of a series of tricks, but this does not necessarily imply a view of life as a "dirty trick" or a "cruel joke" or a "terrible hoax." This may even reflect a profound perception of life as similar to a magician's trick that evokes a sense of awe and wonder rather than betrayal or disillusionment. Things come into being out of an apparent nothing, change shape through some magical metamorphosis, proceed along only partially predictable paths, intermingle in a seemingly infinite network of relationships, and defy any final explanation as to why they are this way rather than that, here rather than there, now rather than then, or anywhere at all.

The trickster symbolizes in a primitive fashion the mystery of being, including the mystery of human being, experienced as an amazing and humorous surprise. While by means of a story an attempt is made to account for things being such and such, and the answers proposed suggest some cause or other, still no final *reason* is presented or presentable. Things "just happened" that way.

What, after all, is the "point" or "meaning" to be assigned to even the tiniest wild flower—on the basis of which we might imagine ourselves capable of understanding and perhaps affirming its existence, finding a place for it in the overall scheme of things, and demonstrating the manner in which it contributes to and is caught up in some destiny of the whole—a wild flower that, like the millions of generations that have preceded it, pushes its delicate face up to the sunlight filtering into the forest glade and dares anyone to make sense out of it? Into what cosmic plan does one fit the millennia of dinosaurs who were so long lords of the planet, or the teeming life of the sea? What is the meaning in the meandering path of the mountain stream, or the sermon being given in the babbling nonsense of the brook? What is the purpose of the millions of galaxies and their billions of stars, or the use of the millions of common flies and their billions of eggs? And what of all the waste space in space—if not as a sign of the sheer thereness or not-thereness of things that stubbornly refuse to conform to our rational patterns and designs or to our egoistic presumption that all things should defer to our moral and intellectual requirements?

The fact that we exist at all to ask questions and propose answers—existing without our self-conscious consent, without even a registry of prior opinion as to time and place and parentage, let alone a choice of individual traits, abilities, and surrounding circumstances—has surely always presented itself as the trick of tricks. The result—as modern societies would express it—of a random impregnation of an ovum by one of hundreds of thousands of possible sperms, we eventually wake up, as it were, to find ourselves existing, male or female, and afforded with this peculiar set of capacities and incapacities. And we must now make our way within a particular mix of individuals and situations, among an infinity of other imaginable individuals and situations, most of which we have not chosen and over which we have little or no control.

In Kurt Vonnegut's *Cat's Cradle*, God has just created Adam, who, upon coming to life and looking around blinking, asks, "What is the *purpose* of all this?" God questions in return, "Everything must have a purpose?" "Certainly," said Adam emphatically. God said, "Then I leave it to you to think of one for all this." And God went away.[13] The issue, however, is not purpose versus purposelessness, but extrinsic versus intrinsic purpose. In the comic vision the meaning of life, like the meaning of art, is primarily within itself, within the spirit and process of living. The purpose of life is fundamentally to live, just as the purpose of the dance is to dance—not to arrive at last at some distant point on the dance floor.

This vision does not imply the loss of some sublime meaning and purpose without which life becomes dark and aimless and absurd. It is a gain. It represents the highest level of existence, just as the highest level of art is for itself rather than for some object beyond itself. If matters were otherwise, life would be lived for a goal outside itself and therefore turned into a perpetual means to some other end, rather than being first and foremost a legitimate end in itself. That is, it would be devalued. And its freedom to be for itself would be forfeited, like reducing art to commercial art or playing baseball for the salary and hoped-for induction into the Hall of Fame. Life would be given the appearance of having meaning and purpose, but that meaning—however glorious—would always lie elsewhere, and life would be turned into a passageway to this elsewhere. Then if such meaning and purpose were to be lost or placed in doubt, life would become empty indeed, for life would already have been emptied by the presupposition that it can only have meaning and purpose if it serves some other end.

Mythologies, of course, attempt to give reasons for things being as they are, and attempt to define the significance and value of this or that aspect of life, and even of life as a whole. For example, "Why do human beings—who are so much more like dogs than lizards—have hands like lizards rather than paws like dogs?" "Because," according to the Yokut Indians, "there was a contest between the dog and the lizard, and the lizard won." As a prize the lizard got to choose some feature of the human anatomy and chose hands! The storied explanation makes sense out of the situation. But while a certain cause is assigned and a logic of relationships developed, a fundamental arbitrariness is quite transparent. Whatever the reasons given for some aspect of life having the particular characteristics that it does, one can always ask why it could not have been otherwise, or for some other reason. Sooner or later one comes to the level where no final reasons can be offered. Reasons become either a hat-upon-hat of further questions ("Why did God create the world?" "Because God was lonely and bored") or an admission that no further answers can be given ("God created the world for the hell of it.").

The problem is on the order of Mark Twain's playful speculations in *The Innocents Abroad* about the reason oyster shells were to be found five hundred feet above sea level at Smyrna:

> I am reduced at last to one slender theory: that the oysters climbed up there of their own accord. But what object could they have had in view? What did they want to climb a hill for? To climb a hill must necessarily be fatiguing and annoying exercise for an oyster. The most natural conclusion would be that the oysters climbed up there to look at the scenery. Yet when one comes to reflect upon the nature of an oyster, it seems plain that he does not care for scenery. An oyster has no taste for such things.... An oyster is of a retiring disposition, and not lively—not even cheerful above the average, and never enterprising. But above all an oyster does not take any interest in scenery. He scorns it. What have I arrived at now? Simply at the point I started from, namely, those oyster shells are there.[14]

Though the trickster is credited with a variety of things being what they are, the elements of *arbitrariness* and *sheer thereness* pervade the vision of that which he represents. Most of the things that he is responsible for having invented or set in motion are not the result of some master plan or carefully calculated purpose or unfolding cosmic destiny. They are the result of chance events, accidents, mistakes, decisions of the moment. Things just happened that way. The tales of the trickster personify the ultimate inability to give reasons for things beyond a certain point, reasons that settle once and for all why there is something rather than nothing, or any one particular thing, let alone this incredible variety of things—reasons which would make it finally impossible for someone, even a small child, to ask "But why?" once more.

10

Between Dreams And Dust—The Simpleton

> *I have seen everything that is done under the sun;*
>> *and behold, all is vanity*
>> *and a striving after wind...*
> *In much wisdom is much vexation,*
>> *and he who increases knowledge*
>> *increases sorrow.*
>
> —Ecclesiastes 1:14, 18 RSV

A popular television program of the 1960s, *Candid Camera*, advertised itself as specializing in the humorous circumstances of "people caught in the act of being themselves." Among the seemingly inexhaustible situations of candid comedy was an episode in which an aptitude test had been given to the graduating seniors of a select eastern prep school. *Candid Camera* personnel, in the guise of evaluators of the tests, interviewed some of the students. In one interview, two young men had been called in to receive a firsthand report of the findings. Both were honor students with college and professional futures clearly on their minds. In a very dramatic and enthusiastic tone, the bogus evaluators indicated that after careful examination of the aptitude scores they were pleased to announce the results in person. The tests showed conclusively that the young men were especially well suited to being *shepherds*!

The look of astonishment and consternation was priceless—both for its comic effect and for its indication of our contemporary distance from the pastoral tradition. While shepherds and sheep are prominent images in the cultural heritage of Western civilization, they are so remote from most moderns as to be almost unthinkable. The kind of experience and outlook that the shepherd represents is nevertheless available to us, both as a problem that will not leave us and as a perspective symbolized for us in other forms. One of these is that of the comic tradition itself, particularly the image of the simpleton, with its primitive suggestion of childlike innocence and simplicity.

The simpleton is one who stands, by and large, outside the competing forces and tragic collision of the day and who from the standpoint of these movers of history is literally quite "out of it"—much like the contemporary Bedouin tribesmen in the Middle East who live in the same hard and happy simplicity on the desert fringes of "where the action is," as have their goat- and sheep-herding forebears for several millennia. The simpleton is a Forrest Gump or Elwood P. Dowd (*Harvey*) representing certain truths about ourselves which are as universal as the truths they counterbalance. The simpleton is "out of it" in the same sense children and clowns and fools seem "out of it," yet privy to a larger wisdom.

The Recovery of Simplicity

Sometimes one has to turn to children's tales for this wisdom. In Munro Leaf's now classic story of Ferdinand the bull,[1] we find an especially charming modern instance, with its own peculiar comic perspective on human nature and tragic fate. The bull is the great ancient symbol of masculine virility and ferocity. He is strength and war and blood and sex in heroic proportions. But young Ferdinand was no ordinary bull. Ferdinand had no interest whatsoever in running and jumping and butting heads like all the other adolescent bulls in the Spanish countryside. He just liked to sit under his favorite cork tree and smell flowers. To accentuate the anomaly further, as the years went by Ferdinand grew into a very large, very strong bull. Still he preferred his cork tree and flowers to the tests of valor that were fashionable among the other young bulls who hoped to fight one day in Madrid.

On the basis of this comic inversion, the story proceeds. One day five men came scouting for the most splendid and spirited bulls for the bullring. All the other young bulls began to run about, challenging and charging and putting on their fiercest displays. But not Ferdinand. He ambled across the pasture to sit under his tree and watch others impress the scouts. But when Ferdinand went to sit down, to his misfortune he sat on a bumblebee and was stung, whereupon Ferdinand jumped up with a great roar and began running about wildly, snorting and bellowing, butting the air and pawing the ground in a most impressive manner.

And when the five scouts saw the performance, they all exclaimed that Ferdinand was clearly the most ferocious bull of the lot. So they took him away in a cart to Madrid.

Suddenly Ferdinand had been awakened from his Edenic bliss. His cork tree had become a Tree of Knowledge. In heroic terms (Campbell)[2] the "call to adventure" had been given. And while he had at first "refused the call," now fate had thrust it upon him. He was transported out of his pastoral paradise into the very center of urban life. There he was to play the ritual role of the hero in a tragic fight to the death with another hero, the bullfighter. On the day of the bullfight a huge crowd was assembled, all expectantly awaiting Ferdinand, who was said to be one of the mightiest bulls ever brought to the arena. When the gate was opened Ferdinand walked out to the center of the ring to the wild cheers of the crowd. But when Ferdinand got to the center of the ring, he looked around and saw all the beautiful flowers in the hair of all the beautiful ladies. And he just sat down in the middle of the ring to enjoy them. No matter what the matador and the picadors did, no matter how unmercifully they poked him and jabbed him and shouted at him, they could not get Ferdinand to fight. So they had to take him back to his pasture, where he sits to this day under his favorite cork tree, smelling flowers.

While Leaf's story uses some of the same patterns and themes as other heroic tales, it abruptly and humorously moves in an opposite direction. All heroic values and virtues are completely reversed. Proponents of the "monomyth" of the hero might attempt to classify Ferdinand as a variant of the universal type.[3] But Ferdinand is clearly no hero. He is the antithesis of the hero. And if there is an archetypal image of the hero embedded somewhere deep in our psyche, here is clear testimony to a counter-archetype, with its own parallel validity.

If anything, Ferdinand is more like the lackluster Adam and Eve of Genesis, who organized no grand rebellion against the gods and made no defiant assault on the heavens or clever steal from divine altars, but who quite unheroically got talked into eating some forbidden fruit by a garden snake in a conspiracy of circumstances. We are in the world of pastoral simplicity. But the questions being raised are still the same basic questions: What is human nature and destiny, and where is true life to be found? And they are being answered from the peculiar standpoint of the simple delight in the ordinary.

For most of Ferdinand's friends, life was to be found in Madrid, in the bustle of the city, the expectation of new excitements, the adventure of the ring, the thrill of competition, the cheering of the crowds, the heroism of the contest, the tragic fight to the death. But for Ferdinand there was something very special and enchanting in all those common things immediately about him in his humble pasture, like cork trees and grass and flowers and the occasional gyrations of a butterfly—excepting, of course, bumblebees. If his companions lived in the push-and-pull world of a *yang* aggressiveness, Ferdinand understood the strength and beauty of a *yin* passivity: stillness, tranquillity, immediacy, nonstriving, humility.

A story like this cuts deeply against the grain of the kind of "bullishness" that characterizes civilizations and their enterprises. It seems particularly subversive of the progressivist mythology of "onward and upward forever" that has dominated the modern West and now seems destined to dominate the whole world. To such an ideology of competition and advancement, Ferdinand cannot help but evoke images of lazy bums, loafers, and clods who will never get anywhere or make anything of themselves. He has no stirring sense of vision, no grand scheme, no consuming passion. Ferdinand is not even *tempted* to leave Eden. He has to be thrown out. And even when thrown out and dazzled by the progress of the city and cast into the midst of an electrified mob and egged on by every conceivable enticement and prodding, he sits down and insists on turning the bullring into a pasture.

Ferdinand is no hero, but he is a very remarkable bull. He has none of those dramatic qualities that would attract the attention of pioneering, competitive, and conquering temperaments, and he performs none of those marvelous feats that might give him a name and turn him into a stirring legend. He climbs no mountains, plunges into no watery abysses, slays no dragons, rescues no maidens, outwits no gods or demons, and engages in no tragic confrontations. Yet one suspects that in a peculiar manner all his own he is already where the hero is trying so valiantly to get.

It would be only too easy to dismiss this as a romantic pastoralism or sentimental primitivism or nostalgic regression to *A Child's Garden of Verses*. And both Marxists and capitalists could cry, "Palliative for the masses." But such would miss the subtler and more mature perceptions being symbolized. Alien though this may be to the official cultural image of ourselves as doers of great deeds and shapers of some "manifest destiny," there is a certain wisdom here. It is a wisdom that finds contentment in the familiar periodicities of life: the ceaseless round of day and night, the waxing and waning of the moon, springtime and harvest, the encircling years, the day-by-day repetitions that never get anywhere and in which there is "nothing new under the sun."

Comedy has always fit in well with the natural and biological rhythms of life. It moves with special ease among the perennial themes of children, love, sex, marriage, food, drink, sleep. It welcomes without cynicism and without weariness those successive waves of blossoming trees and nesting birds and young lovers in which the same old process repeats itself for the trillionth time, yet in each instance as if for the very first time. The comic image of time is not that of a spiral staircase to the stars. Time is cyclical, liturgical, and centered in the present. Its sense of space is likewise "present," as if one need not engage in some cosmic struggle, or build high towers to the heavens, or journey to the center of the earth, or make pilgrimage to some holy city in order to gain meaning, worth, and direction. One is already *there*. And relative to this sense of arrival, heroic quests have the appearance of grand detours, romantic distractions, perhaps even impending disasters. As Joseph Meeker has commented,

> To people disposed in favor of heroism and idealistic ethics, comedy may seem trivial in its insistence that the commonplace is worth maintaining. The comic point of view is that man's high moral ideals and glorified heroic poses are themselves largely based on fantasy and are likely to lead to misery or death for those who hold them.[4]

King of the Birds

Consider the ideology of progress. In the archives of the Circus World Museum is a newspaper advertisement dated at Rockford, Illinois, September 26, 1879. It announced the coming of *The Great London Circus and Sanger's Royal British Menagerie*, the spectacular feature attraction of which was "The Dazzling Electric Light." The text is as follows:

> Night turned into sunlight! A scene of unparalleled beauty! It melts steel without apparent heat! It burns brilliantly under water! It causes a jet of gas to show a shadow! It is like 10 concentrated suns! Look at the apparatus in successful operation! Creating a spectacle of most entrancing loveliness, ravish beauty, and supernatural splendor; transforming the very earth into a paradise of bliss; and carrying the imagination to the realms of eternal heaven; it brings to the soul of

202 The Spirituality of Comedy

every human witness a sense of imperishable ecstasy and enduring charm. And it gilds every object within a radius of 2 miles, animate and inanimate, with subdued enchantment that realizes in every intelligent person the silver dreams of a beauteous fairyland!

Not even the Prometheus of Aeschylus was so effusive in his praise of the acquisition of fire! Yet this, to repeat, is a description of the newly invented electric light.

Human progress is almost embarrassingly relative. A simple chipped-flint tool in its day was a great achievement, and probably greeted with awe and rejoicing. Yet once anything, however momentous has been achieved it becomes so normative and expected that, in relation to the years of struggle and planning and anticipation, the exhilaration of discovery and triumph quickly slides back into the commonplace. Thus the same "dazzling electric light" that evoked rhapsodies of lyrical enthusiasm in 1879 has now become more taken for granted than a Neanderthal stone ax. Thus the rapt attention and ecstatic celebration that accompanied the first lunar landing were soon exchanged for a matter of fact ho-hum of acknowledgment in subsequent missions, if they were noticed at all.

Other relativities are equally persistent. In our own time the same science and technology that heroically set foot in the heavenly sphere of the ancient gods have also developed an astronomical awareness that has reduced the size of the solar system to the head of a cosmic pin, pushing the vault of the heavens some 15 billion or so light years away! Stepping on the moon may have been a giant leap for mankind relative to ancient technologies and cosmologies. But it is only a baby step relative to the new vastness that surrounds us. The bullfrog that formerly held sway over the puddle may now be lord of the pond; yet in the course of his various leapings he has discovered the sea.

Such is the irony of human progress in the heroic "godlikeness" of Adam and Prometheus. The closer we approach both galactic and atomic universes, the more we expose their secrets, the more distant do their horizons become, and the more removed are they from ordinary levels of experience and discourse. The tremendous explosion of knowledge and power in recent centuries, while leading initially to a heady adolescent sense of budding omniscience and omnipotence, and a defiant challenge to the gods, in our more mature moments leads to a renewed sense of marvel and wonder, of awful infinity, and the bewildering immensity of the whole. The very moment of our understanding and mastery is the moment that offers a new awareness of our ignorance and smallness and powerlessness. The opening of each door opens up several other doors and trapdoors, leading into larger and larger rooms and anterooms. If only we could have landed on the moon when it was still near the edge of the canopy of the medieval sky! If only the telescope that brought the planets into earth's orbit did not also notice quasars! If only archaeology had unearthed Adam's bones and not those of Pithecanthropus and Australopithecus, let alone 150,000,000 years of dinosaur remains! What lords and masters of that cozy kingdom of our early imaginings we could have been!

Perhaps history is mercifully relative. There is little evidence to support the thesis that we who see ourselves as soaring on the leading edge of an advancing humanity are any happier or more enthusiastic over our circumstances and successes than the most primitive tribal societies who do not even have the benefit of transfer T-shirts. And one could just as easily argue the reverse by pointing, as the primitivists and pastoralists have always done, to the intrinsic uneasiness and dissatisfaction in the requirement to be always exceeding oneself and others in a grand spiraling of knowledge, power, and achievement. The results of our attainments too often have the look of Donald Barthelme's image of an eight-foot-tall youth (progress in nutrition and healthcare), wearing a cape woven of two hundred tiny transistor radios, each tuned to a different station!

The comedian Dick Gregory has summed up the ironic relativity of "civilized" and "savage" as well as any. "You gotta say this about the white race: its self-confidence knows no bounds. Who else could go to a small island in the Pacific where there is no poverty, no crime, no unemployment, no war and no worry, and call it a primitive society!"

In the ancient world it was not long after Aeschylus' words of praise in defense of a Promethean humanity that Aristophanes offered his own comic version of the Promethean temperament in *The Birds* (414 B.C.). For Aristophanes the plain truth of the matter was that the virtue, so prized and vaunted by a proud Athenian civilization, of *polupragmosune* (inquisitiveness) was both a blessing and a curse. Positively it manifested itself in energy, drive, ambition, enterprise, imagination, daring, leadership, organization. Negatively it became restlessness, impatience, discontent, insatiability, meddlesomeness, intrigue. In *The Birds* this

Promethean ambiguity is satirically developed relative to the general problem of greed, possessiveness, and the struggle for power—especially the political ambition of Athens to dominate other city-states.

The two principals in the comedy, Plausible and Hopeful, have become disenchanted with Athenian life, where the latest madness is suing everyone, and where men are "free to pay taxes." They have left the frantic complexity and vain avarice of the city to return to the simple life of the birds, the paradise of *apragmosune*. But before long the same old human story replays itself—in feathers. Though the birds are initially and rightly suspicious of the bird-men's intentions, the Athenian refugees are accepted as "harmless ornithologists." Yet no sooner are they accepted among the birds than they begin organizing the bird-world into a new and more glorious Athens-in-the-sky, Cloud-cuckoo-land. Primitive simplicity lasts for about twenty minutes.

Plausible quickly elevates himself to King of the Birds, and sets about, like Prometheus, to rescue the birds from their lowly estate—the estate that had been the original object of human envy and "flight" from the city. Through sophistic argument Plausible persuades the birds that they have forgotten their noble primordial status as kings of creation, higher than all the gods, even than Zeus himself. Mythologically it is demonstrated that the birds were hatched before the gods came into being. And various common sayings are marshaled as proof that they are the central powers in the cosmos. The possession of wings alone is evidence enough of a higher origin and destiny. So the birds follow the bird-men into "a vision of glory, a dream so fantastic as to stagger the mind," a promise of "bliss, utter and absolute."

The utopian fantasy becomes more "plausible" and "hopeful" when Prometheus himself appears with news of a tumult among the gods over the fact that the birds have gotten so involved in their own enterprises that they have been ignoring the sacrifices. As a result the gods are starving and are threatening to riot. Prometheus, helpful as ever, suggests a means of taking full advantage of the situation. Drive an uncompromising bargain with Zeus: sacrifices will be resumed only on the conditions that the divine scepter be restored to the birds—via, of course, King Plausible—and that the king be given a divine queen as a bride.

When a delegation from the gods comes to negotiate with the birds, King Plausible wins all his demands, is given a cosmic bride, and their marriage is celebrated as ushering in the new Golden Age of Birds. Plausible is hailed as "the greatest god" and "lord of all." And as the new King and Queen of the Universe prepare to ascend, *deus ex machina,* into heaven, there is a great fireworks display of thunder and lightening. The supreme power of the Olympian gods is now the possession of the bird-man of Athens, who grasps the lightning bolts of Zeus, takes up his heavenly bride, and dons the diadem of God.

Despite the totally successful ending, Cloud-cuckoo-land turns out to be but a heavenly reflection of many of the same fantasies and follies of city life from which Hopeful and Plausible had originally fled to wear feathers and don wings. That is, they have really been in the same old world of insatiable curiosity (*polupragmosune*) and vain pride (*hubris*) all along. The concluding victory and wedding celebrations thinly veil the transparent truth that the bird-men are only feathered repetitions of their former Athenian selves. In fact the wedding feast is a feast of fowl!

Our heroes had set out to realize the primitivist dream of returning to nature and nature's ways. But before long they were moving in the opposite direction, trying to rise even above the gods. They have been aided in disguising this contradiction by the ambiguities of the bird-metaphor itself. To be bird-like is both to be animal-like and to have the divine-like capacity of soaring flight. Images of animal innocence are combined with images of divine transcendence. Thus the goal of becoming "free as a bird" moves in contrary directions simultaneously like the clash between hippie and yuppie cultures in the 1970s. The ending of Aristophanes' play comically intensifies the contradiction between these idealizations of birdlikeness and their irreconcilable utopias. Midst the clash of ironies, the new King of the Birds ascends with his Queen, pulled skyward in a basket, accompanied by paeans of outrageous praise, when they should have been tarred and feathered! We are indeed suspended between dreams and dust, gods and pigeons.

The Clever and the Simple

The mediating wisdom of simplicity is quaintly articulated in the Yiddish tale of the Clever Man and the Simple Man.[5] According to the tale, two neighboring sons have been orphaned. The one is clever, the other simple. The clever son sells his father's property and goes off to seek his fortune. His considerable intelligence and skill give him resounding success in everything he tries. He masters not only the world of trade and finance, but also the science of medicine, the art of sculpture, and the craft of the goldsmith. But the same lofty standards and high ambitions that have carried him to a surpassing excellence in every endeavor leave him perpetually dissatisfied with others and with himself. The least imperfection infuriates him, and the perfection of his accomplishments bore him once they are achieved, endlessly causing him to search out new worlds to conquer, which in turn bore him when conquered.

The simple son remains in his father's house and becomes a shoemaker. He is not perpetually imagining new forms of life for himself, but is quite satisfied in being a simple shoemaker. He becomes, in fact, a rather poor shoemaker; his shoes come out looking like triangles! Yet though he is without special talent and accomplishment, and though he is poor and life is hard, he takes great pleasure in what little he has. He eats bread as if it were roast beef and drinks water as if it were fine wine. He lives and enjoys each day as it comes and in the form in which it comes.

After many years, the king, having heard of these opposite types and desiring to meet them, sends a summons to each. The clever son, clever as always, scrutinizes the summons and its messenger. This might not be from the king at all, and no one is going to fool him or make a fool of him. He has always gotten the better of everyone and every situation and is not about to be duped now. So he refuses to go. The simple son, however, goes immediately. And when the king sees what a simple person he is, and how little he is concerned about cleverness or power or wealth or self-importance, he makes him his chief minister.

A similar wisdom was expressed by an eighth-century Chinese sage, Layman P'ang:

> How wondrous this, how marvelous!
> I carry fuel, I draw water!

The poem, brief as it is, manages to contain a very odd mixing of terms. We are hardly inclined to think of such daily tasks as carrying wood and buckets of water as being particularly wondrous or marvelous, let alone "meaningful." This despite the fact, and perhaps because of the fact, that most of life consists of such inconsequential and recurrent events, just as most of human labor is menial and repetitive. It is possible that an advancing senility had dimmed P'ang's powers of discrimination between significant and insignificant duties. And it is conceivable that

Layman P'ang suffered a severe blow on the head the week before and ever since had been confusing categories like "marvelous" and "ordinary." But it is also possible that he had touched on the delicate inner secret of carrying fuel and drawing water, a secret that is the special wisdom of small children and great sages and simple fools.

It is a secret that an age, like ours, of great sophistication and great achievement, and consequently also of jaded sensibilities, has some difficulty in grasping. And it is a secret that tragic heroes have never understood. Our search after the wondrous and marvelous is everywhere *but* in the simple acts of carrying fuel and drawing water. For us the ecstatic moment is to be found where the term itself literally suggests it is to be found: in *ecstasis*, standing outside, going beyond, being beside oneself.

The ecstatic quest has really become the overpowering myth of our time, the Holy Grail of both our most sublime aspirations and most subliminal forms of abandon. That which is Real, that which makes life worth living or at least endurable, is to be found up there or down there, back there or out there, on some far perimeter of existence, beyond the dull, trivial, boring, humdrum recurrences of life.

Herbert Read's description of one of the impulses of fantasy in modern art is a typical modern restatement of the problem rather than its solution: "The inner world of the imagination becomes more and more significant, as if to compensate for the poverty and drabness of everyday life."[6] The imagination is, of course, capable of proposing endless other worlds, more paradisal or monstrous, or at least more exciting and challenging, than the current one. In this lies both the strength and weakness of fantasy. By means of a cultivated dissatisfaction with whatever forms of life are immediately available, everyday life becomes a matter of poverty and drabness, whether it is or not, and even for those who live in the palaces of other people's imaginations.

One is perpetually led to suppose that true satisfaction and true being and truth itself are somewhere else. Life is therefore, like Plato's cave, seen as so many shadows cast by the real and forgotten radiance beyond. Or, like *The Pilgrim's Progress*, life is turned into a tortuous, labyrinthine pilgrimage to some distant City of Light. Existence is always being postponed and awaited: at the end of the tunnel, over the last mountain, beyond the far horizon. All immediate circumstances are ignored or despised or turned into so many stepping-stones to the grand kingdom of elsewhere.

In a sense, it makes little difference whether this magical-mystical-mysterious moment is imaged in terms of the heroism of soaring flight (eagles and hawks) or subterranean descent (serpents and frogs). It makes little difference whether the desired goal is envisioned in terms of the eurekas of scientific discovery, space conquests, and technological wonders; or the triumphs of market coups, military supremacy, and sexual exploits; or the adventures of gambling casinos, state lotteries, and cocaine trances; or the paradises of revolutionary utopias, otherworldly mysticisms, or heavenly abodes. In structure and spirit the questings are quite similar. Hence the plausibility of a mono-mythology of the hero. Vitality, Completeness, Fulfillment, Real Life—these are not to be found among the immediate circumstances of life, but in transcending them or escaping from them or in that peculiar form of excess, *exceeding* them. The end result is also much the same. Instead of being revitalized, the world of the commonplace is rendered even more commonplace.

Beyond Oedipus, Dionysus, and Apollo

When one speaks of fantasy and ecstasy in a post-Freudian generation, the first thing that usually comes to mind is sexual ecstasy. We therefore come to it last. No doubt sex, and the relations between the sexes, and all the tensions and awkwardnesses generated by this dimension of our being are frequent themes in joking, clowning, and comedy. And there are those enterprising Freudians, beginning with Freud himself in his *Wit and the Unconscious* and especially *Totem and Taboo*, who have dreamed of crediting most of humor and most of religion and most of art, music and literature to the surplus of this account.

Not even Ferdinand the bull is safe from sexualist interpretation. According to one Freudian analyst, Ferdinand is a pre-Oedipal and narcissistic figure who is refusing to grow up and enter the Oedipal world. The soft corks on his favorite tree represent the limp phallus of boyhood. The flowers are his attachment to mother. His disinterest in preparing for the bullring is his unwillingness to rebel against, castrate, and kill the father. The sting of the bumblebee is an external attempt at awakening sexual desire and an aggressive will-to-power. But when the sting wears off, he is still not interested in murdering father-figures (the bullfighter and picadors) or raping mother-substitutes (the beautiful ladies in the stands). So he is taken home in disgrace, still infantile, sexually impotent, socially powerless, and in effect castrated.[7]

For those with smaller Freudian enthusiasms, such ready-made categories of interpretation may seem as humorous as the fact that King Oedipus himself had no apparent desire to kill his father or wed his mother, while the realization that he had done so became the basis of his torment. But even in Freudian terms, what is missed is the trans-Oedipal and post-Oedipal character of the symbolism. Ferdinand has a secret, and this secret is not narcissism, attachment to the mother, castration, or regression. it has something to do with going beyond the Freudian Oedipus and the Sophoclean Oedipus. It has to do with the nature of maturity.

When one is disposed, for whatever reasons, to approach even so simple a defense of simplicity as *The Story of Ferdinand* in the ominous terms of murder and rape—or, failing these, the choice of infantilism and regression to the womb—it is time to bring forth the Greek god Comus, from whose name the term comedy probably derives. In the first place, Comus was not one of the great gods who played a major dramatic role in Greek mythology, and that in itself is symbolically significant. He was not party to the bloody power-struggles, the court intrigue, the sexual exploits, or the titanic conflicts of these gods and goddesses. While he *was* a fertility god, he was not such in the grand manner of Dionysus or the goddess Aphrodite, let alone in the sense of representing Oedipal jealousy of the father and desire for the mother. He was not noted for or supportive of excess, whether in the realm of power, sex, or family.

Comus was the god of fertility in that relatively unexciting, intramarital, down-on-the-farm, barnyard sense. He was not a god of heady wine, fantastic sexual exploits, and inflamed passions. His province was that of the basic, around-home concerns of life: sexual companionship, begetting children, family welfare, productive fields, and healthy animals. As a god of fertility, Comus was inevitably like Dionysus in some respects, and was also represented by a phallus. But his sex was something normal and ordinary and essential to survival, not something abnormal or frenzied or orgiastic. As Joseph Meeker has commented,

> Comus was content to leave matters of great intellectual import to Apollo and gigantic passions to Dionysus while he busied himself with the maintenance of the commonplace conditions that are friendly to life. Maintaining equilibrium among living things, and restoring it once it has been lost, are Comus's special talents, and they are shared by the many comic heroes who follow the god's example.[8]

While Greek comedy has its origin in the Dionysian festival, it shows itself even in its Dionysian context, and dedicated to Dionysus, as belonging to Comus. Even in the act of giving vent to revelry and license, comedy does so, after all, comically. Comedy is concerned with relieving and moderating tensions, not supercharging them. This principle continues to be followed even today in film comedies, by making exceptionally beautiful and sexy blondes dumb, or desired by blundering males. The extreme physical displays of comedy are simultaneously a matter of joke and parody. When "country boy" in an old Japanese print comes into town to show everyone how it is really done, he comes with a penis so gigantic that it requires a procession of several wagons to carry it. That is the comic perception of excess and ecstasy.

Both Aristophanes and Kratinos "honored" Dionysus in their comedies by portraying him as a bit of a fool, with a penchant for getting into uncomfortable and humiliating situations—as sex, and passion generally, seem to have a tendency to do. The ribald humor and phallic exhibition in the performances of their plays had the same import. Sex can be rather awkward and complicating. Since the phallus was so conspicuously depicted as a Dionysian symbol and generously displayed at his festival, humor was invited and needed. All the Athenian colonies, furthermore, were required to send phalli in special procession to his festival. The rationale was that the local phallic symbol would be recharged at the temple of Dionysus with sexual potency, bringing a new abundance back to the village. If one can imagine the scene of groups of men, coming from all directions, each group parading a large phallus to Athens, one can readily see how comedy might have developed from the "revel songs" (komodia) and ribald witticisms of those carrying the phallus in grand procession or catcalling from the sidelines.

When one turns from Dionysus to Apollo and his dedication to law and order, rationality and principle, one finds the same result, only in reverse. The extremes of Dionysian frenzy are matched by the extreme value placed upon order and orderliness in society. This, in Greece, was the province of Apollo with his dedication to law, organization, rationality, and principle. While comedy is commonly associated with disorder, this is only half the story, for comedy is also a champion of order vis-à-vis the excesses of Dionysian enthusiasm. The picture that emerges from ancient comedy is one of moderating the excesses to which both Apollo and Dionysus are susceptible, thus mediating the tragic clashes between reason and passion, order and abandon, sublime heights and subliminal depths. The extremes of such polarities are parodied as opposite forms of folly. And they are brought under the rule of the small kingdom of Comus, where the most lofty and most profound values are the ordinary ones. It is the kingdom of cork trees and water buckets and hungry kids, of sand castles and triangular shoes and plain beans, of bees and minnows and the lice of elephants. It is the kingdom of nothing special.

David Miller has suggested that, as in ancient Greece, "there are two paths in our time, alternative mythologies for a period of crisis: *up and out* (the rational, heroic, masculine way) and *down and in* (the mad, mystical, feminine way)."[9] And as a report on the fantasies and ecstasies of the day, this is certainly correct. It can hardly be disputed that the *extra*ordinary, in whatever form, is the great preoccupation of our time. We have been spirited away by high-flying birds and low-flying pornography, ideological fervor and occult powers, nationalistic loyalties and charismatic intoxication. We have been accosted by drug peddlers, sorcerers' apprentices, demons needing an exorcist, witchcraft revivals, satanic cults, flying ghosts and flying saucers, astrologers, chariots from the gods, and other visitants from outer space. We have been spurred on by dreams of greatness and number-oneness, new frontiers, new worlds to conquer, and all the sundry ladders of success, while visions of superheroes, superstars, supersalespeople, and supersex have danced before us.

But the truly heroic person in our midst is no longer the hero. We have been bombarded by the most incredible variety of heroes and counterheroes imaginable. We have been stampeded back and forth between the "up and out" and the "down and in," as if herded into the to-and-fro of an accelerated Hegelian dialectic. The real hero of our time is the common person, the cipher in the faceless mass, who may be buffeted and bewildered and often caught in the struggle between eagles and serpents, but who somehow through it all manages to remain relatively sane, simple, ordinary, and human. Our hero is the simple non-hero, like Ferdinand the bull, who is content to sit under his cork tree and sniff flowers. And though he may be stimulated to the most heroic displays and frenzied abandon by the sting of some bumblebee, he will return to the simple wonder of sniffing daisies under his marvelous tree.

The truth is that the Apollonian passion for order and perfection, as well as the boisterous abandon of Dionysus, are the forms of our *ecstasis*, not just the wild, mad, irrational surfacings of subterranean excess. The elaboration of ritual and the intricacies of ceremonial pomp, the compulsion of the meticulous person, the relentless drive for possession, the ambition of comprehending or conquering the world, the restless quest for progress and improvement, the perennial fabrication of new utopias—all this is also *ecstasis*, and the excess of constantly exceeding and succeeding. It is the *ecstasis* and excess of the "up and out."

This is not to dismiss either form of ecstasy. We need our visions, our hopes, our grand imaginings, our impossible dreams, our revelries, and our moments of escape. These are a part of both the greatness and the foolishness of our existence. But their function is not simply to carry us outside ourselves, and in that act to devalue or empty the present moment and our common life of its intrinsic power and mystery. It is to revitalize and revalue the here and now. We stand outside in order to stand more profoundly and deeply within. Even heroes must spend most of their time, like the rest of us, in that valley that lies between mountain heights and ocean depths. The essential human problem is to come to terms with that valley, its own marvels and miracles, not just to invent more and more ingenious methods of escape.

Above may be the Apollonian heights, and below the Dionysian deeps. And there we wander now and then in our fantasies, our festivities, and our follies. But our real home, and the true center of our being, is not to be found in either place. It is here, now, everywhere before us at all times.

> ...We shall not cease from exploration
> And the end of all our exploring
> Will be to arrive where we started
> And know the place for the first time....
> Quick now, here, now, always—
> A condition of complete simplicity.[10]
>
> —T. S. Eliot, "Little Gidding"

The Art of the Commonplace

This counterpoint has not been without its instances on the contemporary scene. It is apparent in the recurrent themes of returning to nature and the natural, to the soil, to simpler forms of life, and to the elemental experiences of common people that have manifested themselves in the renaissance of folk music, handcrafting, and classes in organic gardening. It is apparent in those secular gospels that have insisted on reaffirming the integrity of the "profane." It is apparent in an art that is capable of turning even Campbell soup cans into objects of artistic representation (Andy Warhol), or in a music that discovers aesthetic value in common noises and listenings to silence (John Cage), or in a photography that captures the beauty of doorknobs and cracked walls, driftwood and dandelions, thistles and wrinkled faces (Morton White).

The Spanish painter Joan Miró used to go to the beach to pick up odd bits of things washed up overnight by the tide, take these treasures to his studio, search out their special personality and wonderment, and then rearrange them into some new creation. Similarly, German artist Kurt Schwitters took scraps of this and that—paper, cloth, buttons, tickets, old nails—things discarded, rejected, of no value, rubbish to be turned into a "cathedral." Such an artistic sensitivity—which from the standpoint of "high" art is of course unworthy of the name—is moving in an opposite direction from art that attempts to express the sublime. It is closer to the ridiculous, the absurd, the comic. Commonplace items are now elevated—like Marcel Duchamp's notorious bottle rack. They are placed on a pedestal and exhibited, surprising and perhaps shocking us, challenging our aesthetic categories, and being granted an opportunity to "speak."

This is not an art that attempts to express some ideal attribute or heroic virtue or momentous circumstance in its most glorious form. It does not freeze in a posture of finished perfection instances of youthful beauty, romantic love, patriotic zeal, maternal bliss, or pious devotion. This would be too much like family portraiture, with everyone in the stiffness of Sunday best, properly arranged and unmoving, waiting with twitching smiles for the invisible magic word "Cheese." Such an art inevitably—like such a literature or religiosity—calls forth the comic impulse to tell the rest of the story. It mentions the little matter of twitching and cheese, displays the rest of the person and the situation, and comes to the defense of lesser forms.

The art of the commonplace is likewise the opposite of that art which, also in flight from the real world and perhaps with some disdain or despair over it, takes delight in abstract forms. The early abstractionist Kasimir Malevich referred to his pioneering black square on white as the result of his "desperate struggle to liberate art from the ballast of the world of objects." The words are remarkably similar to Henri Bergson's description of the Platonic experience of the body as an "irksome ballast which holds down to earth a soul eager to rise aloft." Such an art, and such a spirituality, has difficulty with toy chests and kitchen scenes, street corners and slum-dwellings, barnyards and vegetable gardens—let alone weeds and mice and insects. Alcibiades said of Socrates in the *Symposium*, "Listen to him talk! Why, his language is like the rough skins of the satyrs—nothing but talk of packasses and smiths and cobblers and curriers, and he is always repeating the same things."

The comic protagonist is a defender of all those simple basics of life and survival that tend to be spurned by soaring spirits and heroic visions and wild excursions of fancy. This simplicity is not, however, a rationalization of poverty. Comedy is not, per se, another opiate of the people, a clever strategy for maintaining the status quo by praising dog meat instead of mutton. What is offered is not a religion of the poor, a baked-beans beatitude for Chaplinesque tramps. It represents rather the capacity to enjoy the *whole* of life, including plain beans and rice. Regardless of the fortunes of one's existence, it is the capacity to take pleasure in simple things, common things. And this is a freedom that no amount of increase in one's general welfare can bring.

This is a perspective on life that comes to some after a serious illness or personal tragedy, as in the case of psychologist Abraham Maslow whose busy professional career was abruptly halted by a near-fatal heart attack. Later he commented,

> One very important aspect of the post-mortem life is that everything gets precious, gets piercingly important. You get stabbed by things, by flowers and by babies and by beautiful things—just the very act of walking and breathing and eating and having friends and chatting. Everything seems to look more beautiful rather than less, and one gets the much-intensified sense of miracles.[11]

Ironically it is Maslow who was noted for his study of people who had what he termed "peak experiences"—extraordinary experiences that become "the ultimate goals of living and the ultimate validations and justifications for it."[12] Such people he had concluded were the most mature, self-actualized and developed people compared with "non-peakers" who seemed caught in a rather ordinary, humdrum, unimaginative existence.

Whether a heart attack may be said to be a peak experience, at least it is not one that dulls all other experiences by comparison, devaluing the simple, common events of everyday life. A heart attack can be only one thing: a jolt, a bit of internal shock therapy, awakening one to what has always been there, immediately available but unnoticed, or only half-noticed, the sort of experiences that everyone, everywhere, has before them at all times.

> Tell me, my brethren, what the child can do, which even the lion could not do? Why has the preying lion still to become a child? Innocence is the child, and forgetfulness, a new beginning, a game, a self-rolling wheel, a first movement, a holy Yea.
>
> —Nietzsche, *Thus Spake Zarathustra*[13]

Epilogue

Education as Fun and the Fall into Serious Work—The Player

What, then, is the right way of living? Life must be lived as play: playing certain games, making sacrifices, singing and dancing. Every man and woman should live life accordingly, playing the noblest games.

—Plato, *Laws* vii, 803

The irony of all play is that it can be turned into work. The irony of all work is that, while it may be work for some—even drudgery—it may be play for others. Work and play are interchangeable, and are often modes of the same activity. The distinction between work and play, therefore, is largely subjective rather than objective. That is, it is psychological. The distinction has to do with attitudes, feelings, perceptions, mental states, mood swings, rather than with what one actually is doing. This recognition brings the subject of work and play within the immediate purview of psychology in general, and of reversal theory in particular, with its distinctions between *telic* and *paratelic* states.[1] The *telic* mode is goal-oriented, serious-minded, structured, and willing to suspend present enjoyment for hoped-for rewards. The *paratelic* mode is playful, light-hearted, spontaneous, centered in the immediate moment, and focused on the process rather than the anticipated result. Tragedy, therefore, belongs to the *telic* and carries it to the extreme, while comedy is *paratelic*.

These modes do not depend upon the objective nature of what is actually being done but on the subjective state of the worker/player. What is objectively classified as play activity (e.g., golf) may well be work for some people, including even the professional who has mastered the game but for whom it is now a job. On the other hand, what many would consider to be work (e.g., writing an essay) may largely be play for those who pursue it as "love's labor"—even if it proves to be "love's labor lost." The fact that a particular sport is labeled a game does not necessarily make it a play activity for all, or even for any one particular person all the time, despite the fact that the origin and primary stimulus of games is playfulness. For some, the game may even be fair agony. Conversely, the fact that an activity is labeled work does not mean that it cannot be played or should not be played. For some, the work may even be a positive delight.

We therefore see, as a common feature of our experience, a frequent reversal of both mood and value in relation to both kinds of activities, conventionally labeled work and play. We sometimes approach work as work, and play as play; and we sometimes approach work as play and play as work. But since all human activities may be turned into either work or play, one may go one step further and suggest that the ideal state to be realized is that of play—whether one is involved in an activity normally labeled work or play. If "all work and no play makes Jack a dull boy," what would all play and no work do for him?[2]

Cultural Games

A telling example and test case for this thesis is *education*. Like most fields of human endeavor, education is commonly perceived as being work, both by professionals for whom it is their "life's work" and by amateurs (students) who usually view it as temporary labor from which they hope to be graduated.

For most students, the word "study" is synonymous with work. The studious student conjures up images of furrowed brow, reclusive habits, midnight oil, and nearsightedness. Study has long since lost its original Latin meaning of "zeal." *Studium* thus becomes the polar opposite of *stadium*, where soccer and rugby are played. Play is what one does outside the classroom and library and laboratory; in recreation periods, on weekends, in dorms and student unions, at parties and pubs, on park benches and dance floors. Play in its multitudinous forms, from unstructured romps to highly structured chess matches, is seen as a release, a temporary reprieve from the *business* at hand which is variously termed class*work* and lab*work* and home*work*. It is play, not study, that one expects to do zealously.

Education, therefore, is placed from the start in the category of work. Linguistic usage alone biases attitudes and expectations in that direction. Education is perceived as a matter of requirements, assignments, testings, certifications, ordeals, toil. When one adds the usual motivations for entering the halls of higher education—namely, to train for a professional career, and preferably one that is high-paying—education becomes serious work indeed. When one further adds a tightening job market, economic uncertainties, tuition costs, parental pressures, and attendant student anxieties, the fundamental character of education in its noblest sense is threatened. Even if one shifts the motivation for learning to the ideological level of training for some worthy cause, education is subverted.

The origins of education, whether in the liberal arts, the fine arts or the sciences, is not in work but in play; not in pedantry or scholasticism but in zest for learning; not in training for a craft or employment or ideological warfare but in love of wisdom. Education is, in the first place, a leisure-time activity. It is, in its origins, *paratelic*. The student is exempted from the work force and freed from the immediate necessities of providing food, shelter and clothing in order to enter the *studium* of learning. Education is a luxury enjoyed by those who, for the time being, and within socially sanctioned protective frames, do not have to work and can enter for a season the adventures of the mind in the play of learning and the interplay of minds and voices.

More importantly, education is born out of play, the spirit of which it is the task of education to inculcate and preserve. The search after knowledge and wisdom is the result of the capacities of the human mind to go beyond sheer biological rhythms and physiological necessities, even beyond real or supposed psychological and sociological necessities, to play with existence: one's individual existence, collective existence present and past, projected existence in some imagined future, and existence as a whole. One can become a philosopher and play with the very concept of existence. Most, if not all, culture is the result of this capacity for play, not necessity for work or preparation for battle. Culture, not in the fine arts sense of high culture, but in its broadest anthropological sense, is a superaddition to the basic physical requirements of survival and preservation of the species. Education, in turn, is the examination, critique and re-creation of this human culture.

To be sure, animals evidence some capacity for play—especially the higher the intelligence—as among whales, dolphins, monkeys and apes;

but, comparatively, the play is limited and of limited creative consequence. Humans, however, have managed to play with every aspect of their existence and of the universe. This human playing with all areas of life opens up an infinity of possibilities of behaving, perceiving, and interacting. As Johan Huizinga argued so masterfully in *Homo Ludens*, culture in all its incredible variety of forms is the result of the capacity for playing with existence. Practically all human activities that come to be considered as work have dimensions that are superfluous to our basic physical requirements, if they are not entirely superfluous. The intricacies and the multiplicities of "the games people play" are the result of the enormous creative potential opened up by this seemingly limitless human capacity for play. Give a dog a box and it will chew on it, providing good exercise for teeth and gums and immediate release of energy, tension, or aggression. Give a child a box and it will be transformed into a doll-house, a castle, a toy chest, a zoo for stuffed animals, an automobile, an airplane, or a boat.

Education, as both the transmission and invention of culture, at its best is education in the inexhaustible variety of play-forms, past and present, and in the playfulness that gave them birth. But—and here's the fly in the soup—insofar as the sense of play is lost, education becomes work or—in the tragic mode—war. It becomes serious business, *telic* in its orientation, while the very imagination and fascination and delight which made these forms possible is forgotten. Education ceases to be what it literally is: re-creation and recreation. Creativity, whether as creative re-enactment or creative reconstruction, is absent; and in its place is found imitation, boredom, or conflict. Eating of the tree of knowledge turns into a laborious toiling by the sweat of one's brow, beset by thorns and thistles, or surrounded by enemies.

Ever since Max Weber's publication of *The Protestant Ethic and the Spirit of Capitalism* (German edition, 1905), it has been common to associate a "work-ethic" with Protestantism, especially Calvinistic Protestantism. While Weber was making specific historical connections, the association of work with meaningful activity and of play with nonproductive and perhaps wasteful activity has a much longer history. Within the Judaeo-Christian tradition such associations go back to "the beginning," wherein the creation of all things is assigned the metaphor of work rather than play: God *worked* for six days, then rested on the seventh from all these labors. In Hindu mythology, by contrast, the god

Vishnu is pictured as creating the universe in the exuberance and prodigality of divine play (*lila*).

The consequences of opting for a mythology of work rather than play are far-reaching. Not only is religion "serious business" but so are all fundamental questions of "the good, the true, and the beautiful." The spirit of play and laughter is moved to the periphery of life, with its main justification being that, after a brief respite, one will be able to work more diligently and fight more fanatically. Otherwise one should rightfully feel uneasy and perhaps guilty about it. To the center of life belongs the spirit of gravity, sobriety, studiousness, quarrelsomeness. It is not surprising to find, in the vast literature of the West, that not only theologians and moralists but academicians and educators have had a great many serious and laborious things to say about the responsibilities of seriousness and hard work, but very little about the responsibilities of laughter, playfulness, and enjoyment. Yet if life becomes simply serious business, if one loses a sense of humor and play, one joins the ranks, not of sages and saints, but of militants and Scrooges.

Those ancient Greek philosophers are much to be preferred who characterized human beings as laughing animals (*zoion gelastikon*) and saw in playfulness (*homo ludens*) and a sense of humor (*homo risens*) distinctive badges of humanity. It was Lucian of Samosata who in *Sale of Creeds* went on to describe the special genius of the peripatetic philosopher as that of being able to distinguish a man from an ass, the one capable of laughter and playfulness (*risens* and *ludens*) and the other capable only of braying. It is, after all, seriousness that we share with the animals. It is in laughter that we laugh alone, and only to a preliminary extent with chimpanzees. By and large, animals take everything "straight." They neither invent nor comprehend double meanings, exaggerations or understatements, paradoxes or ironies. The most highly trained or domesticated animals do not get the point of the simplest pun or witticism, or devise any of their own. They do not even, like the proverbial Englishman, get the point and laugh a day later.

Similarly, we may share in a preliminary way in the playfulness of young animals. Tiger cubs can be quite playful, but as the tiger matures the playfulness diminishes and the struggle of life becomes quite serious business. While many people's lives follow the same pattern, humans have a capacity for play that can be just as alive at age eighty as age eight. It may be more on the side of mind than body, but it is thereby able to become even more creative and enriching. The comedian George Burns in his nineties may not have been able to move about as spryly as he did in his thirties with Gracie Allen, but the twinkle in the eye, the quick wit, the clever imagination and gay repartee were as lively as ever, along with the same cloud of cigar smoke. Burns was even, in his mid-eighties, capable of playing God (in the film, *Oh, God*). One thinks also of Alfred North Whitehead who, when he retired from an illustrious career in the field of mathematics, took up a position in philosophy and had an equally illustrious career to the age of eighty-six.

Finite and Infinite Games

In a remarkable book, *Finite and Infinite Games*, James Carse suggests that all human activity, by virtue of being human, is involved in one or another game.[3] Human culture is itself an intricate kaleidoscope of games being played, consciously or unconsciously. Carse distinguishes, however, between two kinds of games, finite and infinite. These are not two different types of games, such as chess and croquet, but two ways of playing what may very well be the same game. Finite gaming has a specific and definable goal, and one plays the game in order to achieve it (the *telic* mode). Infinite gaming is a playing for the sake of playing (the *paratelic* mode). Though there may be temporary goals, these are neither the original nor the immediate reasons for playing. One plays the game because one enjoys doing so—as in dancing, where the objective is not to get to the other side of the dance floor, or to win a dance contest, but to dance. The psychological result (or cause) of these different modes of playing is that finite play typically becomes very serious, whereas infinite play is primarily playful and lighthearted.

One may see the spirit of finite gaming "at work" in the average university classroom. Despite all our talk about the privileges and advantages of higher education, the opportunities to explore new frontiers of knowledge, to broaden horizons, to discover hidden treasures, to soar on the wings of imagination, to dive into the depths of oceanic profundities, or to eat at the banquet table of wisdom—to cite the kind of embellished prose that graces many an admissions' catalogue—despite all such rhetoric, the honest truth is that much of the time we insist on turning this scintillating play of ideas into work. Collegiate review committees may come forth at regular intervals to shuffle and reshuffle requirements and programs, revise catalogue statements, purchase the latest equipment, plan new buildings and enlarge libraries and their holdings. Yet the central issue remains: How does one preserve or rekindle the play element in learning? When the spirit of play (in Carse's terms, infinite play) is gone, regardless of the number of ingenious and expensive improvements, enthusiasm is exchanged for tedium, marvel wanes into boredom, the excitement of new discovery becomes the ho-hum of yawning acquaintance, thoughtful reflection is reduced to note taking, imagination is limited to imagining what the next examination will be like, and the sense of wonder shrivels to wondering whether one will pass a course of study or not. In short, the *paratelic* becomes *telic*.

Even a small child knows that education is fundamentally play. It is learning for the sake of learning. If it is not this, if it is not intrinsically valuable, then it is not education but training. Children are also potty-trained; but this is not education. Training is essentially work—in Carse's terms, a finite game. The work of training is *extrinsically* motivated. It requires rewards and punishments in order to succeed. And the reason it does is because the trainee is not engaged in the activity for the primary reason of just doing it. The animal trainer trains ponies and lions and tigers to learn and repeat the precise motions devised for them by rewarding them with food when they obey, and by striking them with a whip when they do not obey. These are not activities which they have a burning desire to engage in for their own sake.

In the academic world, such incentives are known as the examination and grading system leading to the diploma and the job market. Or one is enlisted in some ideological cause which legitimates and gives relevance to education. Such necessary evils should not obscure the fact that education is its own reward. It is entered into for its own sake. Learning itself is enjoyment and enrichment. While training is a means to an end, education is an end in itself. We study the stars because there are stars; we study Shakespeare because there is a Shakespeare, and because we have the *studium*, the zeal, to do so. In *Homo Ludens*, Huizinga points to this difference when he notes that:

> According to one theory play constitutes a training of the young creature for the serious work that life will demand later on. According to another it serves as an exercise in restraint, or in the desire to dominate or compete. All these hypotheses have one thing in common: they all start from the assumption that play must serve something which is *not* play. Yet Nature, so our reasoning mind tells us, could just

as easily have given her children all those useful functions in the form of purely mechanical exercises and reactions. But no, she gave us play, with its tension, its mirth, and its fun.[4]

Though students matriculate ostensibly for an education, what is often settled for is a kind of animal training. Even the small child is able to go beyond animal training because, for the child, learning is play and learning is fun. Learning new words is fun; learning the names of things is fun; learning to read is fun; learning to make things is fun; learning in fantasy and wonder is fun. Like the "babbling instinct" of the infant which leads to an endless playing with sounds—and perhaps as an extension of that early experimentation—play opens out to unlimited possibilities. Carse makes the interesting observation that "to be prepared against surprise is to be *trained.* To be prepared for surprise is to be *educated.* Education discovers an increasing richness in the past, because it sees what is unfinished there. Training regards the past as finished and the future as to be finished. Education leads toward a continuing self-discovery."[5]

To be sure, there is an element of training involved in learning. To learn to play a Beethoven sonata one must develop various technical skills. But if the spirit of play is not the basic motivation, if the sonata is not intrinsically worth doing, then one will never succeed in *playing* a single sonata. This also does not mean that learning has no difficulties or hurdles. Some of the most rewarding accomplishments are those which are struggled at, puzzled over, sweated out. A part of the play is the risk, the intellectual challenge, the sense of adventure, the feeling of achievement.

An example from the world of sports is instructive. It is true that participants in a game may feel it necessary to justify their particular sport and all the time, energy and money expended upon it, by arguing that certain external goals are in fact being achieved: teamwork, physical fitness, character development, sportsmanship, group pride, school spirit, even good citizenship. A variety of physiological, psychological, social, even ethical reasons may be offered to legitimate the sport and argue for its "relevance" to life. Yet these are rationalizations for what requires no special reasons or purposes to function, or to come into being in the first place. The purpose of a game is to play the game, and the motivation is that one likes to play that sort of game. One may play football, for instance, for the money and acclaim or the

Notre Dame tradition, but if that is the point of playing, the heart of the action is lost.

Extrinsic and Intrinsic Value

In a similar way, one may imagine a number of worthy goals for the learning enterprise, and they have been imagined: improvement of character, development of critical faculties, achievement of skills, service to the state, overcoming injustice, contributing to the revolution, bringing honor to one's family or nation or race, becoming more marketable, having a six-figure income. But when education is inundated with such extraneous, yet overwhelming motivations and their resulting perceptions of learning, education is either drowned or turned into so many crash courses in the techniques of intellectual swimming. The great need is to reaffirm what William Dean has called "a pedagogy of purposelessness." Such a pedagogy rejects an instrumental and utilitarian understanding of the values of learning, insisting instead on intrinsic values. "Education may be valuable in the way that football and movies are valuable...not in the way that calisthenics and brushing one's teeth are valuable." Such education, like a concert, "would be appreciated, as concerts ordinarily are, primarily for its present hearing."[6]

Such a view does not imply that education, to be play, must be converted into a form of entertainment. The temptation here is great, given the entertainment orientation of contemporary culture. "Educate me" often gets translated as either "bore me" or "entertain me." The solution to the routine and monotony of what is often perceived as training is thought—both by teachers and students—to be one of amusement and divertissement: peppier, spicier, and more popular approaches to learning, of the same order as marketable television programming. While such may have some value in priming the pump of imagination and enthusiasm, this alone is offering an external solution to what is essentially an internal problem. Boredom is primarily a subjective matter, even though it is usually rationalized by crediting it to exterior sources that are said to be "boring" or "drudgery": books, lectures, subjects, courses, assignments, professors. Education is not a matter of trying to amuse those whose principal contribution to the learning situation is that of bringing dullness and apathy with them, like hollow cups waiting to be filled by some bubbling elixir. The goal is not to achieve a momentary fever pitch of excitement, but to cultivate inquisitiveness and fascination. Education is not a kind of show business juggling, but a juggling with ideas and possibilities.

Curiosity may kill cats, but the absence of curiosity kills education. When the only questions the instructor happens to receive are "How much of this book do we have to read?" or "Will this be on the final exam?" or "What is the relevance of this to the cause?" one senses that education is dead, and that the dream of the well-educated person has faded in the light of common day. Even if graduation is achieved, and with distinction, or the intellectual battle is won, or the cause is victorious, the soul of education has been lost. Education is based on the thirst for knowledge, the joy of learning, the play of ideas and interplay of competing convictions, the sense of marvel and wonder, the love of wisdom, the gift of imagination, the liberation of the spirit. To cite Carse again:

> To be playful is not to be trivial or frivolous, or to act as though nothing of consequence will happen. On the contrary, when we are playful with each other we relate as free persons, and the relationship is open to surprise; *everything* that happens is of consequence, for seriousness is a dread of the unpredictable outcome of open possibility. To be serious is to press for a specified conclusion. To be playful is to allow for unlimited possibility.[7]

It is true, of course, that those who play at what they do have less of a problem with tension, anxiety, depression, tedium, apathy, or a sense of meaninglessness than mere trainees, and that they are happier, more imaginative, creative, productive, and fulfilled. It is also true that students who have entered the spirit of education are more enriched, well-rounded, sensitive, prepared for life, and likely to continue to play the game beyond graduation. But let us say such things in a whisper and as an aside. Though these grand results are the bait and delight of university Admissions, Development, and Placement offices, they smell strongly of training exercises and utilitarian sweat. To emphasize such goals as the purpose of education, worthy as they are, and therefore presumably worthy of all the time and money invested in them, is still to lose sight of the intrinsic values to be found in the learning process itself, and in the sheer enjoyment in whatever is being learned. Education at its highest and best is for its own sake. It is the creation, appreciation, and celebration of knowledge. In short, education is fun, and the

delight in the subject is what must, more than anything else, be commu-
nicated. Education is among the noblest of games.

> The time has come, the walrus said,
> To talk of many things,
> Of shoes and ships and sealing wax,
> And cabbages and kings;
> And why the sea is boiling hot,
> And whether pigs have wings.

Notes

Introduction: Comic Hero With a Thousand Faces

1. Michael J. Apter, *The Experience of Motivation: The Theory of Psychological Reversals* (New York: Academic Press, 1982), and *Reversal Theory: Motivation, Emotion and Personality* (London: Routledge, 1989).
2. Peter Berger, *The Precarious Vision* (New York: Doubleday and Co., 1961), pp. 67ff. A similar complaint was made by William Cameron, *Informal Sociology* (New York: Random House, 1963), pp. 79–94.
3. Joseph Campbell, *The Hero With a Thousand Faces* (New York: Pantheon, 1949).
4. For an excellent critique of Campbell's methodology, see Robert Segal, "The Romantic Appeal of Joseph Campbell," *The Christian Century* (April 4, 1990); also *Joseph Campbell, An Introduction* (New York: Garland Press, 1987).
5. I have also explored these comic figures and themes in an oriental context in Conrad Hyers, *The Laughing Buddha: Zen and the Comic Spirit* (Wolfeboro, NH: Longwood Academic, 1989).
6. Nathan Scott, Jr., *The Broken Center: Studies in the Theological Horizon of Modern Literature* (New Haven: Yale University Press, 1966), p. 90.
7. Robert W. Corrigan, ed., *Comedy: Meaning and Form* (San Francisco: Chandler Publishing Company, 1965), p. 3.
8. Paul H. Grawe, *Comedy in Space, Time, and the Imagination* (Chicago: Nelson-Hall, 1983), p. 59.
9. *Ibid.*, p. 74.
10. *Ibid.*, p. 76.
11. Wittgenstein's position has been applied specifically to art and literature by Morris Weitz: "The Role of Theory in Aesthetics," *Journal of Aesthetics and Art Criticism* (September, 1956), pp. 27–35.

Chapter 1. Tragic Weights and Comic Balances

1. W. C. Fields, *W. C. Fields by Himself: His Intended Autobiography*, Ronald J. Fields, ed. (Englewood Cliffs, NJ: Prentice-Hall, 1973), p. 235.
2. John D. Barbour, *Tragedy as a Critique of Virtue* (Chico, CA: Scholars Press, 1984), p. 1.
3. This wording is based on an oral tradition stemming from Twain's lecture tours. The written version, in slightly different wording, is to be found in Mark Twain, *Letters from the Earth*, ed. Bernard DeVoto (New York: Harper and Row, 1962), pp. 227–28.
4. Ernest Hemingway, *Old Man and the Sea* (New York: Scribners, 1952).
5. Thomas Kuhn, *The Structure of Scientific Revolutions*, 2nd ed. enl. (Chicago: University of Chicago Press, 1970).

6. Robert Heilman, *Tragedy and Melodrama* (Seattle: University of Washington Press, 1968), p. 291.
7. Bertrand Russell, "A Free Man's Worship," in *Why I Am Not a Christian, and Other Essays on Related Subjects* (New York: Simon and Schuster, 1957), p. 116. Copyright © 1957 by Allen and Unwin. Reprinted by permission of Simon and Schuster, Inc.
8. W. T. Stace, "Man Against Darkness," *The Atlantic Monthly* (September, 1948).
9. Graham Greene, *A Sort of Life* (London: The Bodley Head, 1971), p. 72.
10. Roger Sharrock, *Saints, Sinners, and Comedians: The Novels of Graham Greene* (Notre Dame, IN: University of Notre Dame Press, 1984), p. 179.
11. James Thurber, Interview in *The New Republic* (May, 1958).
12. E. T. Eberhardt, *In the Presence of Humor* (Salem, OR: Pilgrim House, 1984), p. 2.
13. Arnold Van Gennep, *Mythes et legendes d'Australia* (Paris, 1906), pp. 84–85.

Chapter 2. The Agony and the Golden Mean

1. Charles Chaplin, *My Autobiography* (New York: Simon and Schuster, 1964), p. 364.
2. Maurice Charney, "Comic Premises of *Twelfth Night,*" *Comedy: New Perspectives,* Maurice Charney, ed. (New York: New York Literary Forum, 1978), p. 152.
3. Northrop Frye, *The Anatomy of Criticism: Four Essays* (Princeton: Princeton University Press, 1957), p. 166.
4. Walter Kerr, *Tragedy and Comedy* (New York: Simon and Schuster, 1967), p. 17.
5. Henry A. Myers, *Tragedy: A View of Life* (Ithaca, NY: Cornell University Press, 1956), p. 45.
6. Chaplin, *Autobiography*, p. 399.
7. W. H. Auden, "Notes on the Comic," *Comedy,* Robert Corrigan, ed., p. 62.
8. Daniel Gerould, "Tyranny and Comedy," *Comedy,* Maurice Charney, ed., p. 3.
9. Peter L. Berger, *The Sacred Canopy* (New York: Doubleday and Co., 1961), p.138.

Chapter 3. Tragic Castles and Comic Cottages

1. Umberto Eco, *The Name of the Rose,* trans. William Weaver (New York: Harcourt Brace Jovanovich, Inc., 1984), p. 152.
2. The first English version of this tale appeared in Antwerp in 1492. See Enid Welsford, *The Fool: His Social and Literary History* (Gloucester, MA: Peter Smith, 1966), pp. 35–37, n. 331. See also Ewald Flügel, ed., *Neuenglisches Lesebuch* (Halle, 1895), p. 285.
3. Kerr, *Tragedy and Comedy*, p. 125.
4. *The Dramatic Character of Sir John Falstaff,* cited in Israel Golancz, commentary on *Henry IV* (New York: The University Society, 1901), p. 16.
5. Susanne K. Langer, *Feeling and Form: A Theory of Art* (New York: Scribners, 1953), p. 342.
6. Anne and Henry Paolucci, eds., *Hegel: On Tragedy* (New York: Harper & Row, 1962), pp. 52–3.
7. Luigi Pirandello, "The Art of Humor," *Massachusetts Review* (March 1952), p. 518.
8. *Ibid.*, p. 519.

9. Welsford, *The Fool,* pp. 324-26.
10. Alan W. Watts, *The Way of Zen* (New York: Random House, 1957), p. 147.

Chapter 4. A Voice Laughing in the Wilderness

1. Ken Kesey, *One Flew Over the Cuckoo's Nest* (New York: Viking Press, 1962), p. 65.
2. Friedrich Nietzsche, *Thus Spake Zarathustra,* trans. Thomas Common (New York: Random House, Modern Library, n. d.), pp. 40-41.
3. C. S. Lewis, *The Screwtape Letters,* rev. ed. (New York: Macmillan, 1982), p. ix.
4. Konrad Lorenz, *On Aggression,* trans. Marjorie K. Wilson (New York: Charles Scribner's Sons, 1922), p. 138.
5. William Austin Smith, "The Use of the Comic Spirit in Religion," *Atlantic Monthly,* vol. CVIII (August 1911), p. 188.
6. Georg Friedrich Meier, *Thoughts on Jesting* (1794), ed. Joseph Jones (Austin: University of Texas Press, 1947, pp. 55-56.
7. George Santayana, *Soliloquies in England and Later Soliloquies* (New York: Charles Scribner's Sons, 1922, p. 138.
8. Pat F. Garrett, *An Authentic Life of Billy the Kid* (Santa Fe: NM Printing and Publishing Co., 1882), p. 5.
9. Will Rogers, *A Will Rogers Treasury,* compiled and edited by Bryan B. Sterling and Frances N. Sterling (New York: Bonanza Books, 1986), p. 190.
10. Anthony M. Ludovici, *The Secret of Laughter* (London: Constable & Co., 1932).
11. Cited in Conrad Hyers, ed., *Holy Laughter* (New York: Seabury Press, 1969), p. 255.
12. Sören Kierkegaard, *Concluding Unscientific Postscript,* trans. D. F. Swenson and W. Lowrie (Princeton: Princeton University Press, 1941), p. 413.
13. Bartholomaeus Anglicus, *De Proprietatibus Rerum* 5.41.61.
14. Arthur Koestler, *The Act of Creation* (New York: Dell Publishing Co., 1964), pp. 58-59.
15. *Ibid.,* p. 63.
16. Al Capp, "The Comedy of Charlie Chaplin," *Atlantic Monthly* (February 1950), pp. 25-29.
17. Koestler, *Creation,* p. 52.
18. Gordon W. Allport, *The Individual and His Religion* (New York: Macmillan, 1950), p. 93.
19. Reinhold Niebuhr, *Discerning the Signs of the Times* (London: SCM Press 1946), pp. 99-100.
20. "Sense of Regain," p. 22.
21. Campbell, *Hero,* p. 28.
22. Robert Blake, *101 Elephant Jokes* (New York: Scholastic Book Services, 1964), pp. 8-9. Used by permission.
23. Christopher Fry, "Comedy," in Corrigan, ed., *Comedy,* p. 16.
24. Daniel Keller, *Humor as Therapy* (Wauwatosa, WI: Med-Psych Publications, 1984). See also Cal Samra, *The Joyful Christ: The Healing Power of Humor* (San Francisco: Harper and Row, 1986); Raymond A. Moody, *Laugh after Laugh: The Healing Power of Humor* (New York: Lippincott, 1978).
25. Koestler, *Creation,* p. 46.
26. Jean Strange, "Famous Last Words," *Time* (August 1, 1983), p. 69.

27. James Thurber, *Lanterns and Lances* (New York: Harper & Bros., 1955), p. 61.
28. A. C. Bradley, *Oxford Lectures on Poetry* (Bloomington, IN: University of Indiana Press, 1961), pp. 262, 269.
29. G. F. Hegel, *Philosophy of Fine Art*, trans. F. B. B. Osmaston (London, 1920), vol. IV, p. 348.
30. Sypher, ed., *Comedy*, p. 214.
31. Northrup Frye, *The Anatomy of Criticism*, p. 166.
32. Joseph Campbell, *The Masks of God: Primitive Mythology* (New York: Viking Press, 1959), pp. 39–40.
33. Johan Huizinga, *Homo Ludens: A Study of the Play Element in Culture* (Boston: Beacon Press, 1955), p. 119.

Chapter 5. Will the Real Adam and Eve Please Stand Up?

1. George Steiner, *The Death of Tragedy* (New York: Alfred A. Knopf, 1963), p. 247.
2. Henri Bergson, "Laughter," in *Comedy*, Wylie Sypher, ed. (Baltimore: Johns Hopkins University Press, 1980), p. 94.
3. Scott, *Broken Center*, pp. 101, 103.
4. Cf. Barbara Swain, *Fools and Folly During the Middle Ages and the Renaissance* (New York: Columbia University Press, 1932).
5. Donald Keene, ed. and trans., *Essays in Idleness: The Tsurezuregusa of Kenko* (New York: Columbia University Press, 1967), p. 7.
6. Quoted in Kerr, *Tragedy and Comedy*, p. 152.
7. John Dominic Crossan, *Raid on the Articulate: Comic Eschatology in Jesus and Borges* (New York: Harper and Row, 1976), p. 30.
8. William F. Lynch, *Christ and Apollo: The Dimensions of the Literary Imagination* (New York: Sheed and Ward, 1960), p. 109.
9. Friedrich Nietzsche, *Beyond Good and Evil: Prelude to a Philosophy of the Future* (New York: Random House, 1966), p. 41.
10. Swami Nikhilananda, ed., *The Gospel of Sri Ramakrishna*, abridged edition (New York: Ramakrishna-Vivekananda Center, 1942), p. 23.

Chapter 6. Jester to the Kingdoms of Earth

1. Knud Rasmussen, *The Intellectual Culture of the Iglulik Eskimos* (Copenhagen: Gyldendalski Boghandel, 1929), p. 10.
2. John Doran, *The History of Court Fools* (London: Richard Bentley, 1858), p. 352. See also Welsford, *The Fool*; Swain, *Fools and Folly*; William Willeford, *The Fool and His Scepter* (Evanston, IL: Northwestern University Press, 1969).
3. Erica Tietze-Conrat, *Dwarfs and Jesters in Art* (New York: Phaidon, 1957), p. 70.
4. Sypher, ed., *Comedy*, p. 221.
5. Max Gluckman, *Rituals of Rebellion in Southeast Africa* (Manchester: Manchester University Press, 1954), p. 27. Cf. Max Gluckman, *Customs and Conflicts in Africa* (Glencoe, IL: Free Press, 1955).
6. Tietze-Conrat, *Dwarfs and Jesters*, p. 66.
7. *Sören Kierkegaard's Journals and Papers*, ed. and trans. by Howard and Edna Hong (Bloomington: Indiana University Press, 1976), vol. 6, p. 94.
8. Alfred Metraux, "Voodoo in Haiti," in *Anthropology of Folk Religion*, ed. Charles Leslie (New York: Random House, 1960), pp. 439–40.

9. A. P. Rossiter, *English Drama from Early Times to the Elizabethans* (New York: Barnes & Noble, 1950), pp. 56–60.

10. G. P. Fedotov, *The Russian Religious Mind*, vol. II: The Middle Ages (Cambridge: Harvard University Press, 1966), pp. 316–43. See also John Sayward, *Perfect Fools: Folly for Christ's Sake in Catholic and Orthodox Spirituality* (New York: Oxford University Press, 1980).

11. Erasmus, *The Praise of Folly*, trans. Hoyt H. Hudson (Princeton: Princeton University Press, 1941), pp. 43–44.

12. *Ibid.*, pp. 44–45.

13. *Ibid.*, pp. 46–47.

14. *Ibid.*, pp. 68, 70.

15. Swain, *Fools and Folly*, p. 219, n. 42.

16. *Ibid.*, p. 215, n. 19.

17. *Portrait of Karl Barth*, trans. Robert McAfee Brown and George Casalis (New York: Doubleday, 1963), p. 3.

18. Gerardus van der Leeuw, *Religion in Essence and Manifestation*, vol. II, trans. J. E. Turner (New York: Harper & Row, 1963), p. 680.

19. Reinhold Niebuhr, *Discerning the Signs of the Times* (London: SCM Press, 1946), p. 99.

20. Watts, "Sense of Regain," p. 20.

21. Smith, "Comic Spirit,", p. 188.

22. Paul Tillich, *Dynamics of Faith* (New York: Harper & Bros., 1957).

23. Erasmus, *Praise of Folly*, p. 78.

24. Santayana, *Soliloquies* , pp. 141–2.

Chapter 7. Putting Humpty-Dumpty Together Again

1. Robert Payne, *The Great God Pan* (New York: Hermitage House, 1952), pp. 21–22.

2. *Ibid.*, p. 20.

3. Albert Reagan, "Notes on Jemez Ethnography," *American Anthropologist*, n. s. xxix (1972), pp. 723–24.

4. Elsie Clews Parsons, *Pueblo Indian Religion* (Chicago: University of Chicago Press, 1939), vol. 1, pp. 95, 246.

5. For an extensive discussion of the Pueblo clowns, see Frank Bock, *A Descriptive Study of the Dramatic Function and Significance of the Clown During Hopi Indian Public Ceremony* (Ph.D. diss., University of Southern California, 1971).

6. Reprinted from *Leaves of Grass* by Walt Whitman, ed. Harold W. Blodgett and Sculley Bradley. Copyright © 1965 by New York University Press. Reprinted by permission of New York University Press.

7. Claude Levi-Strauss, *Structural Anthropology*, vol. I (New York: Basic Books, 1963), pp. 202–27.

8. Payne, *Great God Pan*, p. 12.

9. Chaplin, *Autobiography*, p. 144.

10. Wolfgang Zucker, "The Clown as the Lord of Disorder," in *Holy Laughter*, Conrad Hyers, ed., p. 77.

11. Frank H. Cushing, "Outline of Zuni Creation Myths," *13th Annual Report of the Bureau of American Ethnology* (Washington, DC: U.S. Government Printing Office, 1896), p. 402.

12. Elsie Clews Parson and Ralph L. Beals, "The Sacred Clowns of the Pueblo and Mayo-Yaqui Indians," *American Anthropologist*, vol. 36 (October-December 1934), p. 493.
13. Scott, *Broken Center*, p. 90.
14. Gladys A. Reichard, *Navaho Religion*, Vol. II (New York: Pantheon, 1950), pp. 491-92.
15. N. Ross Crumrine, "Capakoba, the Mayo Easter Ceremonial Impersonator: Explanations of Ritual Clowning," *Journal for the Scientific Study of Religion*, vol. VIII, no. 1 (Spring 1969), pp. 1-22.
16. *Ibid.*, pp. 12, 21.
17. Bock, *Hopi Indian*, pp. 274-303.
18. Harvey Cox, *The Feast of Fools: A Theological Essay on Festivity and Fantasy* (Cambridge, MA: Harvard University Press, 1969), pp. 22-24.
19. Adrien Wettach, *Life's a Lark* (New York: Benjamin Blom, 1969), pp. 17, 52.
20. Samuel Clemens, *Mark Twain's "Which Was the Dream?"* ed. John S. Tuckey (Berkeley: University of California Press, 1966), p. 57.
21. Hart Crane, "Chaplinesque," *Complete Poems of Hart Crane*, ed. Marc Simon (New York: Liveright Publishing Corp., 1986), p. 11. Used by permission.
22. Nikos Kazantzakis, *Zorba the Greek*, trans. Carl Wedman (New York: Simon & Schuster, 1952), p. 151.

Chapter 8. A Happy Ending of Sorts

1. e. e. cummings, "i thank You God," from the *Complete Poems: 1904–1962* by E. E. Cummings, edited by George J. Firmage (New York: Liveright Publishing Corporation, 1991), p. 663. Reprinted by permission.
2. F. M. Cornford, *The Origin of Attic Comedy* (London: Arnold, 1914).
3. Northrup Frye, *The Anatomy of Criticism*, pp. 163-86.
4. Langer, *Feeling and Form*, p. 331.
5. Wylie Sypher, ed., *Comedy* (New York: Doubleday, 1956), p. 220.
6. J. Cheryl Exum and J. William Whedbee, "Isaac, Samson, and Saul: Reflections on the Comic and Tragic Visions," in J. Cheryl Exum, ed., *Tragedy and Comedy in the Bible*, Semeia 32 (Decatur, GA: Scholars Press, 1985), p. 8.
7. Dan O. Via, Jr., *Kerygma and Comedy in the New Testament: A Structuralist Approach to Hermeneutic* (Philadelphia: Fortress Press, 1975). Cf. Dan O. Via, Jr., *The Parables: Their Literary and Existential Dimension* (Philadelphia: Fortress Press, 1967), pp. 110, 145.
8. Via, *Parables*, p. 104.
9. Crossan, *Raid on the Articulate*, p. 22.
10. Kerr, *Tragedy and Comedy*, p. 67.
11. Cedric H. Whitman, *Artistophanes and the Comic Hero* (Cambridge, MA: Harvard University Press, 1964), p. 57.
12. James Sully, *An Essay on Laughter* (London: Longmans, 1902), p. 384.
13. Ruth R. Wisse, *The Schlemiel as Modern Hero* (Chicago: University of Chicago Press, 1971), p. 12.
14. Emmett Kelly, *Clown* (New York: Prentice-Hall, 1954), p. 49.
15. Harold W. Watts, "The Sense of Regain: A Theory of Comedy," University of Kansas City Review, vol. XIII (Autumn 1946), p. 23.
16. Crossan, *Raid on the Articulate*, p. 32.

17. Quoted in *Eight Great Comedies*, ed. Sylvan Barnet *et al.* (New York: New American Library, 1958), p. 452.
18. Eugene Ionesco, *Notes and Counternotes: Writings on the Theater*, trans. Donald Watson (New York: Grove Press, 1964), p. 163.
19. Albert Camus, *The Myth of Sisyphus*, p. 91.
20. Christopher Fry, "Comedy," in *Comedy*, Robert Corrigan, ed., p. 15.

Chapter 9. Wandering Within the Great Food-Chain of Being

1. Pierre-Simon Laplace, *Essai philosophique sur les probabilities*, 5th ed. (Paris: Bachelier, 1825), pp. 3–4 Cited in A. R. Peacocke, *Creation and the World of Science* (Oxford: Oxford University Press, 1979), p. 54.
2. Stephen W. Hawking, *A Brief History of Time: From the Big Bang to Black Holes* (New York: Bantam Books, 1988), pp. 10, 13.
3. James Gleick, *Chaos: Making a New Science* (New York: Viking Penguin Inc., 1987), pp. 3, 5.
4. Ilya Prigogine and Isabelle Stengers, *Order Out of Chaos* (New York: Bantam Books, 1984).
5. Gleick, *Chaos*, p. 94.
6. Paul Radin, *The Trickster: A Study in American Indian Mythology* (London: Routledge & Kegan Paul, 1956), p. 164. Cf. Mac L. Ricketts, "The North American Indian Trickster," *History of Religions*, vol. 5, no. 2 (University of Chicago, 1966), p. 328.
7. Radin, *Trickster*.
8. Mark Twain, *Roughing It* (Berkeley: University of California Press, 1972), p. 245.
9. Ricketts, *op. cit.*, p. 335.
10. *Ibid.*, pp. 347–48.
11. Mircea Eliade, *The Sacred and the Profane* (New York: Harper & Row, 1961).
12. Kazantzakis, *Zorba*, p. 152.
13. Kurt Vonnegut, Jr., *Cat's Cradle* (New York: Delacorte Press, 1963), pp. 214–15.
14. Mark Twain, *The Innocents Abroad* (New York: Harper & Bros., 1911), pp. 133–34.

Chapter 10. Between Dreams and Dust

1. Munro Leaf, *The Story of Ferdinand* (New York: Viking Press, 1936).
2. Campbell, *Hero with a Thousand Faces*.
3. *Ibid.*
4. Joseph Meeker, *The Comedy of Survival* (New York: Charles Scribner's Sons, 1972), p. 26.
5. See Martin Buber, *The Tales of Rabbai Nachman* (Bloomington, IN: Indiana University Press, 1962), pp. 71 ff.
6. Herbert Read, *Art Now, An Introduction to the Theory of Modern Painting* (New York: Pitman, 1960), p. 10.
7. Martin Grotjahn, *Beyond Laughter: A Psychoanalytical Approach to Humor* (New York: McGraw-Hill, 1966), pp. 205 ff.
8. Meeker, *Comedy of Survival*, p. 25.
9. *The Christian Century*, May 22, 1974, p. 570.

10. T. S. Eliot, "Little Gidding," *Collected Poems* 1909-1962 (New York: Harcourt Brace Jovanovich, 1963), pp. 208-9. Used by permission.
11. *Psychology Today*, August 1970, p. 16.
12. Abraham H. Maslow, *Toward a Psychology of Being*, 2nd ed. (New York: D. van Nostrand Co., 1968), p. 80.
13. Nietzsche, *Zarathustra*, p. 25.

Epilogue: Education as Fun

1. Michael Apter, "A Structural Phenomenology of Play," in John H. Kerr and Michael Apter, eds., *Adult Play: A Reversal Theory Approach* (Amsterdam: Swets and Zeitlinger, 1991), pp. 13-30. See also M. J. Apter, D. Fontana and S. Murgatroyd, eds., *Reversal Theory: Applications and Developments* (Cardiff: University College Cardiff Press, 1985).
2. See John H. Kerr, "Play, Sport and the Paretelic State," in M. J. Apter, J. Kerr, and M. Cowles (eds.), *Progress in Reversal Theory* (Amsterdam: North Holland Press, 1988).
3. James P. Carse, *Finite and Infinite Games* (New York: Free Press, 1986), p. 33.
4. Huizinga, *Homo Ludens*, p. 2.
5. Carse, *Finite and Infinite Games*, p. 19.
6. William Dean, *Love Before the Fall* (Philadelphia: Westminster Press, 1976), p.33.
7. Carse, *Finite and Infinite Games*, p. 15.

Index